Philosophical Embarrassment

ANTHEM STUDIES IN WITTGENSTEIN

Anthem Studies in Wittgenstein publishes new and classic works on Wittgenstein and Wittgensteinian philosophy. This book series aims to bring Wittgenstein's thought into the mainstream by highlighting its relevance to 21st century concerns. Titles include original monographs, themed edited volumes, forgotten classics, biographical works and books intended to introduce Wittgenstein to the general public. The series is published in association with the British Wittgenstein Society.

Anthem Studies in Wittgenstein sets out to put in place whatever measures may emerge as necessary in order to carry out the editorial selection process purely on merit and to counter bias on the basis of gender, race, ethnicity, religion, sexual "orientation and other characteristics protected by law. These measures include subscribing to the British Philosophical Association/ Society for Women in Philosophy (UK) Good Practice Scheme.

Series Editor

Constantine Sandis – University of Hertfordshire, UK

Forthcoming Titles in the Series

Sense and Value in Wittgenstein's Tractatus

Practical Rationality, Learning and Convention: Essays in the Philosophy of Education

Final Reflections on Wittgenstein and Other Topics

Wittgenstein: Human Beings and Conversation

Iron Pyrite: Reflections on Kripkean Themes

Nightmariners and Wideawakes: The Philosophy of Dreams

Wittgenstein and Popular Culture

The Existential Dimension of Doubt: Sceptical Themes in Kierkegaard, Wittgenstein and Cavell

Freud's Paradoxical Achievement: A Wittgensteinian Perspective

Philosophical Embarrassment

Wittgensteinian Essays in Moral Psychology

Béla Szabados and Peter Campbell

ANTHEM PRESS

Anthem Press
An imprint of Wimbledon Publishing Company
www.anthempress.com

This edition first published in UK and USA 2026
by ANTHEM PRESS
75–76 Blackfriars Road, London SE1 8HA, UK
or PO Box 9779, London SW19 7ZG, UK
and
244 Madison Ave #116, New York, NY 10016, USA

British Library Cataloguing-in-Publication Data
A catalogue record for this book is available from the British Library.

Library of Congress Control Number: 2026937570

ISBN-13: 978-1-83999-766-2
ISBN-10: 1-83999-766-4

This title is also available as an eBook.

In Memoriam
For David Givner

My ideal is a certain coolness. A temple providing a setting for the passions without meddling with them.

Ludwig Wittgenstein

CONTENTS

ACKNOWLEDGMENTS

We thank Alex Rueger for help at various stages of the project and an anonymous reviewer for comments on an earlier version of the manuscript. We are grateful to Andrew Lugg for valuable suggestions and remarks on the Wittgenstein chapters; and to Allen Carlson, Alex Neill, and Roger Shiner for comments on an ancestral version of the chapter "Rousseau and the Culture of Embarrassment." Thanks are also due to Heather Hodgson for editorial assistance and moral support, as well as to Alison Lee Strayer for help with the initial research. First thoughts about the topic appeared in the *Journal of Philosophical Research* with the title "Embarrassment and Self-Esteem." An early and rather different version of the chapter on Rousseau was published in the *British Journal for Aesthetics* under the title "Reading Rousseau through the Eyes of Embarrassment"; and the essay on "Wittgenstein on Self-Deception in Science, Psychology and Philosophy" found a home in *Wittgenstein-Studien*. Finally, we are grateful to Robert Solomon, who, through his pioneering work *The Passions*, initiated a renaissance in the philosophy of emotions in Anglo-American philosophy.

PREFACE

This book consists of diverse chapters held together by the thread of embarrassment that runs through them. We begin with the working hypothesis that the psychology of philosophy can provide insight into the practice of philosophy. This is especially true of modern philosophy, which brings the psychology of philosophy to the forefront partly because of the Enlightenment's new or renewed interest in the primacy of the person. Yet, ironically, the philosophy associated with the Enlightenment provides a diminished conception of the person—unable to live actual lives of persons.

Embarrassment, we aim to show, is particularly revelatory in this regard. Sometimes, it is front and center, as when we discuss its conceptual features; at other times, its presence is oblique, as when we take a closer look at Rousseau's existential outrage at the very idea of a culture of embarrassment; or when we look at Darwin's theory and Eliot's critique of it. We unearth deeply buried embarrassments in the history of philosophy, treating them as useful entry points into the major figures from an unusual if not idiosyncratic angle. We also discuss examples of embarrassment—ancient and modern—and trace their effects on our subject.

All this raises a somewhat different but important line of inquiry, one that is meta-philosophical. Hume and Wittgenstein are our prime examples of philosophers who are aware that they and their subject have undone themselves and thus have been thoroughly embarrassed. What are the upshots, they ask, for philosophers and their subject? Perhaps this issue is the answer to Rousseau's tantrums: embarrassment is useful. Throughout the book we have many things to say about its uses and its abuses. Reality and objectivity catch up to theorists from time to time, and embarrassment is our psychology's signal that the jig is up.

One question this raises for us is how to proceed in philosophy, with equipment that tends to run off the rails with considerable regularity. Do we proceed with all modesty, alive to these facts about us and ready to be embarrassed the next time we get carried away or when our reach exceeds our grasp?

Or do we, as the Vienna Circle and Quine seem to have done, radically revise key elements of the philosophical project—the pursuit of truth and objectivity in all matters, for example—in an attempt to avoid future embarrassments? If you narrow your subject, and if you are competent in that narrowness, you can avoid embarrassment and achieve your modest goals. This is what the early Wittgenstein, Quine and like-minded philosophers seem to be saying with their remarks about professional competence.

Such a course is in keeping with the approach of modern philosophy, since it has taken science as a model of sorts. However, when science exceeds its competence, claiming it can solve any and every problem, it loses its experimental modesty and competence, and we no longer have science but scientism. It should come as no surprise, then, that one of our chapters is a set of reflections on Wittgenstein's cautionary remarks about the embarrassments of scientism. A definition or characterization, Kant remarked, should come toward the end rather than at the beginning of an investigation; hence, in the final chapter, we provide an overview—a conceptual map—of embarrassment.

Our philosophical north stars are Hume and Wittgenstein. And we accept that embarrassment is an inevitable feature of the human condition. With that recognition, we should push along with a corresponding sense of modesty clearly before us. In sharp contrast, we resist those who, in their rejection of the very idea of objectivity, think there exists nothing at all that can embarrass us; that we can create truth, and the only thing to fear is that you find yourself in disagreement with the *bien pensants*. We regard this tendency in our culture as pure hubris and an embarrassment we may not survive.

The chapters may be read in any order, so readers can follow their bent or particular interest. The book's format and punctuation lend itself to slow reading, as if enacting Wittgenstein's friendly injunction: "This is how philosophers should greet each other: 'Take your time!'"

Chapter I

ROUSSEAU AND THE CULTURE OF EMBARRASSMENT

> For a philosopher there is more grass growing down in the valleys of silliness than up on the barren heights of cleverness.
>
> *Ludwig Wittgenstein*

The Moral and Social Importance of Embarrassment

The conventional wisdom is that embarrassment, like some other emotions that we experience, for example, irritation, is a shallow emotion—a feeling on the margins of our emotional life. It does not, we are told, connect up with anything deep in the human condition and is naturally thought to be superficial, even silly.[1] Men and women tend to outgrow it as they get older or wiser, and it is no accident that its high-water mark is in adolescence. Mere youths and the immature continue to be susceptible to embarrassment, but can you picture Socrates embarrassed?

At the heart of this natural reaction is the dormant thought that embarrassment is a form of weakness, even of irrationality: a transient intrusion into our normal lives. If a person continues to be embarrassed about an incident long past, this is a form of neurosis for which he needs treatment or cure. There is, to be sure, an entrenched ideological bias here, namely, the feminization of embarrassment in our culture. Remember: with embarrassment, we cringe; we want to hide, even disappear into the bowels of the earth. And significantly, sometimes we are so embarrassed that, as we say, we could almost die. Can a shallow emotion provoke, perhaps constitute, such deep pools of defacement?

Contrary to the conventional view, we suggest that embarrassment is a significant emotion that cuts deep in our lives; that it is a window on the self;

1 For the conventional view, see Robert Solomon, *The Passions*, Anchor/Doubleday, Garden City, 1976, p. 306.

that its moments and episodes are diagnostic—a personal index to the self's values and concerns, and of its moral and social resources. Now if embarrassment cuts deep, then its wounds should be right in front of our eyes as we read autobiographical literature, our stories of our lives. Yet in retrieving the riches of embarrassment, it is the exceptional writer who offers an embarrassment of riches.

We begin with Rousseau's *Confessions*, and with the understanding that this is, first, a work of autobiography revelatory of Rousseau's moral psychology. But as we shall see, the *Confessions* is more than that. His autobiography is intimately related to his social and political philosophy. The *Confessions*, we maintain, is an existential ground for the social and political philosophy of the *Social Contract*. For Rousseau, embarrassment is an unnatural condition of man created in the opposition between his very essence—free and autonomous—and the heteronomous constraints of an alien culture he finds himself landed in. Man may be born free, but he is everywhere embarrassed—frustrated and misshapen by rules and conventions imposed upon him by others. Rousseau's autobiography, it turns out, is politics dressed up as personal. His social and political philosophy is autobiography in the abstract. If so, his *Confessions* deserves to be lifted from the ghetto of self-indulgent autobiography and kicked uptown where it belongs.

Rousseau's *Confessions*: Autobiography and Embarrassment

Jean-Jacques Rousseau is exceptional. Picture him reciting his *Confessions* to the Count and Countess d'Egmont and their friends. These are Rousseau's final observations on this performance:

> Thus I concluded my reading and everyone was silent. Mme d'Egmont was the only person who seemed moved. She trembled visibly but quickly controlled herself and remained quiet, as did the rest of the company. Such was the advantage I derived from my reading and declaration.[2]

Can one doubt for a moment that Rousseau embarrassed these hapless aristocrats to death? The paralysis, the silence, the ambivalence of embarrassment was thick in the air.

And was this not partly Rousseau's purpose? He speaks of "the advantage"—of the power over others he gained from reading his *Confessions*. Recall the way he begins his story:

2 Jean-Jacques Rousseau, *The Confessions*, Penguin Classics, Harmondsworth, Middlesex, England, 1953, p. 606.

> Let the last trumpet sound when it will, I shall come forward with this work in my hand, to present myself before my Sovereign Judge, and proclaim aloud: "Here is what I have done [...] I have bared my secret soul, as thou thyself hast seen it, Eternal Being." So let the numberless legions of my fellow men gather around me, and hear my confessions. Let them blush for my misdeeds. But let each one of them reveal his heart at the foot of thy throne with equal sincerity, and may any man who dares, say "I was a better man than he."[3]

Well, it seems no one dared to do this at what must have been a long reading. Rousseau managed to reduce them to embarrassed silence by his *tour de force* of textual striptease. Since a confessional autobiography aims at making a clean breast of it, revealing the author's private thoughts and secrets to public scrutiny and, possibly, subsequent judgment, we expect such an undertaking to include particular moments of embarrassment and shame. And we are not disappointed. But who is embarrassed? The person who makes the confession or the audience who hears the confession? Rousseau does not seem to feel embarrassed at all. In fact, as we have seen, he issues a challenge to the audience. His listeners may have various reactions. Some, namely, the empathetic in the audience, "feel with or for" Rousseau and "blush for his misdeeds"; others recall their own misdeeds and feel embarrassed; yet others resent Rousseau imposing his confessions on them.

The *Confessions* constitutes a curious and embarrassing instrument of power. It is meant to bring about a closure to criticism, to invidious competition and judgment. This is at odds, however, with the attitude that issues the dare: "Let any man say, 'I was a better man than he.'" The dare bears the imprint of competition rather than confession, of contest, not contrition, and bodes ill for the project of closure. This tension is unexpected and pregnant with embarrassment, for the attitude appropriate to confession is repentance or at least a certain humility, yet Rousseau seems to be boasting about himself and justifying his mistakes, misdemeanors, and moral shortcomings. Moreover, his confessions have become an accusation that his audience, a proxy for his society, is at fault—is to blame—for causing his pain and suffering.

Mme d'Egmont seems most moved by Rousseau's "final vocabulary." There is an indication of empathetic identification, of solidarity with Jean-Jacques, and this is more than mere sympathetic identification—more than being embarrassed on behalf of Rousseau. For the latter may simply mean feeling embarrassed about the situation someone else is in. Empathetic

3 Ibid., p. 17.

identification, on the other hand, involves an imaginative projection into this someone's skin and feeling the emotion that one perceives him or her to feel. There is textual evidence that this is the form of identification Mme d'Egmont feels: her visible trembling, her need for self-control, and her subsequent quietness all suggest that she feels embarrassed with Rousseau. Or if he does not feel embarrassed, then she imagines that he, like any normal person, would be embarrassed. Some of the other listeners at the reading may have been simply embarrassed by Rousseau—embarrassed to be put in a situation of a private, confessional nature. They might say: Do I have to be confronted with this public breast baring? Their silence may have been that of the cool dispassionate observer or that of someone who casts a cold eye, who mistrusts Rousseau's self-portrait as a paragon of innocence and sincerity.

Rousseau is generous enough to supply us with resources for deconstructing his vaulting ambition: complete sincerity. Must this not be so for someone who thinks of himself as a "transparent crystal"? "Throughout the course of my life, as has been seen," he says, "my heart has been as transparent as a crystal, and incapable of concealing for so much as a moment, the least lively feeling which has taken refuge in it."[4] If so, Rousseau's *Confessions* should reveal not only moments of public, *tête-à-tête* embarrassments, but many moments of self-embarrassment too.

One such moment of "self-embarrassment" is discernible in Rousseau's second thoughts about having disposed of his children by taking them to the Foundling Hospital and leaving them there. He proceeds to engage in a series of self-justifications, apologies for and rationalizations of his misconduct. Then suddenly he comes to a stop, as if he were a jeweler who, while examining his precious "transparent crystal," finds a flaw that blocks his vision. Rousseau says: "I have promised to write my confessions but not to make apologies; so I will stop here. My duty is to tell the truth, my readers' is to be just, and that is all I shall ever ask of them."[5] Did he forget for a moment that, despite the title, this is no act of contrition? It is a contest he intends to win, and he'll not do so by handing his opposition points to use against him. If Rousseau engaged in this self-deceptive soliloquy without an audience, then upon realizing what he was doing, presumably he would have a moment of private embarrassment.

We all know how embarrassing it is to be contradicted, yet it is no less embarrassing to catch oneself in self-contradiction. Rousseau senses that he is doing precisely what he set out not to do, something self-defeating. And of

4 Ibid., p. 415.
5 Ibid., p. 335.

course he cannot resist prowling in the reader's domain, handing out instructions. Of course, he wants more than justice from his "dear reader." He wants the reader's sympathy, compassion, even love. A merely just reader, detached and distant, is unlikely to blush for Rousseau's misdeeds, although he may groan at his depravities. Unlike Mme d'Egmont, a detached, distant reader may observe Rousseau's *faux pas* with quiet contempt or resentment at this self-centered attention seeker. Such a reader is Rousseau's enemy, his judge, his competitor. Against him Rousseau wages war. Such a reader, amused, contemptuous, or resentful, is a catalyst for hiding one's self rather than for self-revelation.

In summary, Rousseau is triumphant, not contrite. Among his purposes is to show the hypocrisy of a society that claims to value individuals and personal autonomy, yet punishes those who are true to themselves, who endeavor to live lives that are fulfilling by their own lights. Shame and embarrassment are among the devices of hypocritical social oppression. And he's also determined to show that, by being frank about all this, he is a better man than those who condemn him.

Nature or Culture, or Both?

The intensity and richness of feeling that a memory brings with it is a criterion for autobiographical inclusion. Embarrassing episodes not only carry an excess of emotional freight, but their structure also contains a crucial tension mirroring Rousseau's discontent. On the one hand, it conjures up a spontaneous, autonomous agent, at home with whatever he is doing. On the other, it includes the critical look of the other, the intrusion into the private of a cool observer perceived as challenging one's self-esteem and passing judgment. Home, for Rousseau, is the innocent spontaneity of the child in nature; hell is other people. Society or culture, according to him, is a corrupting influence on the individual, for man is born free but everywhere he is constrained by rules that are not of his making. To get back to the garden of freedom and spontaneity, we need to cleave these chains. Evidently, for him, autonomy is the supreme ethical value.

Embarrassments, recollected and dwelt upon, are windows through which we, together with Rousseau the narrator, can peer into the inner citadel and re-create Rousseau's inner self. We can catch him unaware and simultaneously experience the sense of violation that any sensitive observer feels when he intrudes on an intimate private scene. Rousseau considers himself in much the same predicament as that of a man who has come in "out of the blue." It is almost impossible for him to talk for a moment without blundering. He is fearful of making a fool of himself:

> Though I am not a fool, I am very often taken for one, even by people in a good position to judge. Unfortunately, for me too, my face and my eyes seem to promise otherwise, and people find my stupidity all the more shocking because it disappoints their expectations. This fact [...] presents the key to a great number of my strange actions [...].[6]

Imagine Rousseau making an attempt at conversation at a party. Mentally rehearsing the norms that govern such a conversation, he is so overwhelmed that he becomes tongue-tied. Sometimes the very fear of making a mistake shades into embarrassment. Having tightened, in his capacity as a philosopher, the informal rules of discourse for such occasions, he is embarrassed to find that the more or less refined guests do not know them yet carry on successfully regardless of the rules. On reflection, he may also be embarrassed for himself for setting up rules that are self-defeating: the high norms he sets for himself, and others make conversation practically impossible. So, there is a noteworthy paradox about conversation in Rousseau. On the one hand, there is a Platonist resonance in that he insists on too high a protocol for conversation, thus making conversation well-nigh impossible. On the other hand, by abolishing requirements for conversation as unnatural artifices that are impediments to his ideal of spontaneity, he makes conversation impossible again, perhaps reducing it to soliloquy, free association, or a jumble of incoherent sentences.

A man who comes in out of the blue, out of nature, into the prison of society with its constraints and conventions, cannot help but display himself "at a disadvantage and in a character entirely foreign to himself [...]. Whenever he has nothing to say, instead of keeping quiet, he has a furious desire to chatter." And "so anxious am I to conquer or hide my ineptitude that I rarely fail to make it apparent. Among countless examples [...]"[7] and he goes on to recite embarrassing and shameful episodes.

Put a plant in the wrong kind of soil and it shrivels. Put a man in the wrong atmosphere and he will be ill at ease, disfigured; nothing functions as it should. He will feel strange even to himself. This is how Rousseau thinks of society as the wrong soil for him—indeed, wrong for everyone. This is why his conduct is strange even to himself. He does not recognize himself in society. If the plant is put back in the right kind of soil, in the right milieu, it thrives and blossoms. So, Rousseau puts himself back "into nature" and hence into solitude.

6 Ibid., pp. 115–16.
7 Ibid., p. 115.

> The role I have chosen of writing and remaining in the background is precisely the one that suits me. If I had been present, people would not have known my value; they would not even have suspected it.[8]

For him, this peculiar solitary confinement is no punishment but a natural condition. Far ahead of his time, Rousseau is a natural social distancer and self-isolator. Yet, notice, he attends the Paris salons and is dependent on others and their generosity! Rousseau lives. How so? Is society not so toxic as he would have us believe?

Rousseau seems unable to play the games of social intercourse. "Unable," "cannot," or "will not"; what does it matter? He did play such roles but does no longer. When he did, he felt as if he were someone else, another, quagmired in artifice, isolated among artifacts. Ironically, such social occasions offer an acute sense of himself as he is placed in sharp relief against the ensemble of social roles that are played out. Rousseau's ambivalence at a social gathering is this: at one fell swoop he betrays himself and others. His fear of faux pas, of forgetting social convention freezes him. His concern with what figure he will cut prevents him from being himself, from spontaneous natural behavior. Instead of facilitating sociability, his excessively high standards for social behavior and conversation, his fear of blunders, become obstacles to it. This is how he sketches his predicament and, in fact, the end of conversation:

> Seeing that I am so little master of myself when I am alone, imagine what I am like in conversation, when in order to speak to the point one must speak promptly of a dozen things at a time. The mere thought of all the conventions, of which I am sure to forget at least one, is enough to frighten me. I cannot understand how a man can have the confidence to speak in company. For not a word should be uttered without taking everyone into account, without knowing their characters and their histories, in order to be certain of not offending anyone.[9]

We mentioned earlier that there is a Platonist resonance in these remarks, as if the conventions for conversation were rigid rather than loose. For in a conversation sometimes one person throws the ball, another catches it and then passes it on. These moves are predictable and boring, precisely because of their well-lubricated mechanical tenor and tempo. But what if a person runs with the ball, or better still, puts it in his pocket? Such an unexpected change, such a source of irritation or delight. Rousseau's conditions for conversation

8 Ibid., p. 116.
9 Ibid., p. 114.

are surprising for an advocate of spontaneity, and they make the possibility of conversation remote. In fact, one suspects this is part of Rousseau's project of dismantling society as a source of artifice, pretense, and corruption. For conversation is emblematic of society. It presupposes a rich social context: standards of appropriateness, conventions of behavior, etiquette, and the tacit endorsement of such things.

It does not seem to occur to Rousseau that the things he loves—writing, literature, language, art, self-expression, music, mathematics—are institutional, rule-governed; essentially social. Moreover, they are agency-enablers, not diminishers. And they are just the sort of things that could not inhabit the rarefied air of a state of nature he professes to prefer. Like that world, the institutions require that we navigate them. And navigation requires knowledge and skill, cooperation and commitment, and the underlying habits and character to sustain them. They require, that is, a culture hospitable to persons.

We might say that embarrassment is the static in the music of our social life. Rousseau wants the static to cease. So, he rids himself of what strikes him as cacophony. Feelings of naturalness, being himself, autonomy, are supreme values for him. Playing social roles violates such feelings of naturalness. He refuses to play this bad game. He wants to be in the right atmosphere: among patches of blue, fields of green, brown earth, gray rock, and Rousseau. When he recollects moments of embarrassment, he is recollecting moments of dissonance: his innocence and spontaneity, his feelings of naturalness, are placed in bas-relief against the artifices, the theater, of social intercourse.

Rousseau is outraged at the very idea of embarrassment, unless it be self-embarrassment. For embarrassment implies norms that are externally imposed and thus violate his preeminent value of autonomy. Embarrassment, for him, is a sign of *mauvaise foi*.

The picture of our social architecture as the theater where we play our scripted roles is a compelling picture. We may, as actors, play lots of different roles. Like Rousseau, we may feel alienated in the course of this game. And we know that at the end of it all, it is we human beings, not the actors, who must die. Rousseau thought: if it is a particular human being, I, Rousseau, who suffers and must die, then let the human being live unfettered by imposed roles. Get rid of the actor by getting rid of the audience. Get rid of the roles by getting rid of the theater. Can Rousseau do this? And if he can, does he thereby rid himself of embarrassment?

As Rousseau goes into isolation, he abandons all roles except one: "The role I have chosen of writing [...] is precisely the one that suits me."[10] Yet this

10 Ibid., p. 116.

unique role reinstates the plurality of roles that he must play as autobiographer: he is protagonist, narrator, reader/writer, lover and critic, judge and judged—an ensemble of roles rolled into one. As he proceeds with his self-exploration, the inevitable burden of trying to do justice to these occasionally conflicting roles brings on a sense of embarrassment. He looks back to discover his inner self, embarrassed to see it scattering into fragments. Little wonder, since his conception of himself is Cartesian—a stand-alone, purely thinking thing; complete, independent, inviolate.

Embarrassment in Cultures: How English Is Embarrassment

Embarrassment's momentary loss of action—its characteristic "I was taken aback" feature; its temporary paralytic effect; its awkwardness; its flustering—makes it an unlikely candidate for autobiographical inclusion or for ideological appropriation in the service of cultural nationalism. Hence, it is refreshing to come across it in Rousseau, as well as in a fascinating exploration of embarrassment in the life and poetry of John Keats by the distinguished critic Christopher Ricks. "Is embarrassment," Ricks asks, "not only a nineteenth-century sentiment but a narrowly English one?"[11] Then he goes on to suggest that while the literature and life of other nations, especially France, pride themselves on unembarrassability, the English not only single it out for attention but give it an importance that seems quaint on first blush.

Ricks is an exceptional critic. He acknowledges that "embarrassment is very important in life; that one of the things for which we value art is that it helps us to deal with embarrassment, not only by abolishing or ignoring it, but by recognizing, refining and putting it to good human purposes."[12] Yet he startles us by echoing the partisan generalization that "one could suggest that English life and literature have had the advantages and disadvantages of embarrassability, and that the French have had the advantages and disadvantages of unembarrassability."[13]

What is embarrassing about this theme is Rousseau, an eighteenth-century figure whose presence in French literature is palpable and who re-creates embarrassing episodes to offer us glimpses into his inner citadel, his lost inner self that he is anxious to recover. Why such a curious blind spot? Could it be that Rousseau pioneers, in the eighteenth century and in a classic of French literature, the very theme that Ricks wishes to promote and elaborate for the

11 Christopher Ricks, *Keats and Embarrassment*, Clarendon Press, Oxford, 1984, p. 5.
12 Ibid., p. 1.
13 Ibid., p. 6.

nineteenth century and English literature? These apparently distinct projects, when considered together, may illuminate each other, even though Ricks seems to erase Rousseau's traces.

What is the deeply buried good that embarrassment is intended to recover in Rousseau? The quarrel and uneasy reconciliation with Grimm in the *Confessions* gives us a clue:

> I was flabbergasted, I did not know what to say, I could not utter a word. The whole scene reminded me of a schoolmaster's reprimand of a student whom he is letting off without a flogging: I never think of it without feeling how misleading are all judgments based on appearances, to which the vulgar attach such weight, and how often boldness and pride accompany guilt, while shame and embarrassment are the attributes of innocence.[14]

Rousseau turns things around and stands them on their head. Although embarrassment—our capacity for and manifestation of it—is characteristically related to our *faux pas* and errors—in some cases it is really a capacity for and manifestation of innocence or moral sensibility. Sometimes, although innocent, we are embarrassed just because we are perceived as guilty by others who ought to know better. Here then is the connection with Ricks:

> It has always been part of the Englishman's objection to foreigners that they are brazen-faced, unembarrassable, and therefore untrustworthy. Especially the French. What the Spaniards said of the South American Indians, the English might say of the French: "How can those be trusted, who knew not how to blush?" What was in the one case false physiology might be in the other true philosophy. "How can you trust a people whose very language does its best to conceal the existence of the blush?"[15]

In remarks such as these we glean the ideology that fuels the strange attempt to appropriate embarrassment as an emotional emblem for a particular national literary culture. What Rousseau does by self-particularization, Ricks performs by an act of generalization whose scope is the English and French literary stereotype. But what is this possibly "true philosophy" that is supposed to provide a basis for Ricks' vast appraisal? Could it be a philosophy of language that scrutinizes the linguistic vocabulary and conceptual resources of English and French and finds that the French language has impoverished

14 Rousseau, *The Confessions*, p. 440.
15 Ricks, *Keats and Embarrassment*, p. 5.

linguistic or conceptual resources for expressions and betrayals of embarrassment? Hence, "it does its best to conceal the existence of the blush"?

But even a cursory look shows this to be false, and Ricks, strangely enough, knows this. He himself cites Robert's Dictionnaire: "*État* de celui qui [...] eprouve une sort de malaise pour agir ou parler. V. Confusion, emotion, gaucherie [...] timidité, trouble; s'embarrasser." These words are used to capture, rather straightforwardly, the senses and uses of "embarrass" in English. Multifarious expressions in both languages amply support a rough equivalence of conceptual repertoire. In any event, if it were true that embarrassment and embarrassability are distinctive of English life, would this not trivialize the emotion? Embarrassment would then be the emotional analogue of an English accent! We suspect that the question "How can you trust a people whose very language does its best to conceal the existence of the blush?" invites a subsequent question: Is this claim not an ideological remark, disguised as a linguistic observation, designed to diminish and manipulate?

But there is more to this, less and less strange as we go along, appropriation. Foreigners are said to be "brazen faced," "untrustworthy" because "unembarrassable." This brings with it a claim of moral superiority and, by implicit comparison, a gradual diminishment of the foreigner. "Brazen-faced" in a relevant context means shameless, unable or unwilling to feel guilt, and hence morally debased. "Untrustworthy" conveys the sense of "deceptive, deceiving, wearing a mask, not showing oneself in one's true colours." The blush of shame or embarrassment is the only redeeming feature of the perceived immoral deed or incongruous behavior: the blush shows your awareness that you violated a norm and thereby you acknowledge the *faux pas*. So, the stratagem is to reduce the foreigner to the moral imbecile or the sociopath, deficient in his awareness of wrongdoing and in his concern for values.

However, the blush of shame, the flush and flustering awkwardness of embarrassment, is somewhat less provisionally distributed than Ricks' picture suggests. The academic who realizes that the love letters that had been left in his desk were read by his sabbatical replacement; the hostess who gives the guests unclean silverware that reveals the lack of hygiene in the household; the contemporary Casanova who goes to great lengths to seduce someone to sleep with him, only to find in the moment of his success the failure of a temporary impotence. Such people may all feel embarrassed, but they do not thereby miraculously become participants in English culture or perceive the world of human relations through a peculiarly English lens!

These cultural caricatures and absurdities make us realize that the observation that English life and literature have had the advantages and disadvantages of embarrassability is best taken as an opportunity to borrow someone else's mirror and see ourselves as others see us.[16] It is like recognizing oneself in another person's autobiographical remark. And one source of greatness in an autobiographical remark is precisely the sort of courage required to acknowledge things that we have a constitutional reluctance to acknowledge. Hence, we owe a great debt of gratitude to Christopher Ricks and his brilliant book.

Might Ricks, however, mean something different? Since the rough equivalence of linguistic resources renders his claim false, might he mean that the French may use the words in question to do or emphasize something different? Perhaps they play a somewhat different language game. And that is a cultural as well as a linguistic matter—a matter of fine shades of meaning or speech act. Perhaps the French, when in a certain context, say "Ah, you are embarrassed!", chiefly perform a perlocutionary act[17] intended more to persuade people to grow up and "get a grip" and compose themselves, to reclaim their self-control, to remind them of their obligations as Frenchmen, and thereby to annihilate or reduce the individual's embarrassment.

Note that we speak of "the French" and "the English" as the cultural stereotypes have it, since obviously there are French people who are easily embarrassed and English people who wouldn't be embarrassed by anything.

We shall read Rousseau as iconic of the French attitude to embarrassment. The reader may be surprised that we regard a Genevan as iconic of the French cultural stereotype. But this shouldn't be all that surprising. After all, Rousseau lived and worked in France most of his life, and his essays and books have had a deep influence in French culture and literature. He seems to be emblematic of the French when he says: "I hate embarrassment [...]."[18] To hate embarrassment as Rousseau does is to hate, not so much its episodes as the very idea of it. Unembarrassability is a triumph of one's psychology over anything heterodox: society, others' rules and standards, objectivity or what have you. Embarrassability, for him, is a character flaw that one should be ashamed of; a failure to comport oneself in accordance with the ideals of the Cartesian self, that purely thinking indivisible thing and therefore unembarrassable and inviolate. Rousseau sees society/culture as a corruption of the

16 "Oh wad some Power the giftie gie us, To see oursels as ithers see us!" Robert Burns, "To a Louse [...]," in *Poems, Chiefly in the Scottish Dialect*, Printed for the author, Edinburgh, 1787.

17 J.L. Austin, *How to Do Things with Words*, Clarendon Press, Oxford, 1962.

18 Rousseau, *The Confessions*, p. 46.

purely autonomous self, a self that is and ought to be the author of any rule that applies to it.[19]

So, in general, the French may hate more the idea of the loss of composure and autonomy, the loss of esteem, the loss of that which is at risk in embarrassment. If so, they may want to deter or minimize embarrassment by being harsher on the embarrassed and the shy. The English, on the other hand, may be more patient and more accepting of it, as well as of timidity and shyness.

If this is so, we would expect the two cultures to tackle the problem of embarrassment somewhat differently. From the French, we would expect more of a "top down" approach, and from the English more of a "bottom up" approach when coming to grips with the dilemmas arising from embarrassing situations. We would expect the French to approach the matter invoking the rules of *a priori* reason, of which we all have an equal share, while we would expect the English to look at the messy situation and see what caused it in the first place and what its effects are.

Rousseau's Children

Rousseau pioneers, through his own life, the project of trans-valuing embarrassment and shame, of tracing their valuations and elucidations of things. Through re-creating embarrassing episodes, he offers glimpses of an otherwise lost, innocent self. But this window is not available to just anyone. Only the sympathetic/empathetic reader, the "dear reader," can see through this window. Readers are implicated in Rousseau's *Confessions*. We are invited to gather around him and blush. He is anxious for the reader's good opinion and regard for his own sensibility and difference. He prowls in the reader's domain, addressing, advising, ingratiating, bragging, embarrassing, manipulating the reader: "What will my reader think if I tell him with my by now customary frankness [...]."[20] The reader is crucial, and there are many

19 Rousseau's conception of autonomy—the idea that persons are naturally and essentially self-governing—that autonomy is a/the prime personal and moral good, that it is categorical, that any constraints on personal autonomy, from society or nature or God, are corruptions of the person—has been remarkably influential. See, for example, the various forms of postmodernism. Interested readers might refer to Chapter 2, to the section on Hume where we draw parallels between what Hume showed us were the consequences of trying to live the philosophical-skeptical life—utter embarrassment—and the consequences of trying to live a Rousseauean autonomous life—an autonomy too far—which not only fails to avoid embarrassment but leads to a terminal form of it.

20 Rousseau, *The Confessions,* p. 385.

different kinds of readers. Even more to the point: Rousseau is also his own reader. Jean-Jacques is a reader of Rousseau before he is his judge!

One sort of reader is distant and detached, haughty and judgmental. Another sort of reader is more like an embarrassed eavesdropper. He happens on the scene, sees the ridiculousness, the absurdity of the situation, senses the acute embarrassment of the person eavesdropped on, and feels embarrassed in turn. Such a person need not identify sympathetically with the narrator, since he may resent the narrator for having put him in a situation where he feels embarrassed. Then there is the sort of reader who feels embarrassed for the protagonist, having put himself in the protagonist's shoes, feeling, identifying with his embarrassment. So, it is a mistake to homogenize the other as reader, as if the other was always a menacing presence.

Picture Rousseau in a moment of self-embarrassment:

> My chief embarrassment was at so fully and openly going back on myself. After the strict principle that I had just proclaimed with so much noise, after the austere rules that I had so loudly preached, after so much stinging invective against effeminate books which breathed love and languor, could anything more unexpected, more shocking be imagined than that I should suddenly with my own hand enroll myself among the authors of these books I had so violently censured? I felt my inconsistency in all its force, I reproached myself for it, blushed for it, I was even angry with myself. But all this was insufficient to bring me back to reason.[21]

The intensity of this moment of self-embarrassment reveals a divided Rousseau in the grip of conflicting inclinations and behavior. It shows him in situations when "I am so little master of myself even when I am alone." He manages to escape from the conventional autobiographical virtue of consistency that is responsible for many false façades. He manages to surprise himself. After all, why can't a thinker leave his "virtues" behind and escape them for a while?

Paul de Man says somewhere that one can dislike Rousseau of the *Confessions*, but one is not inclined to argue with his views. Perhaps this is so because the quality of intimacy is integral to the work? Rational argument does not enter the picture—it is the immediacy of language that seduces the reader. Yet this is not wholly true. Sometimes when Rousseau shifts from the confessional to the apologetic mode, when he contradicts himself, when he quarrels with himself, he is inviting us, albeit indirectly, to quarrel with him. We find this invitation difficult to turn down when we turn the pages relating

21 Ibid., pp. 404–05.

to Rousseau's abandonment of his children and are inclined to draw a limit to such escapes from "virtue."

"My third child, therefore, was taken to the Foundling Hospital, like the others, and the next two were disposed of the same way, for I had five in all."[22] There is a chilling, matter-of-fact attitude pervading Rousseau's recollections concerning his children. He speaks of giving them up "with a calm spirit"; "I really saw nothing wrong with it"; "it seemed perfectly logical to me"; however, in retrospect, "it was an error." "This arrangement," he goes on, "seemed so good and sensible and right to me"[23] that he was tempted to boast of it. It is as if he were giving away a litter of cats. These passages betray a lack of capacity for a sense of loss that Rousseau is so willing and masterly at exercising on behalf of his past selves, his literary children. These children will not be given up; he re-creates them and nurtures them in memory; yet he has a *laissez*-faire attitude to his biological children.

Later on, however, Rousseau's retrospections take a different turn:

> The attitude I had taken with regard to my children, logical though it had seemed to me, had not always left me easy in my mind. While thinking out my *Treatise* on Education, I felt that I neglected some duties from which nothing could excuse me. So strong did my remorse finally grow that it almost drew from me a public confession of my fault at the beginning of Émile.[24]

These quarrels in Rousseau's family of selves, these appraisals of the same action and the resulting omissions of duty, are at loggerheads and are embarrassing, nay, shameful for the narrator. They highlight conflicting selves. The narrative voice cracks and turns falsetto, creating a jarring dissonance as it speaks in turn for one and then for the other. The empathetic reader who formerly identified with Rousseau feels embarrassed by his equivocations and lies, ashamed for his actions.

But a different reading may take us on the path that Rousseau himself points to. Earlier on, he complains about an inability: "I do not know how to see what is before my eyes [...] I have neither feeling nor understanding for anything that is said or done or that happens before my eyes. All that strikes me is the external manifestation." And then he remarks, as if by compensation, on an ability that is especially valuable for an autobiographer:

22 Ibid., p. 333.
23 Ibid.
24 Ibid., p. 549.

> I can only see clearly in retrospect, it is only in my memories that my mind can work [...]. Afterwards it all comes back to me; I remember the place and the time, the tone of voice, the look, the gesture, the situation; nothing escapes me. From what a man has done or said I can read his thoughts, and I am rarely mistaken.[25]

This serves as a clue for how to look at Rousseau's giving up his children: he did not fully appreciate what he was doing, he did not see (the significance of) what was right in front of his eyes. It was only in retrospect that he would recreate the surroundings of the abandonment, the feelings of remorse, and the real implications and understanding of the disposal. The inexcusable neglect of duty sinks in only later, followed by embarrassment and shame.

These are sad passages, perhaps the saddest, in Rousseau's *Confessions*. They make one cry out with Wittgenstein: "God grant the philosopher insight into what lies in front of everyone's eyes!"[26] What is right in front of our eyes, right before Rousseau's eyes as narrator, as we read these episodes? If we use the clues he gives us, Rousseau had neither feeling nor understanding of what he did at the time he abandoned his children. He "thought of himself as acting as a citizen and a father, and a member of Plato's Republic."[27] Granted Rousseau's views on the state and social institutions and the education of children, how could Rousseau hand over his children with such calm? At one point, he says: "More than once then the regret in my heart told me that I was wrong. But far from my reason having told me the same story."[28]

Oh, usually Rousseau is moved to action by feeling, but now "Reason" is brought in! So, what blindsided him and also enabled him to rationalize his actions and thus deceive himself is a philosophical theory he finds in Book five of Plato's *Republic*. There Plato argues that children produced at guardian mating festivals are to be taken from their mothers, reared together with other children and "held in common." Hence, they would regard each of the guardians as their father or mother and each other as brothers and sisters. Plato's ultimate goal in all this is to promote unity in the state and avoid dissension between the state and individual families.[29] Such is the rationale—"the good and sensible arrangement"—that Rousseau pretends to in giving

25 Ibid., p. 114.

26 Ludwig Wittgenstein, *Culture and Value*, edited by G.H. von Wright, translated by Peter Winch, Blackwell, Oxford, 1994, p. 72e.

27 Rousseau, *The Confessions*, p. 333.

28 Ibid.

29 Plato, *The Republic*, Book V, 457d–464e.

up his children and whereby he becomes a responsible citizen and father and a "member of Plato's Republic."

Nevertheless, he insists that he—Jean-Jacques—was the best of men and was never without the feelings of a natural father, thereby acknowledging an inner conflict that, as we have seen, he tries to resolve by an appeal to Plato's theory in the *Republic* about the upbringing of children. As both Wittgenstein and Nietzsche remind us, in such matters the appeal to theory is often a form of distraction from and lack of loyalty to one's moral values and principles.

> Is it possible that all these gentle feelings can ever dwell in the same soul along with depravity which quite unscrupulously tramples the dearest of obligations under foot? No, I feel and boldly declare—it is impossible. Never for a moment in his life could Jean-Jacques have been a man without feelings or compassion, an unnatural father.[30]

The thirst for rationality, for self-justification, becomes a major source of lies. The conflicted, embarrassed narrator disavows the accusation, yet it is he who thus and with good reason accuses himself. Having unwittingly, albeit successfully, splintered the autobiographical self, Rousseau succumbs to trying to do the impossible: glue the bits together with self-deception. As he argues and rationalizes to and fro, one can sense the narrator's embarrassment and shame as he hides and reveals himself in twists and turns. Such are the ways of disfiguring the self.

Self-Understanding: Reading Ourselves

As we reread our reading, perhaps misreading, of Rousseau, we are embarrassed by its occasional lack of charity. In a moment of ambivalence, we recall the following words of Wittgenstein:

> Someone who in this way opens his heart to God in remorseful confession opens it for others too. He thereby loses his dignity as someone special & so becomes like a child. This means without office, dignity & aloofness from others. You can open yourself to others only out of a particular kind of love. Which acknowledges as it were that we are all wicked children.[31]

30 Rousseau, *The Confessions*, p. 333.
31 Wittgenstein, *Culture and Value*, p. 52e.

This suggests that autobiographical literature hovers between the private and the public; that it is like a face, the best picture of an individual human soul. And this is the spirit in which Rousseau gives us his *Confessions*:

> My purpose is to display to my kind a portrait in every way true to human nature, and the man I shall portray will be myself. Simply myself. I know my own heart and understand my fellow man. But I am made unlike any one I have ever met; I will even venture to say I am like no one in the whole world. I may be no better, but at least I am different. Whether nature did well or ill in breaking the mold in which she formed me, is a question that can only be resolved after reading this book.[32]

Rousseau's private soliloquies are given public expression and thereby he becomes his book: "I shall come forward with this work in my hand, to present myself before my Sovereign Judge."[33] In doing so, he aims to cast away his roles, rid himself of his masks, and present himself as he is: a fragment of nature.

We already mentioned one embarrassment, one impediment that we stumble over when we read Rousseau: his invidious, competitive, and comparative attitude echoing throughout his book: "I am as good as you are if not better." D'accord Rousseau! But this is expressive neither of love nor of affectionate intimacy. It is a kind of sibling rivalry. Such ambition, such competition, is dangerous in the moral life. In autobiographical writing, like in philosophy, "the winner of the race is the one who can run most slowly. Or: the one who gets to the winning post last."[34]

Auden told us that a real book reads us. As we read Rousseau's *Confessions*, we have been reading ourselves too. So not only does an autobiography lay the writer's heart open to the reader, but the reader's heart itself opens up to be read. Rather than being competitive, perhaps Rousseau is shunting his embarrassment and inviting his reader to read himself and "to let each one of them reveal his heart at the foot of thy throne."

Rousseau ends his *Confessions* by reading them to Mme d'Egmont and her friends. As he considers himself in isolation at what is really a public reading, Rousseau does not seem to blush, but others blush for him. For embarrassment ensues and catches on, and, as Erving Goffman observes, "it is contagious,

32 Rousseau, *The Confessions*, p. 17.
33 Ibid.
34 Wittgenstein, *Culture and Value*, p. 40e.

spreading, once started, in ever widening circles of discomfiture."[35] Goffman also appreciates that "when an individual finds himself in a situation that ought to make him blush, others present will blush with him and for him."[36] These implied imaginative identifications constitute a community of readers and writers and force us to realize that to consider a person in isolation we must be regarding him as one of us. This paradox is especially compelling when we consider ourselves as autobiographers in isolation. Here one must think of oneself as situated in a community of readers. Even though Rousseau has the scarcity of uniqueness, he can appreciate this only within the context of a community of readers where contrasts and comparisons are available as resources.

Again, as we read autobiographical literature, we read ourselves. As we feel that we intrude on private scenes of other lives, these books invade our own. As embarrassment ensues, tying the reader to the writer in an awkward embrace, the work of literary art, with its style, grace, composure, or directness, enables us to accept and celebrate each individual life. In autobiographical literature, we come across "the fairest virtue of the thinker: the generosity with which as a man of knowledge he intrepidly, often with embarrassment, often with mockery and smiling, offers himself and his life as a sacrifice"[37] or rather as an instance of what it is to be human.

Up on the barren heights of cleverness we found ourselves suffocating, out of our *milieu*, out of our atmosphere. So, we went into the green valleys of silliness and found ourselves at home.

Scapegoating: The *Confessions* as Political Philosophy

In reading Rousseau, we adopted the principle of charity of interpretation, since it strikes us as the best way to understand a person, an autobiography or the meaning of what a person says. This does not mean, however, that we do not have serious reservations about Rousseau's character or objections to his philosophy—both of which are at times acutely embarrassing. So now we put our objections right up front. Some of these objections are philosophical; others are telling *ad hominems.*[38]

35 Erving Goffman, "Embarrassment and Social Organization," in *"Interaction Ritual" Essays in Face to Face Behaviour*, Aldine Publishing, Chicago, p. 106.

36 Ibid., pp. 99–100.

37 Friedrich Nietzsche, *Daybreak*, Cambridge University Press, Cambridge, 1982, p. 192.

38 In doing this, we are mindful of the vast literature on Rousseau and aim at highlighting objections that are interesting and directly relevant to our brief, without being shopworn.

There is a sense, we argued, in which it is right and illuminating to say that Rousseau is interested in self-knowledge and self-understanding. However, the *Confessions* is not simply an exercise in Socratic self-discovery but equally an attempt at self-redemption. By portraying himself as a victim of his social circumstances, Rousseau blames others for all his misdemeanors, embarrassment, shame, and consequent suffering. So, there is a sense in which the *Confessions* is meant to show others that they are as miserable, conflicted, corrupt, and unhappy as Rousseau is, and most importantly, why this is so. His theory of the pure, natural self, its corruption by society, and the path to its redemption are his main philosophical objectives.

Rousseau aims to reveal human nature through revealing himself. What makes him exceptional is that he has identified the cause of dishonesty, deceit, corruption, and their effects of embarrassment and shame. The philosophical point of his telling of his "confessions" is the indictment of an alienating society. He is exceptional because, despite the obstacles, he figured out why life in such a society is impossible without conflict, corruption, dishonesty, and hypocrisy, thus embarrassment and shame, and he rose above those constraints to show the rest of us the way out.

Is it not characteristic of Rousseau to think of himself as an innocent victim through all of his outrageous escapades? The "dreadful Other" made him do it. He is able to be so candid because he believes that he is a victim of society and of himself, insofar as he is a product of a society that requires him to lie, deceive, engage in corrupt practices, and so on. He is corrupt but blameless because society and others made him that way. We might call the *Confessions* "Indictments and Extenuations," for this title throws light on what Rousseau is really doing aside from his project of self-discovery and self-understanding.

"Extenuations" implies not only that they exist, but what they are, yet Rousseau does not tell us. Let us spell them out. He is embarrassed, ashamed, and so on, in the stories he recounts—indeed, the point of the telling is to show the reader how much this victim of socialization suffers. Just look at the lengths to which he must go to save face. Jean-Jacques, the protagonist of the *Confessions*, is embarrassed, ashamed, humiliated, ridiculous, and so on. Indeed, the point of telling his story is to convey to the reader what a miserable character he is and how he suffered—a victim of socialization. Look at the desperate lengths he goes to try to preserve some esteem—the thing he values most—from harm caused by the traps being sprung on his naïve, natural self.

The exception to this is the sad episode of giving away his children. He is not the least embarrassed about telling of any other event in the *Confessions*. But here he is acutely embarrassed about it. Why is this so? If one of the central points of the *Confessions* is to indict society and its institutions for the trouble they have caused Rousseau, then the episode of disposing of his children is the one case where he cannot shift the blame to others for his actions for which he alone is to blame (although he tries when he says "Philosophy (Plato) made me do it"). He owns it. Ironically, the very possibility of "doing his duty as a citizen of Plato's Republic"—as he rationalizes the disposal—presupposes a charitable institution—the orphanage—which he wants to eliminate.

But Jean-Jacques the author is unembarrassed and unashamed. He is eager to tell us all about these embarrassments and humiliations and so on, because they serve his purpose: to show the reader how a basically good, if foolish, young man is caused to do wrong and to suffer because of "you" and "your rules and social conventions" and so on. The latter distort and corrupt Rousseau's otherwise wonderful, natural self! Notice how gratified Jean-Jacques the author was that Countess d'Egmont was so upset and agitated by his telling. Is his purpose not as much to blame and upset as to exact a measure of revenge or, as he thinks of it, retributive justice?

So, in Rousseau's *Confessions*, autobiography and philosophy are intimately related. The *Confessions* embodies his political/social philosophy: he thinks he gives us a proper account of human nature and tells the story of everyman. And everyman, forced to live in an unnatural society, is therefore wretched. We are naturally autonomous creatures forced to live unnatural lives among governing artifacts whose rules inhibit, embarrass, and corrupt, even thwart agency. Rousseau has risen above all this, triumphant for having identified the source of misconduct, pain, and suffering. The natural life, absent from all these unnatural conventions, is the one he recommends.

What would such a "nature-life" look like? Would there be language? What would become of thought? Could there be conversation? Rousseau could not confess without the rules and conventions—the social institution—of language and conversation that he despises. What about creativity and art? How impoverished would this sort of life be? It does not occur to him that the things he loves—literature, music, language itself, including confession and indictment—would be impossible without the structures, rules, and conventions of society, which the misguided mistake for limitations rather than enrichments. Rousseau has become an enemy of himself—an autoimmune disease.

In the clash of these social artifacts, agency, expression, consideration of others, and so on, are thwarted. Rather than enabling our practices, these artifices, Rousseau believes, make an honest individual and a genuine social life impossible. Far from making conversation possible, these artifacts thwart it. No wonder then that some in the audience at Rousseau's reading might have understood them as indictments, and rather than being embarrassed, took umbrage at it, and gave him a cold reception. Rousseau opposes embarrassment; in fact, he is a banner-carrier for the abolition of embarrassment, yet he embarrasses his audience for "their own good," and for the good of their society, so that they will see what their society has done to him and them. He portrays himself as a Christlike figure who sacrifices himself for the interest of others.

But back to our main concern. We should expect Rousseau, having confessed, to apologize, to seek forgiveness. Instead, he is triumphant. But over what? What advantage has he gained from the telling? The advantage, we suggested earlier, of having reduced his audience to embarrassment and shame. But for what? We argued that his purpose is not only to confess but also to indict, embarrass, and shame his audience. He wants to use the story of his own life to identify what causes the distortions of the self. The cause is society, with its unnatural rules and conventions. Along the way, he lays the blame at society's door and embarrasses and shames his audience for the roles they have played in his torment. They and their society, not Rousseau, are guilty and cause all his and other people's suffering. He is everyman, yet "better" than the rest only for his having discovered the source of distortion and corruption of the individual insofar that he is forced to live an unnatural life in societies. He is forced to live as one artifact among a host of others. Rousseau's *Confessions*, the story of his life, is supposed to provide clinching existential evidence for this thesis.

The account of his treatment of his children sheds light on his final remarks upon the public reading of his *Confessions*. There, rather than the contrition one might expect of a penitent, we instead find Rousseau triumphant. His intention, he reminds us, is to confess but not to apologize, since to do so would be self-defeating, not triumphant. He is triumphant because finally he gets revenge: he paid society back for all the injuries and miseries its rules and conventions caused. Society has forced him to be an "unnatural father," and, despite his protestations, he realizes that his actions reveal either that he was without the natural feelings of affection that bind a father to his children or that he was in deep self-deception about this and used Plato to rationalize his behavior. "J'accuse."

So, Rousseau's philosophy, of which the *Confessions* is an autobiographical embodiment, may seem adolescent—conceived by an intellectual and emotional adolescent and especially attractive to them. For doesn't the adolescent complain: Why are there so many rules? Why do you oppress me with your rules? This tendency to lash out and scapegoat is a salient feature of adolescence. There are others: the tendency to be so impressed by one's newfound attitudes or intellectual capacities that one tends to dismiss, without due care, old ideas and ways of life that form the tradition; that one could easily think up new and improved ways of getting on; the inclination to be blind to the fact that one's thoughts and capacities are built upon and made possible by all that has come before; that we need to start with a fresh slate, a *tabula* rasa, to improve things. Rousseau on the social-political front, like Descartes on the epistemological front, wants to start all over again with a fresh slate, on ground zero. As if that were possible or desirable. The fact that a belief or a practice can be criticized only in light of other beliefs or practices does not occur to them; or if it does, it is not taken seriously enough. This is a major embarrassment for modern epistemology and political philosophy.

There is something of the "*enfant* terrible" about Rousseau. The seeming innocence, the desire to return to nature—or if that is not possible—to start society anew from the bottom up—the insistence that the very essence of a human being consists in absolute freedom. The only truly human life is one of pure, absolute, unfettered freedom: free choice, intention, and action. The child is an incompatibilist on the question of free will. This is the charming, ingenuous "*enfant*," the attractive Rousseau, champion of individual freedom. We say with naïve admiration, there is something right about what this precocious child is saying. The child's dream initially appeals to us, and we forget about context, conventions and rules, out of which freedom grows.

The Problem of the Person in Society

Rousseau's problem of the person in society is born of the contrasts between his conception of persons and the nature of the societies in which they live. The essence of personhood is autonomy—rational self-governance; the ability to self-legislate. That is its essence and its excellence. And autonomy is categorical: absolute; it admits no compromise; no half measures. Persons are either utterly self-governing, or they do not live the lives of persons. Persons are thus "born free," yet everywhere they find themselves landed in societies whose rules and conventions they are obliged to obey, but which they had no hand in making. They may be free by their person-nature, yet everywhere they are embarrassed—thwarted by rules imposed upon them: born free, yet everywhere enslaved by others. The consequent torment of such an intolerable life is laid out in Rousseau's autobiography.

Rousseau's "solution" to the problem, he tells us, came in an epiphany, and he wept in gratitude for its beauty. Despite the apparent incompatibility of personhood and society, persons can live authentic lives among others if, in an act of self-recreation, they freely choose to re-conceive themselves, not as mere individuals among others but, first and foremost, as members of the self-governing group. This subsumption of their individual identity in group membership means that each citizen will abandon pursuit of his own individual self-interest, take as his single overarching goal the best interest of the group, and that he will find the means to that goal. When free, rational, self-governing citizen-legislators unite in this way and legislate on this basis, their legislation will be an expression of what Rousseau calls the "General Will."

Government according to the General Will solves the problem, Rousseau argues, since all rules arrived at in this way are rules that each citizen freely, autonomously chooses for himself. All laws that govern him, therefore, do so only because he has autonomously chosen to be bound by them. He would thus live an autonomous life by abiding by laws he has given himself. His self-recreation as a member of the group delivers him from the tyranny of others because, under such conditions, there are no others, and thus no room for the tyrant, no room for the oppressed. The individual person-citizen is preserved from tyranny by "an excessive dependence on a form of association in which each one unites with all the others and so obeys no one but himself," since "each man, giving himself to all, gives himself to nobody."[39] Thus, autonomy, the full flowering of personhood, is achieved by subsuming the individual in a collective of identically-minded others.

Rousseau's solution to the problem of the person in society requires each person-citizen to adopt the role of citizen-legislator. Each will have a single interest—the best interest of the group—and each will have an equal rational capacity to pursue that single goal. Citizens are identical in these respects. Thus, since they have the same interests and an equal means to pursue them, they will reach consensus. How could they not? For there is nothing about them that could explain disagreement. Conclusions reached under these conditions express the General Will.

Thus, by design, the demands of the General Will exclude from politics what else is true of persons, including their interests in themselves, in their well-being and that of their loved ones and friends, and the self-interested passions that can elude the rule of Reason and which can be the source of conflict and an obstacle to consensus. Those demands also exclude attributes that have been thought to be conducive to civil society, such as a sense of fairness, of reciprocity; the desire for prosperity and peace and the recognition that this requires cooperation; a sense of empathy, generosity and charity, of humility and the need for self-correction; a sense of duty, a sense of shame and embarrassment for one's wrongdoings. Thus do the demands of the General Will erase a great deal of what we recognize as characteristics of persons. It is aspects of human nature such as these that Rousseau thinks must be eliminated, or at least subdued, if self-rule and society are to be made compatible.

39 *The Social Contract*, Book I, Chapter VI.

Notice, however, that this flattening of the individual renders Rousseau's ideal person-citizen featureless but for the single goal and rationality they all share. In such a landscape, individual persons would be unrecognizable. The concept of other would have no extension. There can be no Other, nor any others, in the properly run republic. But if there are no others in the republic, there can be no politics. How embarrassing for a political theorist. His solution to the problem of politics would make persons and politics impossible.

Vis-à-vis citizens, members of Rousseau's republic are indistinguishable. By the Identity of Indiscernibles, they are one. A *polis* of one. No wonder "they," in their single-mindedness, reach the same conclusions; no wonder they must agree; no wonder rationality will be univocal. But if so, the problem of persons in society has not been solved because the absence of conflict is due to the absence of other persons. There is no plurality of views to be reckoned with because there is no plurality of persons to have them. Rousseau's epiphany regarding the General Will only "solves" the problem by so re-conceiving person-citizens and their societies that the problem cannot arise. Rousseau's solution to the problem of persons in society is to get rid of persons. And that gets rid of society. How embarrassing.

At least, that is how things would be in the ideal Rousseauean republic. In real, less-ideal societies, there will be real people who persist in thinking of themselves as individual persons rather than as the abstraction required by the General Will and who will therefore dissent from the consensus. These disagreements, and what would be understood as the *mauvaise foi* from which they issue, will make others of them—a mark of bad citizenship, of non-membership, a form of self-exile.[40] Here, now, is the room for politics, in the space between the polis of one—the consensus—and the backsliding other. And Rousseau assures us the politics here will be brutal. His solution to this inevitability is to argue that the just way to deal with dissenters is to coerce or compel them to abide by expressions of the General Will; to force it upon them. Since the General Will is what all free and rational citizens voluntarily believe, to compel others to comply with it is to save them from themselves, from their recalcitrant human nature, from the folly of their individualism. They will be "forced to be free." What can this mean? Not that they will be made literally free, but that they will be forced to abide by laws they did not choose but which, they will be assured, they would have chosen had they complied with the demands of the General Will, given up their individuality

40 See the section on Rousseau's *Reveries.*

and adopted the abstraction of personhood the General Will demands. This is Rousseau's argument for the justification of tyranny.[41]

But if tyranny is justified, then isn't submission to tyranny also justified, and resistance to tyranny unjustified? A double absurdity, it would seem, from this champion of the individual and one of the main thinkers of the French Revolution. Happily for the cause of value in the individual, Rousseau was not its only advocate:

> If citizens are commanded to join in a war, as often happens, if they are quite clear that the war is unlawful, they ought to abstain. That God is to be obeyed rather than men, not only the Apostles have said, but Socrates also; and the masters among the Hebrews have a saying indicating that even the king, if he commands anything against the law of God, is not to be obeyed.[42]

Rousseau's approach to the political problem is unlike traditional approaches that start with acknowledging the competing claims of individuals and the social/political authority and then negotiating in the space between them for a reconciliation. In Rousseau, the two principles are reduced to one: the General Will. By design, expressions of the General Will are always right, but not because they are wise, or prudent or fair compromise among competing views. They are right because they are freely chosen by single-minded autonomous person-citizens. In Rousseau's scheme, there is no room for compromise because compromise is inconsistent with the categorical nature of autonomy. The Enlightenment conception of the rational, independent self-governing person is gone, traded for an opaque abstraction—the voice of the General Will. What is left of the individual is a thinned-out conception of identically minded citizens who, given the restrictions imposed by the General Will, have lost their individuality. Not surprisingly, since they were designed to guarantee agreement. What Rousseau thought was the full flowering of personhood is the end of the person.

In short, Rousseau's solution to the conflict between two things—person and society—is to demand that one of those things—persons—re-conceive themselves so as to dissolve the conflict. But doing so erases persons and society, the other term of the relation.

---

41 See Isaiah Berlin, "Freedom and Its Betrayal: Jean-Jacques Rousseau," https://podcasts.ox.ac.uk/freedom-and-its-betrayal-jean-jacques-rousseau-1952.

42 Hugo Grotius, *The Rights of War and Peace*, 1625, as quoted by Daniel B. Klein, "When Dictats and Conscience Conflict," *American Institute for Economic Research*, September 21, 2021.

What is the psychology of Rousseau's politics? The psychology of the members of the ideal community is limited to rationality and a single goal: the overall best interests of the group. Should the psychology of actual human beings erupt, the utopian calm of consensus would be destroyed. Thus, the psychology of persons is the enemy of politics and must be suppressed. That is a job for the General Will.

Rousseau thinks persons are unsuited for living together in communities and are therefore unsuited for politics. His solution is to eliminate the problem—individuals and their troublesome, non-ideal nature—and to locate political authority in an abstraction, in the ideal member and the General Will. That ideal is the authority for the rules that make the social life of the ideal republic possible. It is separate from its subjects, and it is unimpeachable. Why? Because, Rousseau argues, it is the law citizens would give themselves were they sufficiently enlightened. But this authority has at best an imaginary relation to actual citizens. It is an abstraction of themselves and has little to nothing to do with their identity. There are no persons among the rule-makers. Persons, with their troublesome personal loyalties and human psychology, are expressly forbidden. The authority is said to be pure Reason, and so unimpeachable. And at the same time, it is said to be personal, and therefore incapable of tyranny.

But how could that be? The rules cannot be made by actual citizens, since their natures would prevent consensus. So, the rule-makers are relegated to a realm beyond the reach of individuals. In what sense, then, are subjects self-governed? You'd need to hold that rationality is the single essential feature of persons, while their identity—their nature and interests—are foreign to them—not really their own. Personal identity would be alien; something to be overcome, subdued, defeated. This is not a politics for persons.[43] It is absurd and embarrassing to suggest, never mind to argue, that the solution to the problem of persons in society is to lead the mind away from personhood.

Rousseau, we have claimed, thinks that persons are unsuited to politics. They must be replaced by an abstract object—a reasoning machine whose identity is exhausted by its membership in the group—designed to produce conformity. The clever move is to assure the reader that this homunculus is in each of us, our essence—it's the real person—and that it should decide all political matters. And would do if only we would get out of our own way; if only we could see past the limitations of our individual identity.

43 Rousseau does for politics what Descartes did for epistemology. Descartes argued that the first step in epistemology is to lead the mind away from the unreliable senses. Rousseau argues that the way to do politics is to do away with unreliable others.

The General Will would not be a politics by or for persons. It would be by and for an abstraction of persons. It would be an attractive arrangement for those who think their superior intellects and character should qualify them as the mouthpiece of the General Will, the deciders of all things political. Philosopher-kings, say.

Kant and Rousseau

If these objections are even partly true of Rousseau, one might wonder why is he held in such high esteem in the history of social and political philosophy. Why, for example, did such a master philosopher as Immanuel Kant have Rousseau's portrait in his office and express admiration for him?

It is well known that Rousseau was "the philosopher of the revolution" who anticipated and articulated the motivational ideals of *liberté, égalité, fraternité* that guided it. He not only exposed the masks we wear in our social and commercial transactions and thus uncovered what lay beneath those masks, but, early on, he espoused the ideals of freedom understood as the right not to be constrained by the will of another and of egalitarianism understood as each individual having equal moral worth. It is hard to deny that these are significant achievements which informed the politics of the Enlightenment and the French Revolution. But lest we forget, Rousseau's utopianism also laid the foundations of the French Revolution's reign of terror and the horrors of twentieth-century totalitarianism. Recall "forced to be free."

What would Kant, who found violent revolutions repugnant, yet sometimes admired the ends they aimed at, take away from this? What did he learn from Rousseau at a deeper level? Consider these remarks:

> By inclination, I am an enquirer. I feel a consuming thirst for knowledge which goes with the desire to progress in it, and satisfaction in every advance in it. There was a time when I believed this constituted the honor of humanity, and I despised the people who know nothing.[44]

Enter Rousseau:

> Rousseau corrected me in this. This blind prejudice disappeared, and I learned to honor man. I would find myself more than useless [...] if I

44 Quoted on p. 165, footnote 4, of Louis White Beck, *A Commentary on Kant's Critique of Practical Reason,* University of Chicago Press, Chicago, 1960. The original source is Immanuel Kant, *Notes and Fragments,* edited by Paul Guyer, translated by Curtis Bowman, Paul Guyer, and Frederick Rauscher, Cambridge University Press, Cambridge, 2010, p. 7.

> did not believe that this attitude of mine as an inquirer can give worth to all others in establishing the rights of men.[45]

Kant came to understand that what was respectable in man was personhood, which all men shared equally, irrespective of their circumstances and their achievements. Personhood, he realized, was the equal and universal basis of respect. It follows that respect is due to all men irrespective of any irrelevancies, such as social status, class, achievements, and so forth. This may strike us today as a moral truism, and it is impossible to appreciate it as a deep insight unless we take into account the social and political context of Rousseau's time. Radical and large-scale structural inequalities between people were a baked-in feature of the feudal political fabric. Under the feudal order current at the time, personhood was enjoyed only by those of certain classes—only by nobles, priests, the aristocracy, men, and so on. What Rousseau showed Kant was that personhood is the universal defining attribute of all persons that admits each of them to the moral universe and makes them, at least to that extent, respectable, irrespective of what else may be true of them.

In Kant's terms, the essence of personhood is rational autonomy. That is the basis of respect. It requires that all persons be treated as self-governing ends, not merely as means to another's ends, since each person is an equally self-legislating member of the kingdom of ends. And each is capable of a good will, the only thing in the world that is good in itself. What does this fundamental insight mean once stripped of its opacity? Kant articulates and unpacks Rousseau's insight in terms of a practical principle for acting, directed to each agent as an individual. Suppose I reject this first-person guide for action. Then I tacitly agree that others may treat me as a mere means to their aims and goals. That is to say, I tacitly endorse my own exploitation as a mere device for facilitating the greater good of society. This is tantamount to moral suicide.

A second way to articulate the depth of the Rousseau–Kant insight is by attending to our moral phenomenology—to the reactive attitudes and feelings that we in general have. Consider our interactions and transactions with one another. It is natural for individuals to resent being used as a means to another's ends—to resent being deceived, betrayed, or held as a hostage and used as a bargaining chip. This sort of thing gets our back up. So, Rousseau's and Kant's views comport with what we think about ourselves from the first-person point of view. We apprehend ourselves this way and so can't help but think of ourselves as mistreated when used by others as a mere means to their ends. And we recognize that others apprehend themselves in just this way.

45 Ibid.

Rousseau's and Kant's view of persons as having unconditional value resonates with each of us. It is the modern conception of persons that emerged during the Enlightenment thanks to Grotius, Descartes, Locke, Hume, Rousseau, and Kant, among others. Did these philosophers invent this conception? Or is it a case of philosophical theorists catching up to the rest of us who understood this even if we may not have articulated it? Thus, the periodic rebellions and revolutions in the historical record were motivated by resentment and the sense of injustice of the social hierarchy. We are inclined to think that this conception of persons was emergent in human consciousness all along and that philosophers articulated and deepened it and spelled out its implications for society and politics. Rather than being a philosophical construction *de novo*, it is presupposed by our ordinary moral consciousness and would have been recognized by the man in the street as a description of himself. If not, Socrates would have been able to drag it out of him with his question-and-answer method of philosophical conversation.

This explains why it is natural for individuals to resent being used as mere means to another's ends. That idea and its implications for the improvement of our personal and public lives, our societal institutions and practices, would have been so compelling that it demanded his allegiance—he would have thought it and its implications worth dying for. See the revolutions and transformations that followed. The idea would have been a very powerful glue that bound like-minded people together.

So, Kant recognized Rousseau's insight that persons have unconditional value beyond their epistemic capacities. As such, societies should respect that value, aspire to it, act, and govern themselves accordingly. Thus, for societies to govern themselves justly, they must place that understanding at the bottom of their governance.

Rousseau's *Reveries*: The Problem of the Person in Self-Exile

We have seen that Rousseau's salient concern was to preserve his self-esteem and therefore to avoid adverse judgments and the emotions they engender—embarrassment, shame, and humiliation. Self-esteem, he thought, flows from living an autonomous life, where that is understood as the unfettered ability to give laws to oneself.[46] Now embarrassment is conceptually tied to "otherness"—internally related, one might say, to societal norms by which one is

46 Or perhaps misunderstood, as we shall argue below.

assessed and sometimes found wanting.[47] The embarrassed may try to mitigate its effects by justifying or rationalizing their conduct. But those are half measures, at best, and they're levied after the fact. Better to prevent it, but how?

Rousseau offers two ways: by reforming society so that embarrassment need not arise, and by eschewing society altogether and living a life of solitude. As to the first: In a perfect society governed by unanimous expressions of the General Will, there is no cause for embarrassment, since there is neither room for error nor impediments to citizens' autonomy. Hence nothing to be or feel embarrassed about.[48] In Rousseau's utopian society of *liberté*, égalité, et fraternité, with citizens "freely" choosing the General Will, there can be no embarrassment. The very idea of difference, of dissent from the General Will, the supreme source of social embarrassment, is made impossible. In arguing for this utopia, Rousseau incurred untold—that is, amply told—suffering at the hands of his fellow men. Why? Just because he showed them a perfect civil society from which otherness has been removed, where they could live better, if not perfect lives.

The second way to elude embarrassment is to retreat: to withdraw from society—his *bête noire*—to a life of solitude. This is the path that Rousseau embarks on later in life. After being "persecuted" by communities and countries, he retired to Saint-Pierre Island near Neuchâtel in order to live in relative isolation, avoiding society's disapproving eyes. No society, no others, no embarrassment; peace of mind was the hope. What is more, solitude would offer space and time for re-examining one's present self, which would no longer be a self caught up in the social and distorting games of invidious comparisons and ressentiment. The suggestion is that once alone, the real self, unadulterated, would be free to emerge. Thus, he would devote himself to a life of solitude: to walks, to the study of botany, and to write *The Reveries of the Solitary Walker*. His *Reveries*, not written for publication, were intended to be read by him alone—for his own joy.

Rousseau, as he relates it, lives a Robinson Crusoe-like existence on Saint-Pierre. This exile, once externally imposed by the authorities, is now chosen as a liberation strategy, and includes liberation from the constraints of Reason, argument and justification, and their rhetorical devices. Since he no longer has an audience, he has no need to argue, convince, rationalize, or

47 *Other* comprises others, norms, judgment, criticism.

48 "And nothing to get hung about. Strawberry Fields forever."

justify, nor to accuse, blame, embarrass, and shame others.[49] Nor can others inflict these devices on him and intrude on his person. And if they do, he is free to be indifferent to them. His former self, Rousseau says, was completely other-oriented, since he wrote out of a sense of obligation to others, to right what he considered wrong. This necessarily involved the Other, including the authorities, since he engaged in public disputes and quarrels in the intellectual life of the salons and on the world stage through his publications. The business of Reason—thinking, arguing, the practice of criticism—were, he felt, just so many onerous duties weighing upon him like heavy metal, someone else's excess baggage which he was at liberty to cast off and be the better for it. Now, in his solitude, he is at peace, joyfully exploring his feelings, sentiments, and reveries, taking pleasure in his independence from society, his walks in nature, and calming botanical studies.

What enabled Rousseau to live such a private life? What impediments and constraints had to be removed from his life? And did such deprivations spare him from embarrassment? There are three layers of protection of Rousseau's privacy. First, he was no longer poor and so no longer subject to the embarrassments of poverty that had tormented him. It was not easy on one's self-esteem to appear like a beggar and ask for financial support from wealthy aristocrats and the well-to-do. On the other hand, however, such a life of relative comfort may confront him with fresh reasons for embarrassment, such as his riches and the guilt that goes with it. If, as he professes, he remains compassionate in isolation, embarrassment may return to haunt him in the privy.

The second layer of insulation was geography. The island itself, no doubt, cut Rousseau off from the busy outside world and enabled him to control the extent and duration of his social contacts. It is worth mentioning in this regard that Rousseau exaggerates his solitude. He was no Robinson Crusoe. There were people around him, including his wife Thérèse, the custodians, occasional visitors, and others to whom he could communicate. Moreover, it was left up to him when, with whom, and how long he would have social intercourse. Should he not be embarrassed when his own description of exile omits the very people who make his alleged solitary existence possible? Embarrassment, not so easily eluded, should haunt him still.

The third layer of insulation was his conception of himself as a philosopher: a detached, disinterested, distant figure, transcending space and time and mundane human interests, seeing the world under the aspect of eternity,

49 Does he abandon this much of morality? In this connection see the embarrassment of riches point, below. Is he beyond such considerations, now that he is in exile? No others, no morality?

from a godlike point of view, a view from nowhere in particular. Rousseau regarded himself as a citizen of no country—ultimately, he disavowed even Geneva—but a citizen of an imagined republic of perfect beings—a republic whose members were reduced to points of comparison with citizens of actual republics; otherworldly citizens of a perfect Platonic Republic toward which actual republics should veer. Such a "wise person" is idle and useless, he says, but harmless.

Is this not a familiar though embarrassing picture of a philosopher? A far out-and-away figure, an outsider who does not share the norms of any community, with whom citizens cannot find common ground to start a conversation, or regret it should they succeed?

As if this were not embarrassment enough, has Rousseau not forgotten about the possibility of retrospective embarrassment and self-embarrassment, where there is no audience except the self? Contradictions abound in the *Reveries* as Rousseau disavows some of the foundational principles of his perspective. When he says that "Man was made for society" and that he himself was the most sociable of men, he contradicts his earlier analysis of natural man's aversion to society, precisely because society constrains and corrupts him. Here he is in his "Sixth Walk":

> The conclusion I can draw from all these reflections is that I have never been truly suited for civil society where everything is annoyance, obligation and duty and that my independent natural temperament always made me incapable of the subjection necessary to anyone who wants to live among men.[50]

Furthermore, the remark made to M. Malesherbes—"I need a friend suited to my heart"—belies his proclamation that he is indifferent to human society and resigned to his solitary way of life. Again, "I have said that the idleness of social gatherings made them unbearable for me and here I am seeking solitude solely to give myself up to idleness." In a moment of self-awareness, Rousseau recognizes his blatant self-contradictions and admits that "I am a walking paradox," blaming human nature for having made him so! "That is the way I am, it is due to nature and not to me."[51] These examples show that Rousseau in solitude was capable of momentary private embarrassments, yet

50 *The Reveries of the Solitary Walker*, English translation with Interpretive Essay by Charles E. Butterworth, Hackett, Indianapolis, 1992, p. 83. An excellent translation with an illuminating interpretive essay to which we are indebted.

51 *Confessions*, Book 12, p. 591. As though his human nature were no part of him, but something alien to which he is attached he knows not how.

when they occur, he conveniently explains them away as due to things being at odds, not he. A form of conscious self-deception? Again, even in the solitude of his *Reveries*, Rousseau remains embarrassable.

Now a question arises: After his renunciation of society, does he still have the resources he needs to pursue his various goals? A number of contrasts come into view between the Rousseau of the *Confessions* and the Rousseau of the *Reveries*. In the *Confessions*, Rousseau was a social being enmeshed in society, marshaling the devices of Reason and persuasion to communicate with and to others. He wrote for others, and this presupposes a concern with others. He has an audience and thus an uptake for illocutionary and perlocutionary acts. In the *Reveries*, on the other hand, he ceases to interest himself in others and is solely self-concerned. Others, whether these be his contemporaries or future generations, "are non-entities," "mean nothing to me," and "everything external is foreign to me. I no longer have neighbours, fellow creatures or brothers in this world." If so, he cannot write for them. Since he is "unperturbed" by others and external things, he is "like God himself."[52]

"I write my reveries," he says, "only for myself."[53] In true Cartesian style, Rousseau the solipsist regards even his body as external to him and thus a possible source of embarrassment. "My body is no longer anything to me but an encumbrance and obstacle, and I disengage myself from it as much as I can." Then he asks the Cartesian question: "But I, detached from them and from everything, what am I? That is what remains for me to seek."[54]

How should we characterize Rousseau's *Reveries*? Despite his statement that they are meant for him alone, are they not communications, nevertheless? Normally when we speak, we communicate and express ourselves through gesture and language to others. But are language and gesture not social institutions, governed by social conventions? What is more, communication presupposes care. Isn't "Who cares" one way to dismiss another or indicate that we do not wish to hear what is being said? A cessation of communication. If Rousseau neither cares for, nor has any interest in, others, is communication not thwarted and embarrassed? Moreover, if he writes, as he says, only for himself, since he cares only for himself, mustn't he be able to understand himself from one moment to the next? Surely that requires rules that he must follow. He is left with fleeting, chaotic impressions, in no order or sequence, without cause or effect. In such circumstances the question "What am I, if anything?" is up in the air, as is the question of communication.

---

52 Rousseau, *The Reveries of the Solitary Walker*, p. 5.

53 Ibid., "First Walk," p. 7.

54 Ibid.

What gives stability to the meaning of Rousseau's words and locutions? How can he overcome "the private language problem," a language that only he understands fully?[55]

Yet it might be asked whether Rousseau is up to something other than the language games of information, description, and so on, which are bound by conventions and rules? Perhaps he thinks of his daydreaming as a form of therapy, like meditation, where the practice is meant to clear his mind, calm himself, regain some of that calm sunshine of the mind; then, contrary to what he says, he is not eschewing rationality. Or perhaps he is trying to come up with or reinvent a form of writing appropriate to Hume's skeptical conception of the self as a bundle of perceptions, seen by the later Hume as a reduction? Perhaps the late Rousseau, writing in late style—the style of an elder preparing for death—is a forerunner of "stream of consciousness" writing: a writing of chimeras that we experience in a half awake, half asleep state; a form of writing without structure, logos, method or system, truly a winged creature, unanchored to the world, that attempts to break out of social conventions and rules, that attempts to break onto the other side, expressive of our desire for transcendence? Such a desire may be admirable, and it is a human tendency we would not want for our lives to disrespect; yet it is an exercise in futility. The political philosophy runs along the same lines.

Rousseau is convinced that living among others is incompatible with a life worthy of a person: an autonomous, self-directed, self-creating life, free of the fetters imposed by others. His remedy is a life of self-exile. But fetters come in more forms than the social. There are the laws of thought—of Reason and argument, laws of consistency and non-contradiction. And these rules are non-permissive. There are the rules of language, meaning, and conversation. Moreover, because he is conscious and enjoys sensory perception, reality, that inhuman other, imposes itself upon his thoughts even against his will. Such thoughts may lead to others, such as thoughts about the qualities of his perceptions and perhaps about what their objects might be, and about what may explain them, and so on. In short, as long as he remains a conscious thinker, social exile does not deliver the freedom he seeks, since he cannot elude the human nature that he believes is foreign to and opposes him. That nature, together with his circumstances, freights his mind in ways inconsistent with his desire for maximal autonomy.[56]

55 See Ludwig Wittgenstein, *Philosophical Investigations,* translated by G.E.M. Anscombe, Blackwell Publishing, Oxford, 2001, #269–75.

56 Why didn't it occur to him that he could do with all this heteronomy what he did with social heteronomy in his solution to the person in society problem? Namely, to identify

And so, he retreats further to a life of reverie; dreams, mere fancies: wool-gathering. Is this what he had in mind for a life worthy of an autonomous man? Is this the apotheosis of a man? Moreover, the very endeavor of self-exile presupposes the fact and the use of the person-nature he relies on to make good his escape. Likewise, the endeavor of "self-seeking": How could there be any kind of inquiry if he eschews the use of our devices of inquiry?

Were Rousseau to succeed in his efforts to elude all constraints, he would cease to be the thing that he is. That would be autonomy too far. It would be, not his triumph over nature, but his demise. A fool's errand. How embarrassing. What's respectable about undoing the very thing—personhood—that he proclaims to have ultimate respect for?

We've made two sorts of criticism of Rousseau's project in exile. The first was that his solitude was not as solitary as he made out. His solitude required the concerted, cooperative efforts of a number of others to mind his worldly affairs for him, on his behalf, and in his stead,[57] working within and making use of the institutions of society so Rousseau didn't have to. Others keep house, pay the bills, run errands for him, and so on, without which there would be no solitude. It's a rather crowded solitude; a rather dependent sort of independence.

Rousseau would doubtless concede the point, and he may respond as follows: Surely, he might say, I can't achieve total solitude all at once, in one go. What I have, initially, may not be the real McCoy, but I can "see real solitude from here," on the island, admittedly with a lot of help. I could not do so were I living in society. This may be true, but it concedes the objection, for it admits that when the genuine article arrives, it will be a solitude that depends for its existence on a society of others who cooperate in ways he eschews and for his benefit. It seems that Rousseau accepts society but only on his terms.

Moreover, his response to our complaint implies that the support he gets from others is merely practical. But is it? This question leads to our second criticism of the exile project. Suppose his "checking out" required that he give someone—his wife, say, or his lawyer—power of attorney or its equivalent, to make decisions for him regarding, for example, the disposition of his property and other assets, decisions which may well include moral judgments. If this were so, he would have achieved self-exile by alienating decision-making

himself with it; to make it his own. Hey, presto! No more heteronomy.

57 When he said that man was made for society, might he have had this sort of thing in mind: that others, but not he, reach their apotheosis when they cooperate in these very useful ways? Or, that society allows the individual to elevate himself beyond mere individuality to something greater: namely, the social. And note that the story of the *Reveries* is that the individual may elevate himself beyond that, to the pure self.

powers proper to his person. He would have subjected himself to another, even if only in a limited domain, who would act, *in loco* parentis, as it were, as Rousseau's master. He would have carved off features essential to his personhood in order to achieve solitude. Had he done so, he would have traded a diminishment of his person for solitude, but a solitude of the remains of his person. This would be solitude that comes at too high a price. Rousseau has diminished and enfeebled himself. He has embarrassed himself to death.

We do not know whether such a diminishment occurred. We raise this question because we do know, from his own hand, that he was willing to give up aspects of personhood for peace of mind in solitude. His exile, he says, will allow him to think and write without the constraints imposed by the fact of others: for example, rationality, consistency, justification, relevance, clarity, and objectivity. In his reveries, he would finally be able to think and write "freely," he claims, as though thinking and writing, seeking one's real self, and freedom could survive such depredations. Moreover, his life would continue, not only unimpaired by these self-diminishments, but improved by so much freedom. However, with the loss of objectivity, his thoughts lose intentionality and meaning. He would lose the ability to distinguish his actions from things that happen to him and from events that are neither, distinctions without which he cannot understand himself as living the life of a person. He would lose the concept of responsibility. Without others, he would lose the concepts of morality. Can Rousseau survive so much "freedom"?

It is useful, we suggest, to understand Rousseau's retreat as a thought-experiment to see what the answer to that question might be. What would result were one to try to elude concepts like judgment, responsibility, praise and blame, just deserts, obligations to oneself and others, the laws of thought, language, conversation, and so on—that set of concepts which we think are inextricably bound up with personhood?[58] Indeed, his retreat is best understood as an inquiry into what becomes of the person who pursues the Cartesian conception of a person as a purely thinking thing—utterly independent, solipsistic, monadic? The method is to carve off what he thinks are merely contingent and encumbering constraints on personhood—mere accidents of personhood, along with constraints and distortions inflicted upon us by our corrupting societies—and examine the result.

Not only does the person survive the experimental abstraction, we are told, but it is improved in the bargain: no longer is he distorted by something external and foreign that imposes itself upon his person, but he is better off

58 And which include, not coincidentally, the conditions of embarrassment.

without it because now he is really free. Free to pursue the ideal of the fully autonomous creator of the self and its life.

We think we have shown that not only are these allegedly constraining elements not foreign, but their removal distorts and detaches the person from essential elements of himself and from the world he, as a person, is enmeshed in. The result—the daydreamer—looks for all the world to be enjoying a form of psychosis. His self-exile was no solution, for it left Rousseau both too dependent on others and too detached, too autonomous.

In conclusion, we submit that what Rousseau sought to elude all along, in both his personal and political philosophies, was otherness: other people, their societies, their human, as distinct from their personal, natures; even, in the end, rationality and objectivity. He would not abide what he took to be the personal insult of otherness. Nor would he abide anything by which he, as a person, could be measured: no objectivity, no ideals, no standards by which he may be judged and found wanting. This solipsism became the main, apparently more attractive part of his legacy. It has been inherited, enthusiastically, by his many "other children" of the twentieth and twenty-first centuries, who rage, now with ressentiment, against cultures, civilizations, and objectivity, for the crime of not being devoted to satisfying their every wish. It's a Rousseauean success story. From a culture of embarrassment to a culture of ressentiment. This, we suggest, is the wrong lesson to have taken from him. Instead, they might have learned that the goal of politics cannot be the self-esteem of its theorists, and that individual freedom does not require solipsism.

The capacity for embarrassment comes with rationality. It arises out of the recognition that, for finite creatures such as we, any endeavor includes the possibility of failure; that success requires that one wield one's agency-nature—one's practical reasoning—according to high epistemic and motivational standards; that one is obligated to oneself to do so, and equally obligated to those one lives with and among to measure up, to live up to one's expectations. This means that, for persons like us, embarrassment is always in the cards.

Otherness is as much a feature of personhood as rationality and freedom. Rationality and freedom are valuable to us because they allow us to cope, to navigate our personal and social lives. They allow us to solve the problems of the person living in a world. Embarrassment is a sign, to us and to others, that we are aware that we've not measured up to our own and others' standards.[59]

59 See embarrassment as an emotion of incompetence in the section titled *Effects and Strategies*, Chapter IX.

Rousseau, we are sure, was aware of this. His response was to attempt to elude embarrassment by re-conceiving personhood and its relations to others and to the world which removed the very possibility of failure and embarrassment. So liberated, Rousseau's person, having eschewed rationality and worldly purpose, was rewarded—"freed," he would say—to live the paltry life of a daydreamer. This, we submit, is an autonomy too far—the person "freed" from all the features of personhood, unhinged from itself and from reality, unable to live or otherwise act: a mere object, something that is acted upon. A pyrrhic victory. This is not the life that Kant had in mind for self-sovereign members of the Kingdom of Ends.

Chapter II

HUME'S *REDUCTIO*: THE EXAMINED LIFE IS UNLIVEABLE

Hume's Embarrassments on Behalf of Early Modern Philosophy

Recall Christopher Ricks' suggestion that embarrassment is a nineteenth-century sentiment and a narrowly English one. How could he forget the glaring counterexample of David Hume, the great Scottish philosopher of the eighteenth century? Hume's revolutionary work *A Treatise of Human Nature* surprises us by moments of philosophical embarrassment. But what has Hume to be embarrassed about?

One source of embarrassment may be that, while traditional philosophy advertised itself as a guide to wisdom and living well, what Hume's skeptical arguments against induction show is that, were we to try to live by philosophy, we could not.[1] If we have no reason to believe that water is wet and fire will burn, and that the sun will rise tomorrow, then we have no reason to believe we can act at all. Our life under philosophy would cease to be. Philosophy, he argues, fails to deliver on the goods it promises. It is false advertising. Instead of wisdom, what you get is rationalization and self-deception. This is not only ironic but acutely embarrassing for philosophy and its practitioners.

Meanwhile, our decidedly non-philosophical nature, including the derided, non-rational habits of mind such as custom and the emotions, happily persists, immune to these doubts and violating the tenets of philosophy at every turn. And despite this, we flourish. For Hume, traditional philosophy is not for the living. But our nature is. No surprise, since it is a nature born and bred within the living. Another reason for embarrassment!

So, we think that Hume is embarrassed on behalf of philosophy. His philosophical inquiries have led him to radical skeptical conclusions about our

1 Hume Texts Online. *A Treatise on Human Nature*, Book 1, Of the Understanding. All subsequent references to Hume's works are to this scholarly resource.

ability to know the world around us. He tells us that we have no reason to believe that the future will conform to the past, and that all we can mean by causation is mere constant conjunction of what we call "cause" and "effect." The skeptical result: All we can know about the world we live in is the content of the present testimony of our senses and our memory. Philosophy has thus shown itself to be unworkable: the traditional picture of the reasoned philosophical life is impossible and there can be no place for it in our lives. Philosophy, Hume concedes, is idle. If Hume is right, philosophy would thwart or bar us from living and so embarrass us. All of this, of course, is embarrassing for Hume as well, given his role as one of its greatest practitioners.

Hume's "Solution"

Happily, Hume has a "solution." It is not a solution that points out some flaw in his skeptical arguments. On the contrary, it is, in his words, a "sceptical solution"—one that is not a solution to his skepticism but consistent with it; one that allows us somehow to elude its effects. He shows us how we in fact live, irrespective of the implications of his philosophy that we cannot. Despite philosophy, life happily goes on. How so?

In his discussion of causation, Hume empties the concept of all its law-likeness. We never perceive the necessity of cause and effect, only their mere conjunction. He asks us to consider the following two propositions: (1) Such an object has always been attended with such an effect. (2) Such an object will always be attended by such an effect. Since his analysis of the causal relation has stripped it of any necessary connection between cause and effect, we cannot reason from 1 to 2. Yet he asserts that 2 may be "justly inferred" from 1. What can he mean?[2]

He cannot mean that one can reason from 1 to 2. For there is no "demonstrative reasoning"—reasoning concerning relations of ideas—that supports "like effects from like causes," since to deny it is non-contradictory, and it cannot be proven false by reasoning *a priori*. And no "experimental reasoning"—reasoning concerning matters of fact and existence—allows the inference to 2. All such arguments proceed upon the assumption that the future will be like the past. But since 2 is an instance of that assumed premise, any such argument would be circular.

Hume's point is that the mind is entirely unaffected by his skeptical arguments. We are not able to reason from 1 to 2. But we have a nature such that,

2 David Hume, *An Enquiry Concerning Human Understanding.* Section IV, Part 1. Hume Texts Online.

given experience of the constant conjunction of some cause C and effect E, we are determined to expect the one from the other. All our so-called inferences from experience are not the effects of rationality, but of our nature, of our custom or habit of mind to expect the future to be like the past. These "inferences"—steps not in reasoning but in mere sequence of ideas—are "just" since they are natural, hence not subject to criticism.

It is these habits or customs of thought that "solve" the skeptical crisis in philosophy. The solution is made possible because of the nature of our mind to expect observed patterns to persist. That nature is impervious to Hume's arguments to the contrary. Habit and custom, developed over time, are our guide to life: they make experience practical and allow us to adjust means to ends. This may be embarrassing to the traditional champion of Reason, but Hume is delighted: The role left for philosophy is of a much more practical nature than we had previously thought.

Hume and the Embarrassments of a Substantial Self

So far, the philosophical reason for embarrassment was that we do not really know the most basic things that we assume we know: that the external world exists; that others exist; that induction works. Nevertheless, one might say, at least the self, the "I"—that which makes each of us the person that he is—exists and is secure from doubt. Cold comfort! From Descartes' "Cogito" we cannot legitimately reason to "*Res Cogitans*." All that logically follows, says Hume, is that there is a particular thought or perception. Therefore, we can't even know the existence of "our own self"—either as an enduring mental or material substance—which we presume underlies the constant flux of perceptions. Consider:

"For my part, when I enter most intimately into what I call myself, I always stumble on some particular perception or other, [...] I never can catch myself at any time without a perception, and never can observe anything but the perception." When Hume looks into himself, he finds no such thing as the self, but simply "a bundle or collection of different perceptions which are in constant flux and movement.[3]

Then he challenges us to try this thought-experiment for ourselves and see if we can find such a thing as the self. We cannot. This is a theory of self that no self survives. It is like his theory of causation that eviscerates the relation.

So, the idea of the self as a mental or material substance is a fiction. No matter how hard we look, there is no substance behind the substantive. No

3 Ibid., Book 1, Part 4, Section 6: Of Personal Identity.

philosophical theory of personal identity can be built on it. Philosophers, quite literally, engage in self-deception when they claim to have found a self. They deceive themselves into thinking that they are something when they are not. This should be acutely embarrassing to traditional philosophers who claim to have proved the existence of the self as a spiritual/mental substance.

In his skeptical argument for the self, Hume begins with the assumption that if the self is an enduring thing, as we tend to think it is, then one should confront that substantial self in thought—upon reflection or thinking about oneself. This is the analog of his assumption that if physical objects are substantial items, then we ought to encounter them in sense perception; and that if causation is a real relation, we should be able to observe it and the causal powers of its relata, and so on. He then argues that we do not confront, or have direct or immediate access to physical objects, causation, or the self. His explanation in every case is that what confronts the mind immediately is always an idea only and never an object that might exist beyond it. As though such ideas can have existence of their own, independently of what they are about. As Reid pointed out, what takes Hume all the way to his radically skeptical views is his theory of ideas, inherited from Locke and Berkeley, that ideas are the immediate objects of perception and that they land before us like a veil, obscuring anything that might exist beyond them. To echo Berkeley: ideas have no exit.

We know Hume's reaction to his skeptical arguments concerning the existence of physical objects and causation. First, it was shock and depression and deep melancholia over the fact that philosophy had taken us to this skeptical impasse. And, we think, he is embarrassed for philosophy that it has taken us there and embarrassed for the role he has played in its having done so. But then, he is over-the-moon delighted to see that all his theoretical reasoning puts not the slightest crimp in the nature of thought, which, despite his best efforts, persists in believing that A will cause B, that the future will conform to the past, and so forth—delighted to see human nature, a nature of creatures that live fully enmeshed in a world like this one, is impervious to his skeptical philosophy that denies it.

But why did "the self" not receive the same skeptical solution that causation, induction, and objectivity receive? Why didn't he say that even though his philosophical analysis finds no such thing as the self, his glorious, blessedly resolute nature insists otherwise: that he cannot but think of himself as a substantial enduring object, the author of all of his actions, and toward whom he is especially sympathetic? And if he did not think this, why didn't he? Is the self significantly different in kind from physical objects that this treatment is unavailable? We cannot for the moment think why that kind of question would get in the way. If the skeptical solution to the non-existence of the self was available to him, why didn't he use it? Was it an embarrassing oversight?

Even if he did not, perhaps as an oversight, use the skeptical solution, might we not offer him a Humean way out of the difficulty we raised for him? Officially, as it were, writing a standard autobiography in the conventional way about the journey of an enduring substantial self is just not on. However, if confronted with this objection, might he not say something analogous to what he would say if you discovered him planning what he would do the next morning: Yes, I have no reason to believe that there will even be a tomorrow, let alone that there be an identical successor to today's self, or that there be something I can plan for, but my nature happily compels me to believe that there will be and that I, the very same David Hume, will be there, God willing, to welcome it. And we cannot but believe that the better we plan for such things, the better off we are. This goes for us and everyone else who shares our nature.

Hume and the End of Philosophy

So, those who thought Hume called for the end of philosophy misunderstood him. He called for the end of philosophy as it had been done—the old academic philosophy—because he thought he had shown it was impossible, unrealistic: an embarrassing overreach. Instead, we should do what we can, which is to muddle through as best as we can, which we had been doing anyhow, but thought it unphilosophical. We had misdescribed philosophy as an activity for gods, as if it demanded perfect rationality, motivated by Plato's divine spark of reason. And in this pretentious misapprehension, nay, hubris, we embarrassed ourselves for not being up to the task. The divine spark is not divine, but it's the best we have.

Hume thinks of his work as a contribution to "the science of human nature." He is doing psychology broadly construed. He continues the Socratic tradition. We are natural creatures with a psychology and limited perceptual, conceptual, and rational abilities. Philosophy is a recommendation, a practice, designed to help us do better what we limited creatures can do. It is a recommendation for the best way for us to proceed, given our limitations. There is still room for embarrassment in philosophy, but it is no longer constitutional—it is no longer embarrassment at our failing to be gods. Now it is for failing to live up to philosophy's more modest standards—for failing to be the best natural, fallible, limited creatures that we are.

Chapter III

LATE MODERN EMBARRASSMENTS: EARLY WITTGENSTEIN, LOGICAL POSITIVISTS, AND QUINE

Wittgenstein: Young and Tractarian

What, if anything, has the early Wittgenstein to be embarrassed about?[1] Quite a few things, it might be argued. First, he should be embarrassed about following, wittingly or unwittingly, in Hume's footsteps without any footnotes to Hume, and claiming he had not read a word of Hume.[2] In general, Wittgenstein should be embarrassed about his dismissive attitude to the philosophical tradition. One remark in particular stands out for its primitive tone, expressing naïve surprise that "all the philosophers he once worshipped in ignorance, are after all stupid and dishonest and make disgusting mistakes."[3] A sweeping generalization, to be sure, about the diverse figures in the history of philosophy, and a logical blunder for a budding logician. Informed readers may be embarrassed for young Ludwig, as indeed he should have felt embarrassed for himself, then and there, or at least in retrospect.

What is more, in an ironic twist, young Ludwig made the remark that he had not read a word of Hume to his friend the mathematician David Hume Pinsent—a direct descendant of the philosopher. Should he not have been embarrassed about offending Pinsent by denigrating his ancestor, especially

---

1 Following David Stern, we speak of the early, middle, and later Wittgenstein, thus distinguishing between the early work of the *Tractatus* and the later work of the *Philosophical Investigations,* as well as marking a "Wittgenstein in transit" between the two lines and styles of thinking. See his "Introduction" to *Wittgenstein in the 30s: Between the Tractatus and the Investigations*, Cambridge University Press, Cambridge, 2018.

2 Wittgenstein mentions Hume in his *Lectures: Cambridge 1930–1932*, edited by Desmond Lee from the Notes of John King and Desmond Lee, Basil Blackwell, Oxford, 1980, p. 73.

3 David Hume Pinsent, *A Portrait of Wittgenstein as a Young Man: From the Diary of David Hume Pinsent*, Blackwell, Oxford, 1990, p. 5.

when that ancestor is a striking counterexample to Wittgenstein's hasty generalization? In any event, after Pinsent's tragic death as a test pilot in the last days of the First World War, Wittgenstein dedicated the *Tractatus* "to the memory of my friend David H. Pinsent."

Nevertheless, his negative attitude to the history of philosophy survived, perhaps in a less unacceptable form, and has become a characteristic feature of his relentless attack on the philosophical tradition.

> "As little philosophy as I have read," he wrote later on, "I have certainly not read too little, rather too much. I see that whenever I read a philosophical book, it does not improve my thoughts at all, it makes them worse."[4]

Presumably, he thought that a traditional philosopher's treatment of a problem only leads to more problems and confusion.

In addition, there is the issue of authenticity. In Wittgenstein's view, a philosopher with footnotes is an academic philosopher who is too much indebted to the past—hence his footnotes—and betrays the present, and is, therefore, inauthentic. Such philosophers neglect the context of their own times and the role their own character plays in their contributions. Perhaps this is why, when Wittgenstein began to read a past philosopher such as Hume, he soon threw away the book and started to think about the problem for himself, configuring the problem in the present context.[5] With such a negative attitude toward the history of philosophy, no wonder the issue of scholarly acknowledgment does not seem to arise for him with any urgency.

There is, however, a principled reason he gives for the dismissal of the study of the history of philosophy. The study of philosophy, he says, is not a matter of choice between rival theories. If it were, it would be sound to teach it historically. But if it is not, then it is a fault to do so, because it is quite unnecessary. We can tackle the subject directly, without any need to consider its history.[6] Hence, the traditional approach to teaching philosophy would not be helpful in solving the problems that trouble us.

Yet in the *Tractatus*, we come across criticisms of the theories of idealism and realism and a qualified defense of solipsism as he tersely articulates his own un-articulable positions.[7] Undeniably, then, the grand theories served as

4 Quoted in Ray Monk, *Ludwig Wittgenstein: The Duty of Genius*, Jonathan Cape, London, 1990, p. 496.

5 Brian McGuinness, *Approaches to Wittgenstein*, Routledge, New York, 2002, p. x.

6 See Wittgenstein's *Lectures: Cambridge 1930–1932*, pp. 74–75.

7 *TLP* 40412; 564; 562; 564.

landmarks to orient himself in the philosophical landscape and as targets of criticism as he took the measure of truth in them.

But does Wittgenstein really defend solipsism, and if he does, what is the caveat? There is strong textual evidence for the claim that he does. In the *Tractatus*, Ludwig speaks of the extent to which solipsism is a truth and says that what the solipsist means is entirely correct, only—and this is the caveat—it cannot be said. He also asserts that "I am my world. (The microcosm),"[8] meaning that the world is identical to my experiences and this "shows itself in the fact that the limits of language (of that language which only I understand) mean the limits of my world."[9] Notice the iteration of the personal pronoun "my" in "my world" and "my language" and "I" in the language only I understand. For the Tractarian Wittgenstein, if a language is to be meaningful, its names need to correlate with objects. If those objects could not be directly known to me, then I cannot meaningfully talk about them; hence, the language could not be my language, and those objects could not be part of my world.[10]

Wittgenstein's later remarks about death lend additional support for a solipsistic interpretation: "So too at death the world does not alter but comes to an end."[11] "Death is not an event. We do not live to experience death."[12] Of course, he refers only to his own death since we witness but do not experience the death of others. What is more, only a solipsist would say that with his death, the world and life come to an end. In contrast, the non-solipsistic idealist would allow that after his own death, the world and life go on in others. So, on the face of it, a straightforward reading of these passages is that young Ludwig was a solipsist or at least sympathetic to solipsism.

It might be argued, however, that Wittgenstein's intent is to critique solipsism rather than support it. As evidence for this interpretation, one may point to Wittgenstein's observation that "solipsism, when its implications are followed out strictly, coincides with pure realism. The self of solipsism shrinks to a point without extension, and there remains the reality coordinated with it."[13] This suggests that the Tractarian Wittgenstein was a realist after all, as

8 *TLP* 5.63.

9 *TLP* 5.62.

10 Here we follow Severin Schroeder's line of argument in his "Schopenhauer's Influence on Wittgenstein," in *A Companion to Schopenhauer*, edited by B. Vandenabeele, Blackwell, Oxford, 2012, pp. 367–85.

11 *TLP* 6.431.

12 *TLP* 6.4311.

13 *TLP* 5.64. See David Pears, "Wittgenstein's Treatment of Solipsism in the Tractatus," *Critica Revista Hispano-Americana de Filosofia*, Vol. 6, 1972, pp. 57–84; Peter Hacker,

does "the picture theory" of meaning, which is after all a realist theory: "A proposition is a picture of reality. A proposition is a picture of reality as we imagine it."[14] Thus there is textual ambiguity. But if so, how are we to reconcile the tension between Wittgenstein's anti-theory stance on the one hand, and his apparent embrace of both the theories of solipsism and realism on the other? Is this not an embarrassing contradiction?

Looking back at the history of philosophy, we see that Berkeley held that his own idealism was not only compatible with realism but "was the most realist doctrine, since it keeps accurately to what we actually experience."[15] This view is echoed by Schopenhauer: "True idealism [...] leaves the empirical reality of the world untouched."[16] So Wittgenstein's remark that solipsism, strictly carried out, coincides with pure realism is not a stand-alone view but has idealist predecessors in modern philosophy.

In any event, if solipsism were presented as an exclusive doctrine in competition with idealism and realism—as if listed on a metaphysical menu from which we are to choose based on their merits—Wittgenstein would dismiss it. For him, the very idea that the grand metaphysical theories could legitimately say something about "the essence of the world" is nonsense; yet from this, it does not follow that they are not insightful.

Consider an entry from his wartime notebook which is suggestive of his approach to relieve the above-mentioned tension:

The way I have traveled is this: Idealism singles men out from the world as unique, solipsism singles me alone out, and finally I see that I too belong to the rest of the world; so that on the one side nothing is left over, and on the other side, as something unique, the world.[17]

Realism, idealism and solipsism are traditionally presented as offering sharp contrasts, while Wittgenstein is keen to blur such contrasts. This is reminiscent of a dialectical approach. Recall that when considering the methods of philosophy with his students, he said of the dialectical/Hegelian method

---

Insight and Illusion: Themes in the Philosophy of Ludwig Wittgenstein. The main textual basis for their interpretation is *TLP* 5.64. For an interpretation that acknowledges the textual ambiguity, but nevertheless comes down on the realist side, see Robert Fogelin, *Wittgenstein*, Routledge & Kegan Paul, London, 1976, pp. 86–87.

14 *TLP* 4.01.

15 Berkeley, Three Dialogues between Hylas and Philonous. Wittgenstein told his friend Drury that "Berkeley and Kant seem to me very deep thinkers." M.O'C. Drury, "Conversations with Wittgenstein," in Rush Rhees, *Ludwig Wittgenstein Personal Recollections*, Basil Blackwell, Oxford, 1981, p. 171.

16 Schopenhauer was an early and acknowledged influence. See Wittgenstein, *Culture and Value*, p. 16.

17 Wittgenstein, *Notebooks 1914–1916*, Basil Blackwell, Oxford, 1961, p. 85e.

that "it is very sound and a way in which we do work. But its goal should not be coming up with a synthesis from a pair of contradictory statements. Its object should be to find out where the ambiguities in our language are."[18]

Brian McGuinness remarks that "Wittgenstein's relationship to solipsism is complicated because he not only began with a sympathy for idealism and solipsism but retained that sympathy throughout the period of writing the Tractatus and beyond."[19] The suggestion is that Ludwig wanted to accommodate solipsism alongside the other theories without dismissing it. On Wittgenstein's philosophical journey, the measure of truth and insight in each of these one-sided theories is not abandoned only to be replaced by a new comprehensive theory. They are not rivals or competitors as they may appear to be. The journey is not such where realism finally overcomes idealism and solipsism. Each has its own measure of truth, and it is this measure that philosophers need to clarify and put side by side.

Understood this way, Wittgenstein can accept and at the same time reject each theory with caveats. Perhaps the best way to characterize the relation of realism, idealism, and solipsism is in terms of mutual corrections.[20] This resolves the perceived tension in the idea of Wittgenstein endorsing contradictory theories, as well as putting the remarks about solipsism in proper perspective: Solipsism is a corrective to the distortions of realism.

We also claim that, in line with his solipsism, the early Wittgenstein still regards a private language as possible. On the face of it, this possibility seems to be excluded by the picture theory of meaning which after all is a realist view of language. Logic and language, remember, mirror the structure of the world. But why could a realist not have a private language? Why should it have been obvious to Wittgenstein, at the time of writing the *Tractatus*, that realism is incompatible with a private language? If elementary sentences, as he says, are a connection of names,[21] the names could still be private. It's only the structure of the world that is reflected in the connection of names.

Be that as it may. Perhaps critics are right that Ludwig's acquaintance with the history of modern philosophy was rather impoverished. Had he been more widely tutored in that history, he would have realized that Hume avoided many of the ground-floor errors philosophers had made in the past.

18 Wittgenstein's *Lectures: Cambridge 1930–1932*, pp. 73–74.

19 Brian McGuinness, *Wittgenstein: A Life. Young Ludwig*, University of California Press, Berkeley, California, 1988, p. 78.

20 For an illuminating treatment of this approach, see David Cerbone, *Wittgenstein on Realism and Idealism*, Cambridge University Press, Cambridge, 2023.

21 *TLP* 4.22: "An elementary proposition consists of names. It is a nexus, a concatenation of names."

For Hume struck many of the same themes, took many of the same positions, in roughly the same words, as Ludwig did in his *Tractatus Logico-Philosophicus.*

This sounds plausible, not least because both Hume and Wittgenstein rejected metaphysics, which is at the core of the philosophical tradition. Hume urged us "to commit to the flames" books of metaphysics since they contain nothing but "sophistry and illusion."

In them, there is no "reasoning about quantity or number nor experimental reasoning concerning matters of fact [...] When we run over libraries, persuaded of these principles, what havoc must we make? If we take in our hand any volume; of divinity or school metaphysics, for instance; let us ask, *Does it contain any abstract reasoning concerning quantity or number*? No. *Does it contain any experimental reasoning concerning matter of fact and existence*? No. Commit it then to the flames: for it can contain nothing but sophistry and illusion."[22]

Similarly, Wittgenstein privileged the propositions of science as meaningful and repudiated the sentences of metaphysics as senseless grammatical illusions that do not add to our knowledge of the world:

> The correct method in philosophy would really be the following: To say nothing except what can be said, i.e., the propositions of natural science—something that has nothing to do with philosophy—and then, whenever someone else wanted to say something metaphysical, to demonstrate to him that he had failed to give a meaning to certain signs in his propositions.[23]

It is surprising that of these two seminal philosophers—the calm Hume and the passionate Wittgenstein—it is Wittgenstein who is calmer in his rejection of metaphysics, while the generally tolerant Hume, uncharacteristically, we hasten to add, advocates book burning. Such advocacy is a mild embarrassment for us twenty-first-century Humeans, since, after the horrors of the twentieth century, book burning has a very different resonance than it must have had for Hume in the eighteenth.

Returning to Hume's influence on the young Wittgenstein: The *Tractatus* echoes Hume's arguments concerning the self, causality, and induction, and it also adopts Hume's fork of dividing propositions into analytic and empirical. What is more, consider these sentences about the self whose target is Descartes' *res cogitans*: "There is no such thing as the subject that thinks or

---

22 Enquiry Concerning Human Understanding. See Hume texts Online, E 12.34, SBN 165. Here we note another irony: Hume eventually became chief librarian at the University of Edinburgh.

23 *TLP* 6.53.

entertains ideas." "The philosophical self is not the human being, not the human body, or the human soul, with which psychology deals, but rather the metaphysical subject, the limit of the world—not part of it."[24] As we have seen, after demolishing the metaphysical self, Hume comes to a full stop; Wittgenstein, on the other hand, does not, but proceeds to reintroduce the solipsistic self "as a condition of the world, value, logic and language." If anything, Hume is more consistent, for he concludes that there is no metaphysical subject either.

And now consider the things Wittgenstein says about causality: "There is no possible way of making an inference from the existence of one situation to the existence of another, entirely different situation";[25] "There is no causal nexus to justify such an inference";[26] "We *cannot* infer the events of the future from those of the present. Belief in the causal nexus is *superstition*."[27] And about induction: "This procedure (induction), however, has no logical justification but only a psychological one."[28] Finally, "It is clear that there are no grounds for believing that the simplest eventuality will in fact be realized";[29] "It is a hypothesis that the sun will rise tomorrow: and this means that we do not *know* whether it will rise."[30]

These quotations show an unmistakable intellectual indebtedness to Hume, yet he is unappreciated, un-flagged, unacknowledged, unmentioned, and never referenced. So, here is a philosopher of the eighteenth century who was the very opposite of "stupid and dishonest and making disgusting mistakes," and whose views and arguments the early Wittgenstein adopted and adapted in the *Tractatus*. But what, if anything, distinguishes Wittgenstein's view of causation from Hume's?

A neglected remark in Wittgenstein's diary entry for 1930 sheds light on this question: "16 years ago when I had the thought that the law of causality is insignificant in itself & there is a way of regarding the world which does not bear it in mind, I felt the beginning of a New Era."[31] However, why is the law of causality insignificant or meaningless? It is "meaningless" (bedeutunglos) because it is not an empirical proposition that describes the world but part of

24 Ibid., 5.641.
25 Ibid., 5.135.
26 Ibid., 5.136.
27 Ibid., 5.1361.
28 Ibid., 6.363.
29 Ibid., 6.3631.
30 Ibid., 6.36311.
31 Ludwig Wittgenstein, *Public and Private Occasions*, edited by James Klagge and Alfred Nordmann, Rowman & Littlefield Publishers, Lanham, 2003, p. 29.

our network for describing the world. "It's about the net and not about what the net describes."[32] So, unlike Hume who saw the law of causality as a matter of psychology, Wittgenstein sees it as a matter of logic—as an a priori presupposition or principle for the scientific description of the world. "The law of causality is not a law but the form of a law [...] Here as it so often happens the a priori turns out to be something purely logical."[33] "If there were a law of causality, it might be put this way: There are laws of nature. But of course, one can't say that: it shows itself."[34]

And why does "not bearing the law of causality in mind" bring about a New Epoch, a new way of looking at things? Because it frees us from the felt tyranny of the "superstition of the causal nexus"—the aura of inevitability—and dissolves the philosophical problems associated with it; for instance, the "free will and determinism" problem.

Notwithstanding these differences, the fact is that Hume influenced Wittgenstein's critique of causation as necessary connection, and it is bad form to use the work of others without acknowledgment—a violation of scholarly ethical norms—and this, if true, should be embarrassing to Wittgenstein, as well as to Bertrand Russell and G.E. Moore, the examiners of his doctoral dissertation titled *Tractatus Logico-Philosophicus*, who failed to point this out.

Speaking of bad form: what about Wittgenstein's abysmal conduct during his defense of the *Tractatus*? When Russell and Moore asked legitimate questions, thus fulfilling their duties as examiners, Wittgenstein responded dismissively: "clapping each of his examiners on the shoulder and saying condescendingly, 'Don't worry, I know you'll never understand it,'"[35] and walked out of the room. This response is deeply embarrassing, even shameful, on many levels. There is the matter of violating the rules and norms of the university and implicitly getting his examiners to do so as well. There is also the matter of gross ingratitude to Russell and Moore who were Wittgenstein's tutors, friends, and supporters. Russell wrote an introduction to the *Tractatus* without which the book would not have been published, and Moore was the one who came up with the title of the book. What is more, they recommended Wittgenstein's appointment to an academic post at Cambridge.

Back to our central issue. Is it possible that, despite the salient Humean themes appearing in his early work, Wittgenstein never read a word of Hume? Well, there are more ways to learn from Hume than by actually reading him.

32 *Tractatus*, 6.35.

33 Wittgenstein, *Notebooks 1914–1916*, p. 41e.

34 *Tractatus*, 6.36.

35 Monk, *Ludwig Wittgenstein: The Duty of Genius*, p. 271.

As a student at Cambridge, he would have breathed the air of British empiricism and absorbed the problems of British philosophy by, as it were, osmosis. Such an immersion in the British tradition would certainly have involved Hume's skepticism about an enduring self, about causality, and induction. Moreover, as a student of Russell, Wittgenstein read Russell's *The Problems of Philosophy* where a whole chapter is devoted to induction with many references to Hume. So, Wittgenstein had absorbed the lessons Hume taught us and assumed them much like we assume the air we breathe, even if, as he says, he had not read a word by Hume. This immersion-osmosis scenario would explain Wittgenstein's lack of embarrassment for not mentioning or referencing Hume. He took what Hume said for common knowledge.

Things, however, are more complicated than this. What of Wittgenstein's shrugging his shoulders at the history of modern philosophy? Would his works be intelligible without the background of the history of philosophy and its theories? It's hard enough for those of us with that understanding. Therefore, should he not be embarrassed about his indifference that borders on contempt? He brings up this ethical issue himself, if only to explain it away, in the preface to the *Tractatus*:

> I do not wish to judge how far my efforts coincide with those of other philosophers. Indeed, what I have written here makes no claim to novelty in detail, and the reason why I give no sources is that it is a matter of indifference to me whether the thoughts that I have had have been anticipated by someone else.[36]

So, the issue of sources and their attribution crossed his mind because he deemed it troubling enough to deserve a cryptic response. The reason for the dismissal, however, is embarrassing. Is a mere subjective attitude of indifference a good reason for flying in the face of scholarly convention, and for omitting footnotes that might help others understand the work?

In any event, the "osmosis scenario" is plausible insofar as it throws light on how Wittgenstein managed to acquire a deep understanding of the essence of the tradition without actually reading the great works in the history of philosophy. However, his condemnation of the tradition is too broad and too strong, for it includes Hume, who was not guilty of the mistakes Wittgenstein condemns the tradition of having made. The long and short of it is that Ludwig read Hume since he refers to Hume explicitly in his lectures when discussing methods of doing philosophy.[37] Moreover, it was the tradition that gave rise to

---

36 *TLP* 3.

37 Wittgenstein's *Lectures: Cambridge 1930–1932*, p. 73.

Wittgenstein himself, and understanding the essence of that tradition enabled him to critique it and think his way out of it. In any case, he could not have written his critique of the tradition without having been fully immersed in it.

It might be objected, however, that it is a one-sided way to look at the early Wittgenstein exclusively through a Humean lens. After all, there is the Kantian influence, and once this is taken into consideration, the proposed Hume–Wittgenstein alliance is undermined. This objection raises several questions: Had Ludwig actually read Kant? Or was the Kantian influence indirect, perhaps by way of Schopenhauer? And how far did that influence extend? We claim that the Kantian influence was both direct and indirect as well as extensive.

There is both anecdotal and textual evidence for the claim that young Ludwig read Kant. Late in life, Wittgenstein told Drury that Kant was "a profound philosopher," while he said to von Wright that "from Spinoza, Hume and Kant he could get only occasional glimpses of understanding."[38] These remarks may be ambiguous or even inconsistent, but they do imply that he had read Kant. In addition, Brian McGuinness tells us that Ludwig "had the normal educated man's acquaintance with Kant." When on leave at Olmutz during the First World War, Wittgenstein, in discussion with friends, "would quote Kant from time to time and say: 'In the words of the great Kant.'"[39]

However, how likely is it that "a normal educated man" could quote pertinent passages from Kant on a particular topic? What is more, a critical remark in the *Tractatus* on Kant's problem of the right- and left-hand glove bespeaks of a more extensive acquaintance with Kant than suggested by McGuinness. The matter was put to rest by Wittgenstein's friend Ludwig Hänsel who confirmed that he and Wittgenstein had read and discussed Kant's *Critique of Pure Reason* together, from beginning to end, in the prisoner of war camp at Monte Cassino sometime between 1918 and 1919.[40]

A more significant matter, however, is the extent and depth of Kant's influence on the *Tractatus*. For that work is, roughly speaking, a Kantian project. Like Kant's transcendental deduction, Ludwig's logical analysis of language has the aim of identifying the a priori form of experience, which form is "shown" in any meaningful language and therefore cannot be put

---

38 See Georg Henrik von Wright, *Wittgenstein*, Basil Blackwell, Oxford, 1982, p. 33.

39 McGuinness, *Wittgenstein: A Life. Young Ludwig*, p. 253.

40 See *Ludwig Wittgenstein: Private and Public Occasions*, Lanham, Rowman and Littlefield Publishers, 2003, pp. 257–58. See also Monk, *Ludwig Wittgenstein: The Duty of Genius*, p. 158.

in a proposition.[41] The question is, in what specific ways does Wittgenstein's project differ from Kant's?

In a notebook entry in 1915, Ludwig wrote: "The great problem around which everything I write turns is: Is there an order in the world a priori and if so, what does it consist in?"[42] If this question is understood as asking whether we have a priori knowledge of the structure of the world, then, for the Kantian, such knowledge would have to be synthetic a priori. For such knowledge is possible only if "the world" means the world of appearances. Of this we can have synthetic a priori knowledge, namely, of that part of the structure that our mind imposes—the a priori intuitions of space and time and the a priori laws of the understanding. In contrast to Kant, young Ludwig not only rejected the distinction between "the thing-in-itself" and the way things appear to us that transcendental idealism depends on, but denied that we can have synthetic a priori knowledge: "No part of our experience is a priori," said he.[43] So, there is no a priori experience of the world's relation to the subject, no a priori order in the world.

So, the fundamental structure of the world is not learned by experience but is a necessary condition for the possibility of language and experience. If "logic," as Wittgenstein avers, "pervades the world" and the laws of logic form part of the "scaffolding" of the world, then this knowledge would be analytic and, a fortiori, a priori. Logic is what makes meaningful language and thought possible. But while logic is prior to experience, there is no experience of logic. "Logical form is not among the things we can describe, for the possibility of description presupposes logical form."[44]

Wittgenstein draws an analogy between logic and ethics. Logic is a condition of meaningful language and thought, while ethics is a condition of the possibility of a meaningful life. A meaningful proposition is either true or false. A meaningful life is happy or unhappy. "Ethics does not treat of the world. Like logic, it must be a condition of the world."[45] So, both logic

41 See Eric Stenius, *Wittgenstein's Tractatus: A Critical Exposition of Its Main Lines of Thought*, Basil Blackwell, Oxford, 1960, Chapter XI, "Wittgenstein as a Kantian Philosopher," especially section 2: "Wittgenstein's Transcendental Deductions," pp. 218–20.

42 Wittgenstein, *Notebooks 1914–1918*, p. 53e.

43 *TLP* 5.634. Rudolf Haller also points to the striking contrast between Kant's view that the conditions of experience are given a priori and the early Wittgenstein's adamant empiricism to the effect that no part of our experience is a priori. See *Questions on Wittgenstein*, University of Nebraska Press, Lincoln, 1990, p. 53.

44 See Hanne Ahonen Appelquist, *Wittgenstein and the Conditions of Musical Communication*, Hakapaino Oy, Helsinki, 2008, p. 35.

45 Wittgenstein, Notebook *1914–1916*, Oxford, Basil Blackwell, p. 77e.

and ethics are transcendental, and hence inexpressible in propositional form. They say nothing and can say nothing informative about the world; their sentences are all tautologies. Logical and ethical "propositions" are pseudo-propositions and cannot be stated but "manifest" themselves.

Perhaps the structural parallel between Wittgenstein's *Tractatus* and Kant's *Critique of Pure Reason* can be made more compelling if we retitle the *Tractatus* as the Critique of Pure Language where "pure language" refers to propositional language.[46] For the *Tractatus* depends on the dichotomy between "sense" and "nonsense," where "sense" is to be construed as what can be said in a proposition—the propositions of science and everyday factual language—and "nonsense" is to be understood as what cannot be said in a proposition, what is beyond language, and has to "show" itself. This sense of "nonsensicality" is the domain of ethics, aesthetics, religion and the mystical. And it is what is of the highest value. In such cases, Wittgenstein insists, silence is the appropriate attitude.[47]

The Tractarian dichotomy between sense and nonsense has a striking similarity to the line Kant draws in his *Critique of Pure Reason* between theoretical reason and practical reason, where Kant limits the powers of theoretical reason (science) "to make room for faith."[48] Questions that belong to practical reason such as God, morals, free will, and the soul, Kant thought, need a different treatment. The salient difference between Kant and the early Wittgenstein is that Kant takes an epistemological approach to ethics, aesthetics, and religion, while the Tractarian Wittgenstein takes a semantic route to the "unsayable." It might be said that Wittgenstein wants to make room for truths that fail the verificationist principle of meaning. Hence the importance of good "nonsense." For Wittgenstein, this sort of "nonsensicality" has a positive ring—it's what makes us human—while for the exclusively empirically minded it means something purely negative.[49]

As if this were not enough evidence for claiming that Wittgenstein was a Kantian philosopher, in his 1930 lectures on philosophical method, Wittgenstein mentions Kant and sides with him against Hume (of Book 1 of the Treatise) and Descartes:

---

46 This insightful retitling of the *Tractatus* was suggested by Peter Geach. See Stenius, *Wittgenstein's Tractatus*, p. 220.

47 Of course, there is plain nonsense that is to be dismissed or appreciated as in the theater of the absurd.

48 See the Preface to the second edition of the *Critique of Pure Reason*: "I have therefore found it necessary to deny knowledge, in order to make room for faith."

49 See Stenius, *Wittgenstein's Tractatus*, p. 223.

> The transcendental method is Kant's critical method without the peculiar applications Kant made of it. This is the right sort of approach. Hume, Descartes and others had tried to start from one proposition such as "Cogito, ergo sum" and work (deductively) from it to others. Kant disagreed and went on to examine the validity of what we suppose we know.[50]

The Kantian influence can also be traced indirectly through Schopenhauer whose name appears on Wittgenstein's list of influences and whose transcendental idealism was the basis for Ludwig's first philosophy.[51] Schopenhauer followed Kant in conceiving of the metaphysical self as a transcendental "I think" that accompanies and gives formal unity to our mental representations. His striking simile compares the self to the eye that does not see itself but only sees our representations of the world. We vanish as we make ourselves the center of the world and our microcosm becomes our macrocosm.[52] Wittgenstein adopts this simile in the *Tractatus*:

> The subject does not belong to the world, rather it is the limit of the world. Where in the world is the metaphysical subject to be found? You will say that this is exactly like the case of the eye and the visual filed. But really, you do not see the eye. And nothing in the visual field allows you to infer that it is seen by an eye.[53]

So, initially it might seem that tracing Wittgenstein's Kantian lineage undermines the Hume–Wittgenstein alliance. We have argued that this is not the case. If we look at Wittgenstein's face carefully, we can see its Humean as well as its Kantian features. The relationship is like that of an offspring to his parents—resembling both, yet different.

At this point in our argument, we bring attention to a broader irony. Wittgenstein's list of philosophers he had read grows, yet his contempt for their work and the history of philosophy in general remains. This requires explanation. Is it consistent? His point might be that no matter how gifted and accomplished the philosophers have been and no matter how good their

50 Wittgenstein's *Lectures: Cambridge 1930–1932*, pp. 73–74.

51 See Severin Schroeder, "Schopenhauer's Influence on Wittgenstein," pp. 367–85; and Alan Janik, "Schopenhauer and the Early Wittgenstein," *Philosophical Studies*, Vol. 15, 1966, pp. 76–95.

52 World as Will and Idea, Vol. 2, chapter 41, p. 491. Translated by R. B. Haldane and J. Kemp. Published by CreateSpace Independent Publishing Platform, North Charleston, South Carolina, 2016.

53 *TLP* 5.632 and 5.633.

work or how much he enjoys reading them—as he did Plato—they cannot succeed, he thinks, because they have the wrong ideas about what they are doing and what their methods are. His point is to show how he and they ought to proceed. Their failures, one might say, are built into what they do. No wonder they fail. And it may also serve to help him to see the virtues of his work and a reminder to himself and others of the benefits of his method. So, not so ironic as one might think.

But back to our main line of argument. So far, we have said little about Wittgenstein's conception of philosophy which perhaps renders plausible the "no scholarly paraphernalia" attitude. He thought of philosophy as an activity, as the logical clarification of propositions, and not a body of theories and doctrines, nor a catalog of philosophical propositions.[54] Ask yourself, he might have said, must a skillful carpenter making a cabinet or a table acknowledge the master carpenters who taught him? And if he did, would that not be a distraction from his task? Similarly, Wittgenstein might have thought that philosophy is best done without any scholarly paraphernalia.[55] No doubt he perceived a radical discontinuity between what he was doing and the philosophical tradition: Wittgenstein wanted to put an end to the old philosophy, while academic philosophers wanted to continue it.

Do all these embarrassments not vanish, however, if only we look at things differently? Suppose that Wittgenstein set out not only to deal with the problems of philosophy but, equally importantly, to compose a work of literary art, something sparse, elegant and beautiful, like a poem. And insofar as a poem must speak for itself, footnotes are over the top, even absurd. The winged creature of poetry is tethered by the heavy weight of footnotes.[56] If Wittgenstein thought of the *Tractatus* as a philosophical poem governed by norms different from those of conventional philosophy—including authenticity and self-expression—the issue of footnotes would not arise.[57]

We are invited to look at Wittgenstein's relation to philosophy by such characteristic remarks as this: "Really one should write philosophy only as one *writes a poem*."[58] In saying this he acknowledged himself "to be someone

54 *Tractatus*, 4.112.

55 For another example of philosophy written with minimum scholarly paraphernalia, see Gilbert Ryle's *The Concept of Mind*. Hutchinson House, London, 1949.

56 *Pace* T.S. Eliot and Ezra Pound.

57 Is this an early instance of Wittgenstein using the notion of a language game? The game of philosophy differs from that of poetry. If so, they ought to be adjudged on different grounds. This is an unlikely scenario. One is hard pressed to imagine that Ludwig would see all that logical apparatus as poetic fragments.

58 Wittgenstein, *Culture and Value*, p. 28e.

who cannot quite do what he would like to be able to do."[59] Undoubtedly, there is a poetic dimension to the *Tractatus,* but since the book is mainly concerned with matters of philosophy and logic, an exclusively poetic perspective is less than satisfactory to a modern reader of philosophy.

Now a neglected but nevertheless important question arises: What does Wittgenstein mean by "authentic self" and "authentic philosopher"? Briefly, his view is that an academic philosopher cannot be authentic or original, since he stands on too many shoulders to be his own man and speak in his own voice.[60] The fact that there are Platonists, Aristotelians, Thomists, Humeans, and even Wittgensteinians in the history of philosophy shows that the inclination to be someone that one is not, is alive and well, and so is the temptation to deceive oneself about who and what one is. For there was only one Plato, one Aristotle, one Hume, and one Wittgenstein, and following them hinders one from being authentic or original. "The seeds of originality," Wittgenstein observes, "are already present in someone who does not want to be someone or something he is not and who does not deceive himself."[61]

Wittgenstein aimed to be an authentic, original philosopher who wanted to break with the tradition and to be independent of it and the work of others.[62] This idea of difference, reminiscent of Rousseau's attitude that he may be no better but at least he is different from others,[63] was very important to him. His work had to display something that was his own, that bore his own stamp. In his view, as we said before, if philosophy is to be done well, it must be done by an authentic self, a self not burdened by a whole lot of others, their lives, books, and teachings. So, for him, the notions of self and authenticity are intimately related. To be authentic, we might say, we need to express something that is genuinely our own despite being rooted in our culture.

Does Wittgenstein, however, present us with a conception of the self that is rich enough to include the potential for authenticity? In the *Tractatus*, he sketches two conceptions of the self. First, there is the philosophical self, which is not part of the world; it is the "metaphysical subject," the limit of the world, where the world leaves off and I begin; ultimately, the solipsistic self. Second, there is the empirical conception of the self—the everyday sense of self as a human being engaged in the world, as a man with a human body, a nature,

59 Ibid.

60 Gilbert Ryle quoted in Monk's *Ludwig Wittgenstein: The Duty of Genius*, p. 495.

61 Wittgenstein, *Culture and Value*, p. 68e.

62 However, in the Preface to the *Tractatus*, he made an exception to this resolve when he recorded his indebtedness to "Frege's great works and to the writings of my friend Bertrand Russell."

63 Rousseau, *The Confessions*, p. 17.

and psychology. This self is essentially inauthentic, since it is dependent on others, pressured and burdened by their books, their teachings, rules, and dogmas. If so, the ground of authenticity must lie in the other self—the philosophical-metaphysical self. But what is this philosophical-metaphysical self? It is not, as we have seen, the man, not the human body, not the human psychology, nor anything in the world. The philosophical self does not require a further ontological commitment. It is really nothing but an extensionless vanishing point—a creature of language, the limit of the empirical world. How could an attenuated self, an "almost nothing," be the ground of an authentic self and its expressions?

The solution to the problem of authenticity is, Wittgenstein says, to see that the philosophical-metaphysical self is solipsistic. In being solipsistic, it is incapable of relations with any other thing, since there are, *ex hypothesi*, no other things to be related to. Such a self could not be affected by others, by their teachings, their dogmas, their rules, institutions, and conventions—in short, by all the sources of inauthenticity, since there are no such sources. This is just the sort of arrangement that guarantees authenticity. What more could one ask for? Solipsism, and idealism generally, are not only not the obstacles they have been thought to be to solving the problem of the self in the world. They are its solution. As Wittgenstein might say, "I love solipsism, because I love authenticity."

Can we squeeze authenticity out of either of these conceptions of the self? The empirical self is essentially inauthentic, since it is utterly dependent on and pressured by others and otherness. On the other hand, the metaphysical conception of the self is a "vanishing point," a creature of language, the limit of the world. This "almost nothing" conception of the self is too thin to be a source of authenticity, since it is unconnected to any other thing, including the world and the worldly self. If so, this authentic self cannot inform the inauthentic, worldly self; and if not, it cannot make expressions of the self authentic. Nor can it play any other role in the worldly world. How, then, can authenticity be a supreme value of ours if it is unattainable? Whither, then, the supreme value of authenticity if it is beyond the limits of thought? To aspire to an impossible authenticity would be as self-defeating as aspiring to turn philosophy into poetry. Finally, to accept the existence and value of something that plays no role and does no work would be to violate Occam's razor.[64]

So, we do not seem able to achieve authenticity on either of Wittgenstein's conceptions of self. And this is embarrassing or should be for someone like

64 The moral would be: Bring your ideals down to earth.

Wittgenstein who laid so much store by authenticity, since it shows that he cannot be or do what he aspires and struggles to be or do.

There is another line of reasoning in the *Tractatus* that supports a solipsism of the self. What does Wittgenstein mean when he says that the metaphysical subject is the limit of the world? My understanding of the world goes only so far as the language I understand takes it. We understand the world through propositions whose structure mirrors the structure of the world. This is the deep truth of idealism. And with this, solipsism enters the picture: "The world is *my* world."[65] If solipsism is understood this way, then "what the solipsist means is quite correct" and in this sense, solipsism is not the problem but the solution.

Wittgenstein, as we have seen previously, is not interested in the impossible task of adopting or justifying solipsism or any other theory. To justify a thoroughgoing solipsism of the self would require that one can see beyond his world and find nothing there, and that would require that he be both inside and outside his world at the same time so as to discern a contrast between himself, his language, and what else is out there, beyond language. And this is impossible. Recall that "what we cannot think, that we cannot think: we cannot therefore *say* what we cannot think."[66] So he takes the measure of what is true in solipsism: "For what the solipsist *means* is quite correct; only it cannot be *said*."[67]

Wittgenstein reiterates the theme of "The limits of my language are the limits of my world" but in a significantly different formulation: "der Sprache, die allein ich verstehen." There are two possible translations: "the language only I understand" or "the only language I understand." The first translation is open to solipsistic interpretation; the second is not. Both are possible translations, given the ambiguity of the German in which "*allein*" can refer to the "I" or to "the language." A natural reading would tie the issue of authenticity to solipsism, for what could be more authentic than the expressions of a solipsistic self? We might not be understood by anyone else, but undeniably we would be fully ourselves. Hence authenticity would be connected to a private language which is uniquely the speaker's own. If this is so, the struggle to articulate such a private language is the closest we can come to an authentic self—whether in the arts or in philosophy—but ultimately un-describable. Yet this seems not only counterintuitive but crazy, for it turns language and

65 *TLP* 5.62.
66 *TLP* 5.61.
67 *TLP* 5.62.

the arts, surely the most shared and shareable of human practices, into something private and elusive.

Consider however another reading which is less crazy. We argued that the empirical self is too immersed in the world to allow a sense of authenticity; and that the metaphysical self, by not being part of that world, lacks the contrast that is necessary for authenticity. If the truth of solipsism can only show itself but cannot be stated, couldn't there be an associated notion of authenticity that likewise cannot be formulated but can only show itself? We then could not say that an authentic thinker is one who does not rely on historical precedence. Such a formulation would ignore the distinction of empirical and metaphysical selves; only the empirical "I" can be said to be dependent on tradition etc., while it does not make sense to say such a thing about the metaphysical "I." Instead, the elusive mixture of independence and dependence that we intend by "authenticity" can show itself in the thinker's work which itself is unavoidably the result of both selves.

This sounds promising. Wittgenstein's remarks from his *Notebooks 1914-1916,* however, not only fail to support such an interpretation but provide support to the opposite which "grounds" authenticity in the metaphysical self. Consider: "What is the objective mark of the happy, harmonious life? Here it is again clear that there cannot be any such mark that can be described but only a metaphysical one, a transcendental one."[68] If there is an analogy between authenticity and happiness, our suggestion of understanding authenticity as composed of metaphysical and empirical ingredients would be wrong.

No matter which way we turn, we see young Ludwig "grounding" authenticity in the world of transcendent values and not in the world of facts. After all, if the self is everything, then there is nothing beyond the self to constrain, influence, restrict, or frustrate it. If so, all expressions of that self would be authentic, and inauthenticity and embarrassment would be impossible. But if inauthenticity is impossible, then authenticity is no achievement. And that does not seem to square with what we think authenticity is. It's all too real a problem.

Young Ludwig argues that for a person or work to be authentic, the worker or the work has to be separated from the influence of everything external. There are, however, external constraints on authenticity: matters of good taste, beauty, morality, relations to other artists, and so on. So, authenticity cannot be a stand-alone intrinsic value that overrides everything else. What is more, to make sense of the concept of authenticity, we need art history: comparisons and contrasts. Otherwise, any attempt to reinvent the wheel may be said to be authentic.

---

68 Wittgenstein, *Notebooks 1914–1918*, p. 78e.

So insofar as the notion of authenticity is tied to the self, the early Wittgenstein has a "separation problem" not unlike Descartes' and Rousseau's. Once you so sharply separate the self from everything external to it, you have a hard time bringing them together even if, or especially if, the self is said to be "a vanishing point" and "almost nothing." Recall that Descartes, to do justice to the mind, made it otherworldly and then had difficulty showing how mind and body work *together.* In his desperation he had to resort to a *deus ex machina* strategy to work the trick. And Rousseau, working in the social and political context, failed to find a satisfactory solution to the problem of the autonomous individual living in society, stopped interacting, decided to become an isolated subject, and to live a "solitary" life. What this shows is that young Ludwig, despite his remarks to the contrary, follows in the footsteps of Plato, Descartes, and Rousseau and ends up with a private language which only he understands; or perhaps we should say not even he understands. He uses the philosophical tools and assumptions of the tradition and reduces the tradition to absurdity and himself and everyone else to silence.

Nevertheless, he and we remain disposed to talk about these most important things—the ultimate meaning of life, absolute value, ethics, aesthetics, and religion—despite the fact that, or perhaps because of it, all such talk is nonsense. This persistence of ours documents the tendency in the human mind, which, Wittgenstein says, "I personally cannot help respecting deeply and I would not for my life ridicule it," despite their "subject matter" being transcendent.[69] Their very essence, says he ironically, lies in their "nonsensicality." That is a mark of their transcendence. For all he "wanted to do with them was to go beyond the world, to run against the boundaries of language; that is to say, beyond significant language. This running against the walls of our cage is absolutely hopeless."[70]

Notice that "the cage view," on the one hand, presupposes the acceptance of the picture theory of language—that all we can legitimately do with language is to describe the world. On the other hand, it flags a palpable and natural dissatisfaction with the limits of our cage, manifest in our repeated attempts throughout the history of philosophy to break somehow out of it. We suggest that this desire to open the doors of our cage and break out is the desire for transcendence most evident in ethics, aesthetics, and religion. In these areas, we do more than state facts or describe the world. We prescribe,

69 Ludwig Wittgenstein, *Lecture on Ethics,* in *Philosophical Occasions*, edited by James Klagge and Alfred Nordmann, Hackett Publishing Company, Indianapolis and Cambridge, 1993, p. 44.

70 Ibid.

recommend, assess, appreciate, pray, forgive, cajole, embarrass, and so on.[71] So apart from the desire to jump out of our skin, the desire for transcendence presents a deeper and more complex picture of language that acknowledges that language is our means of communication and expression—the very opposite of a cage. It is the very thing that enables us to escape our solitude and solipsism.

In any event, in one sense or another, Wittgenstein seems to be committed to the idea of a private language, which marks a contrast between the early philosophy of the *Tractatus* and the later philosophy of the *Investigations.* In contrast to the *Tractatus*, the later work of the *Investigations* treats language as a shared social practice and regards the idea of a private language as problematic or dependent on a socially shared language. If there is language, then there must be a language user. If there is meaning, if there is sense and reference, and intentionality in a language, then there must be something capable of endowing language with those characteristics. That thing can't be any old thing. Language is an institution. A language *user* participates in that institution by following its rules, practices, and conventions to perform the full array of actions that we language users have in our linguistic repertoires. Authenticity, like a private language, will have to be cobbled out of already existing materials, including the work of others, pushing it to the limits and putting one's own stamp on it by performance or through some other means.

If so, it is embarrassing to speak of a solipsistic self as seeking authenticity and originality. Such attributions are intelligible only if there are persons and others embedded together in the world, in institutions, in a history and a culture, and not transcendent metaphysical subjects. But the big embarrassment is the metaphor of the cage of language.

Lastly, the Tractarian theme of silence, of what we cannot speak—namely, ethics, aesthetics, and religion—offers a stark contrast to the Logical Positivists. They took Wittgenstein at his word and dropped from the philosophical lexicon everything that *we cannot speak of and must be silent about.* In their view, all that transcendent "nonsense" was just that. For them, the transcendent objects of Wittgenstein's reverence were embarrassing excess, philosophical baggage.

The Vienna Circle

And now to the embarrassments of the Vienna Circle. Hume and the early Wittgenstein had a powerful influence on members of the Circle, chiefly

71 Is this an early reference to language games?

because they adopted a thoroughly empirical orientation, the analytic–synthetic distinction, and an anti-metaphysical stance. Wittgenstein wanted to abolish philosophy altogether, while the Logical Positivists wanted to abolish metaphysics and translate ethics exclusively into the language of feelings. Between 1927 and 1932, Wittgenstein had conversations with members of the Circle, especially with Moritz Schlick and Friedrich Waismann. Later on in life, Wittgenstein said, perhaps exaggerating somewhat, "And, Hell and Blazes, I founded the Logical Positivists but scoffed at the title 'Wiener Kreis' as a publicity stunt."[72]

The Vienna Circle is not to be thought of as a homogeneous group, although given their manifesto, perhaps it is fair to say that its members were guided by a revolutionary fervor to abolish traditional philosophy and to promote the scientific worldview. They wanted to hive proper philosophy off from what they thought were its historical embarrassments, consistent with the Humean[73] and Tractarian programs. Suffice it to say that these avant-garde practitioners of twentieth-century analytic philosophy worked in Hume's and Wittgenstein's wake.

There is a difference, however. While the Positivists wanted to preserve scientific philosophy and philosophy of science, Wittgenstein of the *Tractatus* aimed to eliminate philosophy, including the philosophy of science, since in his view philosophy and science have nothing to do with one another. In his view, philosophy would just intrude on and interfere with the practice of science. Here was a genuine attempt to put an end to philosophy altogether.

Like Wittgenstein of the *Tractatus*, the Positivists not only made use of the powerful new logic of Frege and Russell but they added to their toolbox the verificationist principle, which they called the "Wittgenstein principle," that the meaning of a proposition is its method of verification. The latter was intended to identify meaningful sentences and separate them from those that, on the surface, simply look as though they have sense; for example, metaphysical sentences. Thus, they followed Hume's injunction to consign the metaphysical guff to the fire. Philosophy, for them, consisted in logic and scientific philosophy, with epistemology still important, but now a part of the science of psychology. This sudden and unexpected contraction of traditional philosophy embarrassed many of its practitioners—much like a shrunken shirt that no longer fits. Not the Positivists, however, since their lack of sympathy with the tradition and its values did not allow much space for embarrassment.

72 Wittgenstein, *Public and Private Occasions*, p. 396.

73 *Treatise,* Book 1 only.

The principle of verification as a criterion of meaning proved to be an overreach and should have been acutely embarrassing for the Circle. It was neither analytic nor empirical, and hence, by their own account, meaningless. When your announced criterion of meaningfulness itself makes that criterion meaningless, surely that should be embarrassing. And perhaps it was, for the objections to the principle drove them to suggest that it should be regarded as a mere proposal. But why accept as a proposal what had been rejected as a meaningless principle? What does demotion from principle to proposal do to alleviate the problem of meaninglessness? Perhaps this is best understood as their way to take back the principle to save face while they continued to employ it. "We couldn't have meant that," they might say in self-defense, "because according to the verification principle, it's meaningless." Which begs the reply "Oh? So, you *did* mean it!" This is an example of what we call "Hitting the nail right on the thumb."

There is yet another reason for positivist embarrassment. Don't you have to understand what a proposition means before you can say whether it is verifiable and how, and to set about verifying or testing it?[74] Doesn't that meaning figure in deciding what would verify or refute the proposition? And mightn't the test uncover additional meaning of an insufficiently well-understood sentence, in a manner not unlike the ways that science and philosophy work? If so, then meaning is logically prior to verifiability and verification. Hence, meaning cannot be reduced to verification or verifiability. This sounds like something the post-positivist Wittgenstein would have thought, and why he understood verification as a useful device, only.

It is not surprising then that philosophers, in general, did not buy into the principle's revised version as mere proposal either. Wittgenstein remarked in retrospect that he had never heard of the Verification Principle until recently; however, he knew about the method of asking for the verification of propositions and that it is useful. "Its main point was to bring out distinctions and to ask what is to be done with the proposition. To show that the method is fruitful, one has to do some philosophy using it. To call this method a principle is," he said, "to make philosophy look too much like mathematics."[75]

On the face of it, this may seem disingenuous since there is evidence for Wittgenstein's "verificationism" in G.E. Moore's detailed notes on

74 For a brief history of this objection, see F.J. Pelletier and Bernard Linsky, "Verification: The Hysteron Proteron Argument," *Journal for the History of Analytical Philosophy*, Vol. 6, No. 6, 2018, pp. 8–35.

75 December 1, 1938, at the meetings of the Cambridge Moral Science Club. See A.C. Ewing: "A Reply to Mr. Wisdom on Meaninglessness." See Wittgenstein, *Public and Private Occasions*, p. 334.

"Wittgenstein's Lectures, 1930-1932" where Wittgenstein is said to have made "the famous statement, 'The sense of a proposition is the way in which it is verified.'"[76] However, later in these lectures, Wittgenstein qualified this by saying that he only meant by this that "you can determine the meaning of a proposition by asking how it is verified," and went on to say, "This is necessarily a rule of thumb, because 'verification' means different things, and because in some cases the question 'How is that verified?' makes no sense."[77] So, he was not a slippery customer but he was attentive to difference and rejected the Circle's application of it as a dogma. He did not propose a theory of meaning but saw verification as *one* way of getting at the sense of a sentence.

Now to the question of whether Wittgenstein founded the Logical Positivists or was his claim an exaggeration or even braggadocio? Here are the relevant facts. When Moritz Schlick first met Wittgenstein in 1927 and invited him, on behalf of his group, to attend their meetings, obviously the group had already existed. Its members called it the Schlick Circle, for Schlick originated the group soon after he was appointed Professor of Philosophy at the University of Vienna in 1924. However, at the Prague 1929 meetings of the Ernst Mach Society in 1929, which Wittgenstein did not attend, the group renamed itself the "Vienna Circle" and at the same time issued a Manifesto—The Scientific Conception of the World: The Vienna Circle. This is the moment that Wittgenstein alludes to as a "publicity stunt." Indeed, the document contains much sloganeering, of which Wittgenstein was critical: "Renunciation of metaphysics! As if that were something new!" Thus, he had already expressed caveats about the Manifesto to Waismann early on when the Manifesto was being planned.[78] How could you claim to be the father of a movement whose Manifesto you disavow? These facts belie Wittgenstein's claim as a founder of the Vienna Circle Logical Positivists.

What could have prompted him to make such a claim? Perhaps he thought he did not receive enough credit for the role he and his work played as an intellectual stimulus to the Circle and its activities. Considering these contributions, he could, without exaggeration, describe himself as a seminal influence on, or an important member of, the Circle. To say this, however, is very different from saying that he had founded the Vienna Circle.

---

76 Ibid., p. 59.

77 Ibid.

78 McGuinness, *Approaches to Wittgenstein*, p. 3. For the Manifesto, see Hans Hahn, Otto Neurath, and Rudolf Carnap, *The Scientific Conception of the World: The Vienna Circle.* https://www.biostasis.com/pdfs/viennacircle.pdf.

The contretemps between Wittgenstein and Rudolf Carnap, a fellow member of the Circle, seems to support this line of thinking. In the summer of 1932, Wittgenstein complained that a recently published paper of Carnap—a member of the Circle—titled "Physicalist Language and the Language of Science" made such extensive and unacknowledged use of Wittgenstein's own ideas that Wittgenstein would soon be in a position where his own work would be considered merely as a reheated version or plagiarism of Carnap.[79]

This incident conjures up Wittgenstein's refusal to acknowledge his debts to Hume in the *Tractatus*. Can he say that what he assumed or borrowed from Hume was not novel, or extensive, or unique to Hume, so that he did not need to cite him? While his ideas borrowed by Carnap were so extensive or unique that they deserved a reference? Otherwise, Wittgenstein's work may come to be understood as a mere footnote to Carnap? No salient difference, unless for the passing of centuries, justifies this omission.

What happened, one might ask, to the young Ludwig who wrote in the "Preface of the Tractatus" that he was completely indifferent whether the thoughts that occurred to him had occurred to someone else and therefore he gave no footnotes? He was not so indifferent when the shoe was on the other foot. This smacks of ethical inconsistency, if not outright hypocrisy. Why does Wittgenstein suddenly assert his intellectual property rights? If he is free to help himself to Hume's work without acknowledgment, why can't Carnap do the same? The flagrant inconsistency between the way Ludwig treated Hume and the way he expected to be treated by Carnap should be deeply embarrassing for Ludwig—at least in retrospect.

And now to ethics—as if the above case was not an ethical as well as a legal one! The Positivists did not concern themselves with normative or virtue ethics but were mainly interested in the analysis of the meaning of ethical sentences, thus reducing ethics to metaethics.[80] Since ethical sentences seemed to be neither *a priori* nor *a posteriori*, there was a distinction to be brought out here. The vast tracts of language which were declared meaningless or unsatisfactorily analyzed—as, for example, "Courage, Hurrah!" and "Cowardice, Boo!"—were embarrassing if only because such analyses reduced the complex meaning of ethical sentences to expressions of mere personal preferences. Most members of the Circle had little or no interest in ethics, apart from Moritz Schlick, who wondered with his students about the verifiability of

79 See David Stern, "Wittgenstein versus Carnap on Physicalism: A Reassessment," 2006. Philsci-archive.pitt.edu/2860/; and Oscar Kuusela, "Carnap and Wittgenstein: Tolerance, Arbitrariness and Truth," 2024. https://www.mdip.com.

80 With the exception of Moritz Schlick.

ethical sentences and made a serious effort to do justice to ethics within a Positivist framework. Eventually, he settled on the view that ethical sentences are empirical statements about maximizing happiness, hence verifiable.[81] He even came up with a maxim: "Increase your happiness," where happiness was to be understood as joy that accompanies actions done for their own sake springing from our talents. The basis of ethical studies, according to Schlick, is the shared human practice of value-ascribing behavior.[82]

Under the Positivists, ethics would be reduced to the anthropological task of describing value-ascribing moral behavior, but without being able to understand what its practitioners think or say about what they're doing and why, since all such value thought and talk is made meaningless by the positivist's criterion. Ethics would become like a description of mysterious, unintelligible practices of a foreign culture. Worse still, even the anthropologist's descriptions would be too much because the verificationist principle would prevent the positivist ethicist from describing what they observe as behavior, since to do so requires understanding the intentions with which one acts, and intentions include ascriptions of value to courses of action. An intention includes a judgment about what one ought to do—unintelligible nonsense to the positivist.

Thus would the anthropologist be reduced to describing mere bodily mechanics. Ethics would be emptied of the concepts and distinctions we have fashioned for explaining and evaluating one another *qua* person-agents. Such a limited vocabulary would deny the ethicist the distinction between intentional and unintentional action, and without that distinction, they could not understand the role of excuses and extenuations in our assessment of human conduct. And that would destroy the concept of responsibility. Ethics would not survive these reductions.

Moreover, were philosophy itself to take up the positivist's recommendations, it would find the evaluative questions at the core of practical and theoretical reasoning meaningless. In all contexts, the questions What should I do? and How should I do it? would be beyond its ken. Philosophy, and rationality with it, would thus be embarrassed into silence about evaluative issues, not only in morality and practical reasoning, but everywhere—in law, politics, religion, etiquette, customs, art and language, and in philosophy, math, logic,

81 Moritz Schlick, *Problems of Ethics*, Prentice Hall, New York, 1939. Republished by Cambridge University Press, 2009; For a first-hand account, see Béla Juhos' entry on "Moritz Schlick," in *Encyclopedia of Philosophy*, edited by Paul Edwards, Vol. 7, Macmillan Publishing and The Free Press, New York, 1972, p. 323.

82 See also the ethical emotivism of C.L. Stevenson in his *Ethics and Language*, Yale University Press, New Haven, 1944.

and science—all those meaningful activities, and the institutions in which they are embedded that constitute the interpersonal lives of persons. Why? Because all such activities would have been declared unintelligible because corrupted by nonsense and therefore unfit for science or philosophy—insufficiently "scientific" and so beyond the scientific and philosophical pale. The positivist philosophers would be unable to understand themselves when they say, approvingly, that such and so a procedure is sound; that some method of inference is reliable; that a scientific philosophy is better than its fuzzy historical alternatives, and so on, for all those enterprises in which terms like "reliable" and "sound" are used evaluatively.[83] Thus would philosophy be embarrassed into silence—diminished by a theory of itself according to which philosophy had been too theoretical. Philosophy would be "Dada-ed" on its own petard.

Unlike the Logical Positivists, Wittgenstein was not dismissive of ethics but carved out a special place for it in the realm of the mystical and therefore of the un-sayable. He took it dead seriously. In the *Tractatus*, there was reverential silence about ethical and religious value. "It is clear that ethics cannot be put into words. Ethics is transcendental."[84] "The sense of the world must lie outside the world. In the world everything is as it is and happens as it does happen: *in* it no value exists—and if it did exist, it would have no value."[85] "And so it is impossible for there to be propositions of ethics. Propositions can express nothing that is higher."[86] So Wittgenstein sends ethics up and, thereby, rejects naturalism in ethics much in the vein of G.E. Moore, for whom *the good* was intuited and unanalyzable.[87]

These two positions present us with the following dilemma: On the one hand, the price of bringing ethics down to Earth seems to strip it of all ethical content, thus losing it. (Logical Positivism) On the other hand, the price of preserving ethics is to make it otherworldly, ineffable, unintelligible, thus apparently losing its usefulness. (the early Wittgenstein) That these are options

83 See John Searle, "How to Derive 'Ought' from 'Is'," *Philosophical Review*, Vol. 73, No. 1, pp. 43–58, 1964.

84 *TLP* 6.421.

85 *TLP* 6.41.

86 *TLP* 6.42.

87 That "Ethics is transcendental" has a Kantian as well as a Platonist resonance since it is concerned with the necessary structure within which we can talk about contingent facts, and since Wittgenstein also talks about a separate realm of value. For Moore's rejection of naturalism in ethics and his open question argument, see *Principia Ethica*, Cambridge, 1903.

forced upon us is a strong indication that something is amiss with the theory that forces them.

This problem is reminiscent of the problem of mind-body dualism: How can two substances with nothing in common interact? In this case, the problem is that ethical value is alleged to be the wrong kind of thing to abide in our earthly lives. The solution is to see our way out of the metaphysical dualism that motivates the dilemma. The beginning of that insight may be to recognize that values, being ours, are as much features of the world as are our thoughts about the material world.

The *Lecture on Ethics* is important, partly because it marks a sharp difference from the views of the Vienna Circle and partly because it signals a new opening through a failed attempt to rescue the Tractarian "silent treatment" of ethics. Readers may be embarrassed for two reasons. First, Wittgenstein revisits ethics as if it had not been done justice—as if it begged for more to be said, in seeming tension with the Tractarian admonition to silence. And second, while in some contexts reverential silence may be an important ethical reaction, since when, one may legitimately ask, is language a limit rather than an enabler of thought, understanding, and communication? Surely, given the glaring importance of ethics, philosophers need to attend to it, if only to clarify its discourse, its conflicts, and disagreements.

Wittgenstein meant what he said in the last lines of the *Lecture on Ethics*, and he would never take it back:

> My whole tendency and, I believe, the tendency of all men who ever tried to write or talk Ethics or Religion was to run up against the boundaries of language [...]. What it says does not add to our knowledge in any sense. But it is a document of a tendency in the human mind which I personally cannot help respecting deeply and I would not for my life ridicule it.[88]

The *Lecture on Ethics* flags Wittgenstein's felt need to expand his discussion of value in more detail, and it seems to lead to the eventual emergence of Wittgenstein's new "language game" approach. As he feels the need to revisit ethics, as he confronts and discusses its questions, the embarrassed Tractarian silence is partly abandoned and the dormant concept of the human form of life (*Lebensform*) emerges ("a tendency in the human mind") and is assumed as background for the discourse of value.

Thus, Wittgenstein, like Hume before him, turns from his old to his new way of thinking, by turning to our social and ethical practices and our ways

88 Wittgenstein, *Lecture on Ethics*, pp. 37–44.

of life in general. We might think of it as a form of philosophical populism.[89] Look at what we do; at how we get along, at the tendencies of the human mind, at our patterns of behavior. We refer to this as Wittgenstein's "Humean turn." Suddenly there is the possibility that there is more to say about the deep "meaning" of silence.

Finally, the philosopher who acquainted English-speaking readers with the Vienna Circle was the young A.J. Ayer. Having been sent by his tutor Gilbert Ryle to Vienna for a year to attend meetings of the Circle in the early 1930s, Ayer was close to the action. Through his book *Language, Truth, and Logic,* he introduced the philosophically minded in Britain and America to the Vienna Circle.[90] Like Roger Fry, who, through his 1910 exhibition "Manet and the Post-Impressionists" in London, brought the French Post-Impressionists to the attention of the British public, Ayer performed a similar service for the avant-garde philosophy of the Vienna Circle. In clear, crisp, highly readable prose, he articulated and argued for the Logical Positivist program, putting the verification principle where it logically belonged, at its very center. The book, at the time, received high praise. No less a philosopher than Bertrand Russell said of the book that he wished he could have written it himself. Indeed, it is still worth reading, if only as a document about a certain movement in the history of philosophy.

"Logical Positivism is dead," John Passmore wrote in 1967, "or as dead a philosophical movement ever becomes." We opt for not completely dead. Nevertheless, it is gratifying to see something of a renaissance of interest in the Vienna Circle as their contribution is carefully reassessed, highlighting their important work in the problems of philosophy of science, mathematics, and logic, and at the same time, downplaying what is perhaps embarrassing: the central role the verificationist theory of meaning played in their program.

It is one thing, however, to correct the mistaken impression that the question of verification was the sole concern of the Circle and highlight their work in the philosophy of science and logic. It is quite another thing to neglect the criterion of meaning (or cognitive significance) the Circle adopted in their Manifesto. That would suggest that Ayer had perpetrated a misconception.

---

89 What is the connection, if any, between this and ordinary language philosophy? See Austin on appropriate forms of behavior. On language: language is a repository of the ideas, descriptions, and distinctions we have found worth making [...] etc. It is not the sort of thing that "you or I are likely to think up in our armchairs on an afternoon." (J.L. Austin, "A Plea for Excuses," in *Philosophical Papers*, edited by J.O. Urmson and G.J. Warnock, Clarendon Press, Oxford, 1961, p. 130.)

90 A.J. Ayer, *Language, Truth, and Logic,* V. Gollancz, London, 1936, where he formulated the principle of verification within the framework of British empiricism.

Such a revisionist reading is embarrassing, since it sidelines verification, which the early documents place at the Circle's center. An additional gripe against Ayer may be that he exploited the hard work done by the Circle when he published his *Language, Truth, and Logic*, a best-seller for generations to come.

Perhaps what is embarrassing about such a revisionist reading is the ambiguous way it references the Vienna Circle. On the one hand, there is the movement that was the Vienna Circle (1922–1936), and then there is its dispersal as its various members emigrated to the United States and Britain. Members of the Circle had moved on, and as they developed philosophically, they realized that the principle of verification was the kiss of death. They had, as it were, "Dada-ed" themselves. They revised or abandoned it; yet, in the heady, ideological, early days, it had served their purpose to abolish metaphysics, which was at the heart of traditional philosophy, and to promote the scientific spirit.

Granted, members of the Circle—for example, Schlick, Carnap, and Waismann—may have been on to the problem with the principle and said, in their own way, all sorts of interesting things about verification. But the revisionist reading, by downplaying verification, does a disservice to their pioneering role on the question of meaning and in the philosophy of language. Some instructors, who teach courses in the history of the origins of analytic philosophy, also make light of verification, practically pass over it in embarrassed silence, and dwell on the other achievements of the Circle. And that is embarrassing. But it is worse, surely, for the Vienna Circle or their followers to later disavow the officially meaningless criterion of meaningfulness at the center of their earlier work, having used that criterion to get philosophers to shut up about things—morality and metaphysics—that they thought should be no part of philosophy's ambit.

Quine: A Brief Encounter

At the same time as Ayer, Willard Van Orman Quine, a young American academic, attended the meetings of the Vienna Circle.[91] Both breathed the fresh avant-garde airs of Vienna, but what contrasting characters. On the one hand, we have Ayer: clever, quick-witted, incisive, and highly social—Oxford don by day, man about town by night. On the other, there is Quine: penetrating, highly original and, by his own admission, inept at *Sturm und Drang*. Reading his works, one can see how the Circle, especially Rudolf Carnap, shaped his philosophical perspective, despite the fundamental criticisms he

91 Our treatment of Quine is not intended to be comprehensive but aims to be narrowly focused on our brief.

later leveled against the Circle's tenets of the analytic–synthetic dichotomy and the verificationist theory of meaning.

Quine had several things to be embarrassed about. First, his attack on analyticity presupposes that we understand analyticity. Second, his goal of eliminating the corrupting influences of thought, language, and mind on our accounts of reality—really, he wants to move thought out of the way—occurs in thought—how else?—and presupposes our recognizing the goal should it be achieved. Thus, his project, if it were achieved, would, by reintroducing all that he endeavors to eliminate, fail.

Third, the embarrassment stemming from Quine's scientistic naturalism. To save philosophers from embarrassing themselves through armchair speculation, Quine turns to science. In his hands, philosophy becomes "continuous" with the natural and social sciences: epistemology with psychology; cosmology with physics and astronomy; ethics with social psychology and anthropology. "Philosophy of science," he famously declared, "is philosophy enough."[92]

Quine's naturalism is haunted by an embarrassing ambiguity. He often speaks as if he were a philosophical revolutionary advocating a reductive naturalism according to which only the natural and social sciences could play an explanatory or justificatory role. Is this not a scientistic view of philosophy, where the theory of knowledge would become part of natural science, leaving no room for traditional questions such as the nature of knowledge and the standing of science? At other times he speaks as if he were for a non-reductive naturalism, according to which our presumed empirical knowledge, including our everyday empirical beliefs as well as our scientific beliefs, plays a role in the process of justification.[93] Will the real Quine stand up?

Quine's embarrassing scientism is on full display in his remarks about epistemology, and it is evident in his lifelong behaviorism. Reporting in the early 1930s on his rapport with the psychologist B.F. Skinner, he said: "Fred and I met on common ground in our scorn of mental entities. Mind shmind; on that proposition we agreed. The things of the mind were strictly for the birds. To say nothing of freedom and dignity."[94] And later in 1969, in reply to Gilbert Harman: "I am as much a behaviorist as anyone in their right

92 "Mr. Strawson on Logical Theory," *Mind*, Vol. LXII, Issue 248, October 1953, pp. 433–51.

93 See Susan Haack, "Two Faces of Quine's Naturalism," *Synthese*, Vol. 94, 1963, pp. 335–36.

94 Dagfinn Follesdal, "Developments in Quine's Behaviorism," *American Philosophical Quarterly*, Vol. 48, 2011, p. 273.

mind can be."[95] Does this quote reaffirm his (methodological) behaviorism or place limits on it? To be sure, the goal of his methodological behaviorism is to jettison the Cartesian baggage of "the mental"—including intention—and provide a scientific explanation of behavior in terms of public, observable patterns. However, this still leaves him with significant difficulties: how to account for the first-person point of view, the "absent qualia" problem, for privileged access, and for morals.

And now to Quine's remarks about epistemology. The old epistemology—basically the Cartesian epistemology—involves the idea of proceeding from certain beliefs about the self to our picture of the world through the guarantees of deductive logic. However, as Hume showed us, this is a "lost cause" despite all the self-deceptive, and thus embarrassing, intellectual effort wasted in its aid. Quine sides with Hume, proclaiming that:

> The Humean predicament is the human predicament [...] Why all this creative reconstruction, all this make belief? The stimulation of our sensory receptors is all the evidence anybody has to go on, ultimately, to arrive at his picture of the world. Why not just see how this construction proceeds? Why not settle for psychology?[96]

On first thought, one is inclined to say "Bravo, Quine." But doesn't this remark chastise us? Isn't Quine enjoining us to put away our prejudices, stop being such sticks-in-the-mud, and get out of the way of science instead of being so old-fashioned? Shouldn't we just "get on with the program" and see what happens?

But wait a minute. Philosophy, in Quine's hands, is "naturalized" and is continuous with science. Like Hume, who turned from philosophy to "the science of human nature"—psychology, Quine is turning from philosophy to natural and social science. The best way, according to him, to avoid professional incompetence, and thus embarrassment, is by doing what he calls "scientific philosophy." Indeed, most of the time what he means to be doing is science or helping science along. So, perhaps it is no good criticizing him for philosophical shortcomings, for what could we possibly mean by that? We can be embarrassed, it seems, only about not doing scientific philosophy. Quine is mildly embarrassed about traditional philosophy and philosophers who do not do "scientific philosophy." He does not come out and say it, but

95 Donald Davidson and Jaakko Hintikka (eds.), *Words and Objections*, Reidel, Dordrecht, Netherlands, 1969, p. 296.

96 W.V.O. Quine, "Epistemology Naturalized," in *Ontological Relativity and Other Essays*, Columbia University Press, New York, 1961.

it is, we suspect, there. Philosophers who do not do scientific philosophy, he thinks, are not competent players of the game, since they do not operate from within science, having been blinkered by the tradition.

If Quine means, however, to reduce philosophy to science, is he not thereby getting rid of philosophy and succumbing to scientism—regarding science as an idol—thus signaling that he is a victim of the deep and embarrassing confusion of mistaking philosophy for science? He seems to think that, with the language of science—mathematics—and the language of philosophy—formal logic, now a part of science, plus the special sciences, we have finally succeeded in stripping away all that corrupting, human, personal stuff from our accounts of the world. That with those two languages we can really get to accounts of things in themselves, how things really are independently of how we perceive them, independently of our distorting perceptions of them? But if so, who will understand those languages? And if and when they do, would that very act not reintroduce the dreaded, distorting personal stuff? Isn't he reaching for something he cannot grasp?

Toward the end of his essay "Has Philosophy Lost Contact with People?" Quine turns to the question of ethics.[97] "Ethics as an afterthought," one might say. Such a placing of moral philosophy and ethics is in sharp contrast with Hume, who puts philosophy on the right path by turning it away from the blind alleys of universal skepticism to the passions and to human nature. Hume regards moral philosophy as first philosophy, while Quine views philosophy of science as first philosophy. Is this sort of scientism not a reincarnation of metaphysics? Philosophy as the handmaiden of science? So, hold that "Bravo." To echo the early Wittgenstein: "Logic (philosophy) has to take care of itself."

Quine wants to change the subject matter of philosophy from its central concern with human nature and the self-understanding of the human agent as he is engaged in the world. This is in sharp contrast to Hume's focus on human nature as the primary goal of such a study. Quine, in a sense, sidelines ethics, religion, politics, and aesthetics, and tasks the "social sciences" of sociology, anthropology, political science, and cultural studies exclusively with their study. Thus, no meaningful normative questions can be asked in everyday situations or in scientific endeavors. To be clear, Quine is, and takes himself to be, doing science.

We think Quine is mistaken in thinking that we can do without such concepts as meaning and intention. Suppose that metaphysics is the enterprise

97 W.V.O. Quine, *Theories and Things*, Harvard University Press, Cambridge, MA, 1981.

of uncovering the fundamentals of thought—the things we can't describe our way out of.[98] We believe these fundamentals would include the idea of ourselves as rational agents acting in an objective world alongside others with whom we share, not just our nature, but certain interests, including an interest in our own welfare and that of our loved ones. They also include what Peter Strawson called "reactive attitudes," which include resentment toward those who wrong us, a sign that it is of our nature to apprehend others as persons.[99] If these features of persons are fundamental, then we could neither describe nor modernize our way out of them without losing personhood itself. We have been arguing that embarrassment is another reactive attitude, and that it would be difficult to recognize a life as human without all that goes into it: fallibility, self-correction, goal-directedness, rationality and its standards, the grammar of conduct, and so on. Not impossible to imagine, perhaps, given all the many examples of shamelessness that we increasingly see around us.

Aren't some of the things Quine mentions as hopelessly confused—meaning, idea, concept, essence, and therefore things ripe for the philosophy's ash-heap—things that we could not describe our way out of without undermining our sense of ourselves as person-agents? And if we cannot, what does this say about us? That we lack imagination or the courage to give up our bad old habits and convictions? Or does it mean that there is, after all, a metaphysics of personhood that we cannot do without?

Since there is not enough identification with the tradition, perhaps, after Quine, a certain sort of philosophical embarrassment is impossible. "Competent scientific philosophers" are so deeply steeped in the *a posteriori*-empirical that for them the idea that philosophy may raise meaningful normative questions in everyday life as well as in scientific endeavors, and thus survey and assess science, is unthinkable. For unlike philosophy, which respects and learns from its traditions and history, embarrassing warts and all, science is indifferent to its history of embarrassment. In fact, it buries them. They no longer play a role; they no longer matter. Science moves on; in fact, it has perfected the art of moving on.

Yet a feature of human nature is that, despite our best efforts, we are inclined to repeat our mistakes and errors. Our explorations must take this

98 S.C. Coval and P.G. Campbell, *Critique of the Liberal Conception of Persons*, Edwin Mellen Press, Lewiston, New York and Queenston, Canada, 2010.

99 Peter Strawson, "Freedom and Resentment," *Proceedings of the British Academy*, Vol. 48, Carlton House Terrace, London, England, 1962, pp. 1–25.

into account and include, à la Hume and Wittgenstein, a study of human nature and its passions. It is a significant fact that Hume called his book *A Treatise of Human Nature* and that Wittgenstein remarked that "My ideal is a certain coolness. A temple providing a setting for the passions."[100]

100 Wittgenstein, *Culture and Value*, p. 2e.

Chapter IV

DOING PHILOSOPHY AFTER THE DEATH OF THE TRADITION

Hume's Turn: Books 2 and 3 of the *Treatise*

In our narrative of philosophical embarrassment, Hume is pivotal for two reasons. First, in Book 1 of the *Treatise*, as we have seen, he put an end to the Rationalist tradition by pushing it to its limits. As he writes, he really discovers things, and it becomes painfully clear to him that there is no way out of the contradictions and impasse that skeptical Reason leads to. What is more, he really feels the weight of the problems—the loss of the world, the destruction of the self, the dissolution of fellowship and community. No wonder that feelings of despondency and melancholy overwhelm him as he shows that pure demonstrative Reason—"the divine spark"—designed to solve our common problems such as how to live better lives and bring about a measure of contentment and happiness—accomplishes the very opposite effects. In the whole history of philosophy, there is no better and more moving description of the pathetic and embarrassing state that the philosopher who follows Pure Reason finds himself in: a strange beast who doesn't fit in, is out of sync with every thing and every one.[1] That's what happens when we follow Plato's and Descartes' recommendation to appoint Pure Reason as the master of human instinct and passion.

In Books 2 and 3 of the *Treatise*, Hume turns this picture of Reason on its head and asserts that "Reason is, and ought only to be the slave of the passions."[2] In saying this, he takes a turn in a completely new direction, toward a new way of philosophizing, opening up philosophy to the study of human nature. Reason, once the master of our lesser faculties, is naturalized, it is brought down to Earth where it is subject to human nature and psychology. Such a demotion opens a way to integrate the non-rational passions into

1 *T* 1.4.7.2, SBN 264–5. Hume texts online. All subsequent references to Hume's works are to this resource.

2 *T* 2.3.3.415.

our cognitive life and to appreciate their complex role in our moral and social lives and in understanding ourselves and others.[3]

The Role of Self and Other in the Indirect Passions: Pride, Shame, Humility, and Embarrassment

With the idea of the substantive self demythologized, strict personal identity "as it regards our thought and imagination" is, strictly speaking, excess metaphysical baggage. The self is not a simple unitary thing but is instead a mere succession of perceptions united only by their membership in that succession. Ironically, pure reason, rather than proving the existence of the self, shows it to be a piece of fiction—a product of rationalization.

But this metaphysical housekeeping creates new problems. If there is no stable self, how can we account for the passionate concern we take in ourselves and the self-conscious emotions of pride, shame, and embarrassment? How can we make sense of responsibility, praise, and blame? For there is an intimate connection between personal identity and the passionate concern we take in ourselves. Witness our regrets and remorse about our past actions and our concern about future events such as sickness, decline, and death. We can't regret or have remorse for another's actions, and we are, in general, more concerned about the decline or death of ourselves, our families, and loved ones. These psychological facts about us presuppose an enduring conception of the self. Without it, a significant portion of our lives would be meaningless, even pathological.

Moreover, how would the selfless self make sense of certain passions? Hume takes up the issue of "the indirect passions" in Book 2 of the *Treatise*, and his discussion of these reads much like contemporary philosophy of emotions. Our passions, Hume observes, are either "direct" or "indirect." What makes a passion direct is that it "arises immediately from good or evil, from

3 Books 2 and 3 of the *Treatise* were rarely studied in depth by early twentieth-century analytical philosophers. It was Hume the skeptic of Book 1 of the *Treatise* who had influenced Wittgenstein of the *Tractatus* and the Vienna Circle, mainly because their primary concern was epistemological with an anti-metaphysical thrust. This view was shared by many later Anglo-American philosophers, until the pioneering work of Páll Árdal (*Passion and Reason in Hume's Treatise*), of Terence Penelhum (*Hume*), of Annette Baier (*A Progress of Sentiments: Reflections on Hume's Treatise)*. These authors initiated a renaissance in Hume studies and generated a new understanding of his philosophy. The newly established Hume Society, with its journal *Hume Studies* and its annual meetings, were instrumental in this shift of focus.

pain or pleasure."[4] Moreover, a passion is direct because its cause is identical to its "object"—what the passion is about. For example, fear of the bear is caused by and is about the bear. On the other hand, the object of an indirect passion is not identical to its cause, and this indirection is due to the essential role played in the indirect passions by the idea of the self.

Hume's main explanatory examples of the indirect passions are pride and humility.[5] Darwin, who acknowledges Hume's influence, called them "self-conscious emotions." To be proud of one's house, Hume would say, is to enjoy pride's characteristic sense of elation about the quality of one's self which one perceives to have been elevated by the qualities of one's house. Thus, pride is evaluative of, and mediated by, one's idea of one's self, and it is anchored in the psychology of the self. Pride is a self-conscious emotion, not merely in the sense that we are aware of it, but more importantly in the sense that pride is always about the self and its value.

When we are proud of our accomplishments, or proud of the accomplishments of our children, students, friends, or country, it is the self that we feel good about because of its relationship to those causes of pride. Likewise for the man who feels dejected with humility by the shabby nature of his suit. "It's always self, which is the object of pride and humility [...] and when self enters not into the consideration," Hume declares, "there is no room either for pride or humility."[6] To be proud is to feel elated by the fact that the value of the self is greater than it would be otherwise—if it were not suitably related to its objects and their properties. "He is proud of his house" is an elliptical way of saying that he is proud of himself because of his house.

We know the distinctive phenomenology or feel of pride from being or feeling proud. It is a sense of elation over the belief that our value as a person has been elevated. And we know what it is to be humbled from the sensation of feeling dejected over the fact that the value of our stock, as it were, has been deflated. But in every case, it is our sense of self and its worth that is inflated or deflated. That sense of self is always intimately present to us.

Now the value of the self varies as the value of the objects attributed to it vary. Our stock goes up because our account includes the beautiful house, or the son having won the skateboarding competition. Our stock falls because it includes the shabby suit. In general, the self's stock goes up when bathed in

---

4 *T* 2.1.1.1. "Division of the Subject."

5 *T* 2.1.2.4. "Of Pride and Humility, Their Objects and Causes." The indirect passions include "pride, humility, ambition, vanity, love, hatred, envy, pity, malice, generosity, with their dependants."

6 *T* 2.1.3.2.

the reflected light of valued objects; it goes down when one's attributes and things "take the shine off" the self. Because our stock is so affected, we are especially alive to the value of objects to which we are related.

In Book 2 of the *Treatise*, Hume observes that of pride and humility "it is impossible we can ever, by a multitude of words, give a just definition of them [...] The utmost we can pretend to do is a description of them by an enumeration of such circumstances as attend them."[7] And again, like love and hatred, "they are sufficiently known from our common feeling and experience, provided a description is given of the circumstances which accompany each passion."[8] This is one juncture at which objectivity enters the content and therefore the identity of the emotion. For such a description of the circumstances of each passion that Hume alludes to must include, in the case of pride, how the causes of pride are related to us. We cannot be proud of just any house, but only of one that is "appropriately related" to us: a house we own, or designed, or built, or financed, and so on—some relation that allows its value to be reflected in our own person. To feel proud of a house absent some such relation, say, only because we walk by it every day or take pleasure in looking at it, would be, to say the least, weird, a kind of pathology, perhaps, a form of megalomania. In such cases of "false pride," where an appropriate relation to the cause of pride is lacking, the pride is unjustified and hence inappropriate.[9]

In light of his analysis of pride and humility, Hume makes a telling remark about our emotional psychology in general, our concern over esteem in particular, and how that esteem may be measured by the objects around us: "Whatever other objects may be comprehended by the mind, they are always considered with a view to ourselves."[10] So the object of the indirect passions of pride and humility is the self. Its value varies as the value of objects attributed to it varies. Because our stock is so affected, we are especially alive to the value of objects to which we are related.

Another juncture at which objectivity tends to play a role is where other persons confirm our being proud, humiliated, or embarrassed. Thus, pride and humility are not entirely self-regarding and require affirmation from others for their stability. "Even the other causes of pride, virtue, beauty and riches, have little influence, when not seconded by the opinion of others."[11]

7 *T* 2.1.2.1.

8 *T* 2.2.1.1, SBN 329.

9 Are there cases of vicarious pride and humility, analogous to sympathetic and empathetic embarrassment?

10 *T* 2.1.2.2, SBN 277.

11 *T* 2.1.11.1.

In Books 2 and 3 of the *Treatise*, Hume takes a social turn and affirms "the other" and society, giving them an important role to play in the formation of particular passions such as pride, humility, shame, and embarrassment of self and "other." So, to form the idea of the self and engage in the practices of Socratic self-knowledge, we need sympathetic and concerned others to enter the fray: parents and friends. That is the norm.

Small wonder, then, that Hume's account of the indirect passions—the self-conscious emotions of pride and humility—have a role for others. Pride and humility, Hume says, would not be stable emotions, were they "not seconded by the opinions of others";[12] nor would embarrassment make sense without the existence of standards—a "grammar of conduct"—to which we are held, by ourselves and others. Thus, the idea of the self requires objectivity. Our psychological states earn their content and function in the interplay between mind, body, and world.

What is true of pride and humility is, we submit, also true of shame and embarrassment and of the other self-regarding emotions. Without a sense of self, there would be neither shame nor embarrassment. Similarly, without a concern for the self's respect or esteem, the possibility of shame and embarrassment would be remote, to say the least. Shame and humility are essential for identifying and correcting our errors and faux pas with a view to maintaining a well-founded pride.

Hume singles out the important roles these passions play in our moral and social lives. He not only approves but thinks highly of a certain sort of pride: "A genuine and hearty pride or self-esteem, if well concealed and well founded, is essential to the character of a man of honour, and [...] there is no quality of mind which is more indispensably requisite to procure the esteem and approbation of mankind."[13] Similarly, shame and embarrassment are essential for identifying and correcting our errors and *faux pas* with a view to maintaining a well-founded pride.[14]

The obvious difficulty here is that if there is no such thing as the "self," as Hume the skeptic argues in Book 1 of the *Treatise*, then a necessary condition of the self-conscious emotions—of the indirect passions—is missing and we could neither experience pride, humility, shame, or embarrassment, nor make sense of our practices of self- and other-assessment, responsibility,

12 Ibid.

13 *T* 3.3.2.11.

14 For Hume, embarrassment as such is not a subject of inquiry. He uses "embarrassment" a few times in the *Treatise* and in each case, he uses it to mean a "bar" or an "obstacle" to agency. But it is clear from his treatment of pride and humility that his account of embarrassment dovetails well with our own.

and forgiveness that employ them. To own this paradox must be acutely embarrassing. Is there anything Hume can do to dispel this embarrassing contradiction?

The Problem of the Self: Hume's "Sceptical Solution"

The problem of the self arises again only for those philosophers who think the philosophy of Books 2 and 3 is a continuation of the philosophy of Book 1 and inherits the problems that Book 1 established. Instead, we believe, the philosophy of Books 2 and 3 is philosophy by other means rather than philosophy done by "pure reason." Hume's solution shows how nature, our passions, and objectivity are constraints on pure rationality and philosophy.

Hume's "sceptical solution" to the problem of the self is analogous to his skeptical solution to the problems of causation, induction, and objectivity. Echoing a theme we already struck: It is open to Hume to say that, while philosophy has shown him that there is nothing more to the self than the current, fleeting contents of experience, at the end of philosophy he nevertheless cannot but believe that he is a substantial, enduring thing, the author of his actions—the object of his pride—and someone toward whom he is especially sympathetic; that his psychology which compels these beliefs is a product of the history of that self-same self going about the business of living in a world of objects, others, causation, and the rest; and it is resolutely impervious to his skepticism. After all, this nature of his was born of the business of living.

So officially, as it were, writing an autobiography may not be on for Hume the skeptic for the same reasons that no action of any sort is on, nor any reasoning from present to future, nor from effect to cause. But this "sceptical solution" concedes that, while he has no discrete conscious experience of an enduring self with a past and future and abiding interests, his experience-hewn nature compels in him the habitual, irrepressible passion that he is just such a thing; that his life is something that he lives; and that things turn out much better for him if he plans on the basis of his experience of how things have gone in the past. And, of course, his life is just the sort of thing he is in a privileged position to write about! Who better? Moreover, the writing, Hume the historian might add, is not a work of philosophy. If it were, there would be precious little—even less—to write about. There would be no autobiography, and no biography either.

Hume's Autobiography Without Embarrassment

A critic, however, might say: "not so fast." For if we hold Hume to his Book 1 skepticism about an identical and enduring self, and hold him to his view that the self is nothing more than a succession of ever-changing perceptions, then we have to ask how could such a thing write an autobiography, let alone anything else? Ironically, Hume's "My Own Life" bleaches the self precisely of what he says it consists of—a succession of related ideas and impressions united only by their membership in that succession.

Furthermore, Hume surprises us with external verifiable facts about himself and others, employing a conventional autobiographical narrative, with stable character traits and dispositions that should be unavailable to Hume the skeptic. Consider: "My studious disposition, my sobriety, and my industry [...]; and was seized early on by a passion for literature, which has been the ruling passion of my life."[15] And he concludes: "I am, or rather was [...] a man of mild dispositions, of command of temper, of an open, social, and cheerful humour, capable of attachment but little susceptible of enmity, and of great moderation of all my passions."[16]

These self-ascribed attributes cannot be analyzed away as a succession of perceptions in constant flux. Rather, they are stable character traits that he owns and add up to a sketch of Hume's self-portrait. Critics may cry foul, for they feel a palpable tension between Hume's autobiography and his philosophy of the self. If Hume, the consistent Cartesian skeptic of Book 1 of the *Treatise*, were to enact his philosophical program of personal identity in his autobiography, we would have a description of a lively inner life of perceptions that he remembers and is conscious of. But he does no such thing. Given his "no self" theory of Book 1, such critics may say, Hume has no right to narrate the story of his own self using the language of self that he himself discredited. Is this not a serious embarrassment to Hume and his admirers?

Hume's skeptical solution irons out these wrinkles and does not raise further philosophical problems. To reiterate, Hume, in Book 1 of the *Treatise*, is doing something very different than what he does in Books 2 and 3. In Book 1, Hume is attacking a thick conception of the self—a metaphilosophical theory of the self as an individual mental substance. Not only is such a substance not experienced or grasped, he claims, it is not systematically elusive either, for there is no such thing. In Books 2 and 3, Hume does not put forth a competing theory of the self to the "no self theory." He sticks to what is experienced by him and everyone else: "that succession of related ideas and impressions of which we have an intimate memory and consciousness."[17]

15 Hume Texts Online, *My Own Life*, MOL 3, Mil xxxii–iii.

16 MOL 21, Mil xi–i.

17 *T* 2.1.2.2, SBN 277.

Notice the absence of skepticism about memory and the editing out of those impressions and ideas which cannot be verified by records and others.

If there is a tension in our understanding of Hume's views in the *Treatise*, it is our tension, not Hume's. The notion of the self is contested only in Book 1 where the target of attack is the Cartesian substantive self. It is not contested in Books 2 or 3 where he gives the same "thin" empiricist account of the self that is admittedly presupposed in all of our everyday living and practices. If philosophy questions this, it simply interrupts the smooth flow of everyday life and embarrasses itself.

So, if one senses a tension in Hume's autobiography, it is not because Hume is conflicted, but because the reader may be. Acutely aware of Hume's devastating argument against the Cartesian conception of the self in Book 1 of the *Treatise*, the reader may not fully realize that Hume moved on. If there were such an inconsistency between the philosophy and the autobiography, it is unlikely to have escaped Hume's notice, yet he pays it no heed and writes his autobiography as if it is business as usual. Hume is not doing philosophy in his autobiography.

The issue of autobiography and the issue of the indirect passions of pride and humility, we suggest, are connected in that both are motivated by a passionate concern for the enduring self, past, present, and future. What Hume says about pride in the *Treatise* lends textual support for this claim: "Our reputation, character, and name are considerations of vast weight and importance; and even the other causes of pride, virtue, beauty and riches, have little influence, when not seconded by the opinion of others."[18] Readers of his works are these "others" whose opinions matter and sustain his reputation and good name, both in the present and future. The "indirect passions" of pride, self-respect, and self-esteem heighten, sustain, and guard our sense of self. "It is always the self, Hume claims, which is the object of pride and humility, and whenever the passions look beyond, it is still with a view to ourselves."[19] So Hume's autobiography may be seen as a natural extension of his passionate concern for his own person—his reputation and good name—in the eyes of future readers of his works. He expects readers "to second his opinions," to affirm his works and reputation even after his death.

Up to now, we have been referring to Hume's *My Own Life* as an autobiography. It is, however, a unique document, difficult to classify. Is it a philosophical autobiography? If so, it is odd that he never mentions his philosophical views or their origin or those who influenced him, nor does he describe his

18 *T* 2.1.11.1, SBN 316.
19 *T* 2.1.3.2, SBN 280.

philosophical struggles. He might say: If you are interested in my philosophical views, read my philosophical books. Does Hume decide to disavow the word "philosophy" and adopt its practice? This can be immediately ruled out, for we find philosophy named three times, although no philosophy is done. So, there is no disavowal of philosophy. Witness his saying: "I had an insurmountable aversion to everything but the pursuits of philosophy and general learning."[20] Nor is there any self-deprecation as a philosopher manqué.[21] The autobiography, we might say, is itself a skeptical solution to the problem of the self. So is every other aspect of his life.

Is *My Own Life* a spiritual autobiography? If so, it is a poor instance of that genre, since there is little introspection in it, and the little there is, seems to lack the psychological complexity and rich detail characteristic of the genre that we find, say, in Rousseau's *Confessions.* For Hume, facts and the judgments of others based on them are criteria for a sound autobiography as well as for the passions in general, but especially for the indirect passions, the circumstances that give rise to them play essential roles. Hume is cautious, even reluctant to write an autobiography because he does not want to encourage the false idea, so prominent in Rousseau's *Confessions*, that the self is self-authoritative.

Is *My Own Life* an autobiography at all, or is a mere 13 pages of manuscript too brief for that? But is length a reliable basis for deciding to what genre a work belongs? Hardly. In any event, Hume immediately denies that the piece is about him and says that it is about his works: "But this narrative shall contain little more than the history of my writings."[22] Therefore, it may be of interest to students of philosophy, history, psychology, and others. In general, Hume's account of his own life seems designed to provide helpful factual information to readers of his works about the history, circumstances, and reception of his writings. Since, as he says, almost all of his life was spent in literary pursuits and writing, whether philosophy or history, there is good reason to describe *My Own Life* as a brief, elegant, and by and large factual autobiography.

However, is this all there is to the matter? Let us query a little this "little more." Aside from the historical facts, the indirect passions of pride, humility, shame, embarrassment, guilt, and regret enter the picture. Here is a list of the objects of Hume's pride. He is proud of the fact that he comes from a good family; of having influential connections; of his diplomatic posts; of

20 Hume Texts Online, MOL 3, Mil xxxii–iii.

21 See Liz Stanley, "The Writing of David Hume's My Own Life: The Persona of the Philosopher and the Philosopher Manque," *Auto/Biography*, Vol. 14, 2006, pp. 1–19.

22 Hume Texts Online, MOL, Mil xxxi.

having been celebrated in Paris as an intellectual rock star; of being popular with "modest ladies"; of his being of a cheerful disposition; of being moderate in his passions, of being detached, distanced, autonomous, and of possessing a tranquility of mind; of being calm in the face of immanent "dissolution."

On the other hand, he was humiliated and embarrassed by the scant critical reception of his publications. His *Treatise of Human Nature* was hardly noticed, and his other philosophical works had not received the attention they deserved. As to The History of the Stuarts, he was "assailed" on all sides, and "mortified" by its reception.[23] Regret and guilt enter the picture when he reflects on the failure of the *Treatise*, where the problem was not with "the matter but the manner"[24] of presentation and that he made the mistake of rushing it into print.

Does all this help to explain why Hume himself was troubled that his autobiography—"the history of his writings"—may be misunderstood as a sign of vanity or conceit? Is he not skeptical about such an undertaking? Does he not think that often it is an exercise in vanity, excessive pride, and self-deception? There is, in the *Treatise*, a passage which makes it clear why he has misgivings about the genre:

> Nothing is more disagreeable than a man's over-weaning conceit of himself. Every one almost has a strong propensity for this vice. No one can well distinguish in himself betwixt vice and virtue, or be certain, that this esteem of his own merit is well founded.[25]

Like a conceited individual who constantly talks about himself and his accomplishments offends against the social conventions, so an autobiographer may offend against the literary conventions. What is more, self-assessment of one's own merits is untrustworthy, if only because it is inherently vulnerable to positive bias for oneself. And autobiography as a genre is particularly susceptible to these vices of vanity, excessive pride, and self-congratulation. So, Hume has a palpable aversion to the genre because it seldom manages to avoid such vices. Another reason that Hume is dubious about the idea of autobiography may be that it presumes to be telling "the inner" from the point of view of "the inner." Thus, what is told can't be verified by anyone but "the self." In such cases, the likelihood of self-deception looms large. Again, the case of Rousseau comes to mind.

---

23 Hume Texts Online, MOL 11, Mil xxxvi–vii.
24 Ibid., MOL 8, Mil xxxv.
25 *T* 3.3.2.10, SBN 597–8.

Hume begins and ends his autobiography with concerns about the question of vanity. He denies that he is writing a spiritual autobiography á la Rousseau with the thick Cartesian "self" at its core. If this autobiography were about him, he says, rather than his works, then he might be called vain and conceited, insofar as writing such a narrative might be regarded as an act of self-applause and thus be highly embarrassing. But how do you tell the dancer from the dance? When Hume's works are "overlooked, neglected and unobserved, when they are assailed, even detested,"[26] is Hume himself not "overlooked, neglected, assailed and mortified and detested"? So, although his death is imminent, it is more difficult than he imagines to wrench Hume apart from his writings, no matter how detached or distanced he may be.

But what does Hume mean by "vain"? He might mean either of two different things: Is the autobiography useless or futile, nothing more than vain talk? Impossible talk, given his skepticism? Hence, it's a demonstration of his skeptical solutions. Every act of his is a refutation of skepticism of the "I refute thee thus" variety. Or is he showing excessive pride in his own accomplishments, that is, is it conceited? The first sense would refer to the work and the second to the character of the author who wrote it. To dispel the charge of vanity as conceit, he mentions that his first work, The *Treatise*, "fell dead born from the press" and was not such that could possibly be an object of pride or conceit. Nor is the autobiographical note "vain" in the sense that it is useless or futile, since it may be useful to readers of philosophy, history, literature, and others interested in Hume's writings.

Again, why is Hume so exercised by the question of vanity or conceit? For moral reasons, we suggest. Vanity or conceit involves an exaggerated sense of one's own importance and a false assessment of one's own achievements. And these failures of self-knowledge and self-understanding are tantamount to a betrayal of the Socratic imperative of "Know thyself." And that would weigh heavily with Hume. Recall that Hume thinks highly of well-founded, justified pride: "A genuine and hearty pride and self-esteem [...] is essential to the character of a man of honour."[27] Such a pride is merited pride. And of course, he thinks badly of conceit: of unmerited, false, or excessive pride which is commonly accompanied by self-deceit.

At the end of what he refers to as "this funeral oration," Hume concludes, in a dead man writing mode, with a description of his character that we already mentioned: "I am, or rather was (for that is the style I must now use in speaking of myself [...])," and then returns to the possible attribution of

26 Hume Texts Online, MOL 11, Mil xxxvi–vii.
27 *Treatise*, 3.3.2.11.

vanity: "I can't say there is no vanity in this funeral oration but I hope it is not a misplaced one. Matters of fact are easily ascertained."[28] No skeptic he!

In concluding our reflections on Hume, we point to sharp contrasts between Hume's and Rousseau's autobiographies. If we follow the convention and classify autobiographies as interior or exterior, then Hume's is an instance of exteriority, mostly containing matters of fact that are "easily cleared and ascertained."[29] This line itself gives the lie to the attribution of skepticism to Hume. Recall, however, that he immediately denies that it is an autobiography—that would suggest, according to him, vanity, conceit, or excessive pride. Rousseau's *Confessions*, on the other hand, is an avowed autobiography of interiority: "I have bared my secret soul as Thou thyself has seen it."[30] And true enough, he shares with us shameful and embarrassing episodes. However, many of its claims are difficult to verify, since they are revelations of the secrets of his soul accessible only to him and God. Hence readers need to take Rousseau's word for their veracity.

Immediate qualifications are in order. As we have seen, Hume also speaks of his own "inner states": of taking pride in his family background; of his disappointments upon the reception of his publications; of being overlooked, neglected, assailed, and mortified by his critics, and so on. There is more of these emotional reactions than on first glance meets the eye. An inner process stands in need of outward criteria, and a passion cannot be identified simply by its intrinsic feel. To know an emotion, according to Hume, is also to know its "circumstances." As he describes the circumstances in *My Own Life*, there is much "emotion-implicature": the reader can identify the emotions that Hume does not spell out but implies in the circumstances he provides. For instance, his referring to the *Treatise* as having fallen "dead-born from the press" is expressive of intense grief—like for the loss of a child.

Hume can take pride in his brief and reader-friendly, mostly factual "autobiography." As he says at the very start, "It is difficult for a man to speak long of himself without vanity; therefore, I shall be short."[31] In contrast, Rousseau might be embarrassed about his self-indulgent autobiography of some six hundred pages. By the time Rousseau's *Confessions* was published, Hume was dead.

To protect his good name against Rousseau's embarrassing and unfounded slanders, and pathological accusations of betrayal of friendship and so on,

---

28 Hume Texts Online, MOL 21, Mil xl–i.

29 Ibid.

30 Rousseau, *The Confessions*, p. 17.

31 Hume Texts Online, MOL 1, Mil xxxi.

Hume published their correspondence against the advice of his friend Adam Smith. There is, however, no mention of Rousseau in *My Own Life*.

Summing Up: A Philosophy of Human Nature

Philosophy is as natural, as much part of human nature, as are the passions. Reason can be, unless misdirected, as conducive to human flourishing as are the passions. It has a different role than that conceived by Plato and Descartes. Just look at what Reason can do: describe, explain, justify, create, and so on. But as skeptical philosophy shows, it can be destructive and self-defeating. It can, especially if detached from reality and objectivity, lead us into a *cul-de-sac*, rob us of agency, thwart personhood, and thus utterly embarrass us. Recall Hume's final account of the logical culmination of the skeptical philosophy. Why did philosophy derail? Because it was thought to be independent of reality, not constrained or measured by it. Analogously, seeing the self as purely rational and utterly separate from reality is, as we have earlier called it, an "autonomy too far."

Books 2 and 3 of the *Treatise* are cases of application of Hume's skeptical solutions to various philosophical problems where human nature and the passions "solve" the skeptical problems. What can we sensibly talk about in the wake of being embarrassed to death by the skeptical philosophy? It turns out that we can talk about a whole lot of things: the self, others, including others' minds and their contents, including the passions, their nature, and psychology; the world and the relations between minds and the world, including causation, perception, meaning, intentions; the past and the future, facts of the matter, induction, and morality. Just as we can talk about justice without a God-like "mathematical" understanding of it, all without permission from skepticism-proof theories of any of them. In these books, the doing comes before theorizing—it's really first philosophy—and "the strange, uncouth monster" of Book 1, who is lost in his skeptical nightmares, "affrighted and confounded with that forlorn solitude," cut off from the world and unable to mingle with his fellows, is finally recognizable as a fully functioning and flourishing human being enmeshed in moral and social practices.

Chapter V

THE LATER WITTGENSTEIN

Preamble

We have claimed that traditional philosophy is constitutionally embarrassed. Not only not immune to embarrassment but especially vulnerable to it. Does the embarrassment fade or disappear after the death of the tradition? Let us see how this works in the case of Wittgenstein, a prime example among twentieth-century philosophers who challenged the tradition and its norms not once but twice. Did he manage to avoid the constitutional embarrassments characteristic of philosophy, and if so, how? Did he have anything to feel especially embarrassed about?

Public and Private Embarrassments

Critics might say that only the early, but the later Wittgenstein has quite a few things to be embarrassed about. Recall the twin claims that he made in the preface to the *Tractatus* that he had "found the final solution to the problems of philosophy," and that the truth of the thoughts expressed in the *Tractatus* was "unassailable and definitive." Later it dawned on him that both assertions were mistaken. Surely, he would have or should have felt embarrassed, even ashamed of such dogmatic claims, and of the false pride associated with them.

In the preface to the *Tractatus,* Wittgenstein declares that the value of his work partly consists in showing that the solution of the problems of philosophy mean little for our lives. Is this fake modesty about his achievements? Or is he expressing pride in what he has achieved? Both, we suggest, since he is ambivalent about his achievement. On the one hand, he is boasting that he succeeded in solving "the problems of philosophy." On the other, these problems have been blown out of all proportion because they do not possess the sort of significance philosophers attribute to them. "Look," he might have said, "I solved the fundamental problems of philosophy, but it's no big deal. The solution has little or no existential import to speak of. It liberates a few people from being weighed down by what they think are weighty problems when they are not problems at all. Moreover, such people will be free to join the labour market and do useful work."

That was then. Twelve years later, humiliated by events of the First World War and its aftermath, Wittgenstein, in a 1930 diary entry, writes in a different tone. His experience of the horrors of war, his acknowledgment that he was a rather brutal teacher of school children, feeling shame and embarrassment for his denials and lies about their treatment, all took their toll and resulted in a new, modest attitude. "If there were a solution to the problems of logic (philosophy)," he writes, "we should only have to caution ourselves that there was a time when they had not been solved and then too it must have been possible to live and think."[1]

Is this a repudiation of the Tractarian view that the solution to the problems of philosophy mean little for us, or is it an explication of that view? If the former, then certainly it is a fuller and more compelling formulation of it. In any event, we do not see this question as an either/or. Notice the "If" first: Wittgenstein leaves room for the possibility that the problems had not received a definitive resolution. This tentativeness is in sharp contrast with his dogmatic stance before. So, even if there is no negation of the Tractarian claim, there is a repudiation of the dogmatic attitude. At the same time, the remark is also explicated: Traditional philosophers, suffering from hubris, pumped up the claim that the solution or dissolution of philosophical problems are solutions to our existential problems, and thus, are important for our lives. Wittgenstein, however, has shown that having come up with a solution to them is not much to brag about. Just think of the length of time and amount of effort spent to convince students of the proposition that philosophical problems are *their* problems.

So, there appears to be a change of attitude: the dogmatism, arrogance, and hubris characteristic of the earlier philosophy are gone, at least in his writing, and a humble attitude emerges: "If there were a solution [...]" The statement is hypothetical and no longer dogmatic. Suppose that what Russell called "the problems of philosophy" had been solved in the early twentieth century. If we assume that before such a solution people could not think or live a fully human life, as we do now, we are deluded. There were many admirable people who did so, and there were remarkable achievements even then, before such a "solution" was found.

However, young Ludwig certainly depreciated philosophy's stock when he wrote that his *Tractatus* "shows how little is achieved when these problems

1 Wittgenstein, *Culture and Value*, p. 6e.

are solved."[2] Had he been properly chastened by the study of the twists and turns of the history of philosophy, perhaps he would not have thrown caution to the wind and asserted that he had provided the final solution to the problems of philosophy. Maybe he would not even have held that there are such cultural constants as "the problems of philosophy" as described by Russell. Nevertheless, the Tractarian view seems to recur, cast in a style more in line with the later philosophy: "Philosophic puzzles are irrelevant to our everyday life. They are puzzles of language. Instinctively we use language rightly; but to the intellect this use is a puzzle."[3]

It looks as though, at least for the later Wittgenstein, embarrassment about his philosophical errors and his moral flaws were intimately connected. Let's briefly explore this line of thought. Immediately after the war, Wittgenstein was traumatized. Later, he trained as an elementary school teacher and taught in the Austrian countryside. Charged with using excessive force to punish a student, he was put on trial where he lied about the incident, yet his case was dismissed—probably because of his influential family connections. Nevertheless, feeling embarrassed at first, then deeply ashamed of the act and of the lie, he resigned his post and served in various capacities: as a gardener in a monastery and an associate architect for his sister's house in Vienna.

In 1929, Wittgenstein returned to Cambridge with an apparently striking change of attitude. The youthful arrogance and dogmatism were replaced by a spiritual/ethical struggle for humility and modesty. But is such a sudden conversion possible? That it is does not square with the facts and is too simple a story. Militating against it is Wittgenstein's thesis defense in 1929—truly arrogant, and he should have been embarrassed by his behavior. The submitted thesis was the *Tractatus*, which had been published in English some seven years ago. Russell and Moore were recruited as the reluctant examiners. In the discussion, Russell argued that Wittgenstein was inconsistent in claiming he has expressed "unassailable truths by means of meaningless propositions." Unconvinced, Wittgenstein clapped each of his examiners on the shoulder and said condescendingly, "Don't worry, I know you will never be able to understand it."[4] By any measure, this was outrageous and truly embarrassing behavior that offended against the conventions and rules prescribed by the university for such occasions. What is more, his conduct is likely to have offended his examiners—at this time his betters—who were doing their best to support Wittgenstein's application for funding in support of his research.

---

2 Preface, *TLP*, p. 5.

3 Lee, *Wittgenstein's Lectures 1930–1932*, p. 1.

4 Monk, *Ludwig Wittgenstein, Duty of Genius*, p. 271.

It is hard to think that it could have taken place and tolerated anywhere else than Cambridge. This sort of arrogant behavior is reminiscent of his conduct in 1914 when he was thinking of submitting his essay on logic as the thesis requirement for the B.A. Ludwig complained to Moore about the regulations of the thesis requirement that the student should list the influences of past figures on his work. Ludwig lashed out at Moore in an abusive and violent letter for not making an exception of him.[5] This sort of vindictive and intemperate behavior recurs in Wittgenstein's letters to his family, especially to his sister Hermine. Old habits die hard, if they die at all. Later on, he apologized to Moore for his embarrassing and shameful behavior.

So, there is plenty of embarrassing backsliding both on the personal as well as on the philosophical level. Yet, we believe this is no reason to reject the genuineness of the moral conversion. "The edifice of your pride," he later confessed, "has to be dismantled. And that is terribly hard work."[6] The conversion is genuine, but its implementation is gradual, requiring struggle and vigilance. And there was also a recognition that a dogmatic inclination in philosophical work is anti-philosophical, and he should not engage in providing simple answers to complex problems.

Having reread the *Tractatus* later on, Wittgenstein acknowledged its grave mistakes. A central mistake, he said later, was that when he wrote the *Tractatus*, "I had Plato's idea of finding the general idea lying behind all particular meanings of a word. Now I think of the meanings as like the fibres of a rope. One may run the whole way through, but none may."[7] To think that in one fell swoop one got rid of Plato, the father of the tradition, and later realize that one had unwittingly adopted Plato's crucial assumptions about meaning—would this not be embarrassing to most of us, but especially to Wittgenstein?

Who Wants to Be a Footnote?

A consequence of this admission was that despite Ludwig's best efforts, the *Tractatus*, because of its essentialism, was still a footnote to Plato. Thus, he had failed to break free of that labyrinth of footnotes to Plato that constituted the European philosophical tradition.[8] An embarrassing admission for someone who not only hated the very idea of a footnote, but especially his being a

---

5 Wittgenstein, Letter to Moore, in Brian McGuinness, *Wittgenstein in Cambridge: Letters and Documents 1911–1951*, Blackwell Publishing, Oxford, 1995, p. 73.

6 Wittgenstein, *Culture and Value*, p. 30e.

7 Wittgenstein, *Public and Private Occasions,* Conversations with Waddington and Thouless, p. 387.

8 A.N. Whitehead, *Process and Reality*, The Free Press, New York, 1979, p. 39.

footnote. Being a footnote to Plato suggests that we cannot be ourselves and escape the anxieties of the father's influence. As we have seen in our section about the Young Wittgenstein, thinking or writing with footnotes not only distracted him from the task at hand but prevented him from feeling authentic.

In any event, the later Wittgenstein's change in attitude had implications for his work and manifested itself in a change of philosophical perspective. Instead of the single-minded Tractarian preoccupation with representation, Wittgenstein was now also concerned about the many ways of making sense. No more Platonist questions about the nature of meaning, language, and the form of a proposition. Instead, without ditching representation, he is anxious to emphasize the plurality of language games and how people use language. The job of clarification required attention to how language actually works, how we do things with words: "If we had to say anything which is the life of the sign, we should have to say that it was its use." To encourage this, he suggested a handy motto: "Do not ask for the meaning, ask for the use."[9] But meaning is still at the heart of it. The contrast between the old and new approach is between thinking that words have meanings attached to them, and all we have to do is find the attachments, versus, thinking that words have meanings and looking to their employment to see what they are. To repeat, this is not to say that representation is ditched in the later work, since it is front and center in his last work *Remarks on Colour.* Rather, the language games of representation, referring, and naming, occupy a less central place. After having successfully turned the corner, admitting to an error or recognizing a blindsight is no longer embarrassing.

The ethical/spiritual change, from pride to humility, is noticeable in the preface to the *Philosophical Investigations*: "I have been forced to recognize," he said, "grave mistakes in what I wrote in that first book and that the new thoughts could be seen in the right light only by contrast with and against the background of my old way of thinking."[10] This is a deliberate strategy to think with embarrassment and shame, so as to remain modest and avoid former errors due to false pride.

So, there is no absolute repudiation of the *Tractatus*—as if one could put a negation sign in front of the whole book. The common thread running through the *Tractatus* and the *Investigations* is that philosophical problems are caused by a misunderstanding of the logic of our language. The salient difference between the two works consists in how to achieve the goal of proper

9 Ludwig Wittgenstein, *Blue and Brown Books*, Basil Blackwell, Oxford, 1964, p. 4.
10 Wittgenstein, *Philosophical Investigations*, Preface.

understanding. The Tractarian way forward was to distinguish between surface grammar and depth grammar and then invoke and apply the techniques of the newly developed élite discipline of formal logic to the analysis of language. In the *Philosophical Investigations*, the way forward consists in the humbler, yet more demanding practice of careful attention to the uses of everyday language. The latter goal cannot be accomplished once and for all, since we are engaged in a constant struggle against the bewitchment of our intelligence by language. This bewitchment is to be exposed by focusing on how language is used. To put it crudely, attending to the pragmatics rather than the semantics of language.

These two philosophical perspectives, the earlier and later, seem inconsistent. So, was the later Wittgenstein embarrassed about the apparent inconsistency between the essentialism of the *Tractatus* and the anti-essentialism of the *Philosophical Investigations*? And should he have been? Yes, it might be said. After all, there is only one Wittgenstein and he might be embarrassed at so radically turning back on himself, not to speak of his proud ex cathedra pronouncements about having solved the problems of philosophy in one fell swoop, not to speak of his fake modesty about it. Or was he, in turn, joyful that he finally found a way out of the labyrinth of footnotes to Plato that is the history of European philosophy?

No Escape from Embarrassment

How to counter these criticisms? How to relieve Wittgenstein from his embarrassments? We offer, first, a Humean, then a Socratic rejoinder. Recall Hume on the importance of appropriate pride. If Wittgenstein thought that he was really successful in solving "the problems of philosophy" in the *Tractatus*, does he not have, by any reasonable standard, a right to be proud of his work? We say amen to that. And recall that the Positivist philosophers of the Vienna Circle carried on his work for nearly two decades. Now for the Socratic rejoinder: Could it be that traditional philosophers attributed a greater significance to philosophical problems than these problems merited, since they were self-deceived about the perennial importance of such problems and their own importance? Remember Ludwig's remark that it must have been possible for people to live a good life and think well in previous periods in our history too, when the "problems" had not even been formulated, never mind solved.

To continue with the rejoinder, but this time pressing a conceptual point: Is there not a difference between inconsistency and change of mind? Also, between an arbitrary and a justified change of mind? If so, it is outrageous to suggest that the later Wittgenstein's change of mind amounted to an inconsistency—or is arbitrary and frivolous—something that he should feel embarrassed about. His new movement of thought was the result of more than a decade's struggle and has been of momentous significance in the way philosophy was practiced in the second half of the twentieth century and beyond. Again, was Wittgenstein joyful about finding a way out of the history of European philosophy, out of the series of footnotes to Plato? Yes, indeed. Again, all of that is justified.

Occasionally, however, he was concerned he was doing merely destructive work in his philosophical work, at odds with his artistic nature: "It occurred to me today as I was thinking about my work in philosophy & said to myself: 'I destroy, I destroy, I destroy'."[11] So, at times, he needed to reassure himself that he was destroying only grammatical illusions. Consider Descartes' picture of the nature of mind, which regards it as entirely distinct and separate from the human being yet interacting with it like the "captain of a vessel." This picture, Wittgenstein claims, is a grammatical illusion based on a false analogy that leads to absurdities. If you undermine this picture, you destroy nothing of importance.

But not only that. There is also the fact that "it is embarrassing/humiliating for us to have to appear like an empty tube which is simply inflated by a mind."[12] Indeed, Wittgenstein thought that many of the problems of philosophy hinge on grammatical fictions, unreflective use of language, logical blunders. What other embarrassments or shame might Wittgenstein have felt about philosophy and philosophers, including himself? Some of the errors of philosophy are embarrassing because the mistakes are right in front of our eyes—we should know better—yet we are inclined to make them. The pull of essentialism and stereotypes, the obsession with a one-sided diet of examples, the neglect of intermediate cases, the salience of conventional pictures embedded in our language, the neglect of the particular, the oversimplification and unwarranted generalization involved in theorizing, the lack of attention to the employment of our words—all embarrassing. These and other sources of everyday error and embarrassment are vividly depicted in the *Philosophical Investigations*. Was he not exposing our embarrassments and feeling embarrassed himself?

---

11 Wittgenstein, *Culture and Value*, p. 19e. A remark from the transition period of 1931, written after reflecting on a piece of music.

12 Ibid., p. 11e.

Pedagogical Embarrassments

This brings us to pedagogical embarrassments. Wittgenstein was an unconventional teacher. Although he put immense effort into his classes, not for him the ready-made formal lecture.[13] Nor were, for him, the Socratic dialogues, which he regarded as a waste of time proving and clarifying nothing. They were a pretense at conversation, he thought, in which Socrates had the lion's share of the talking and the participants' contribution often consisted of one-liners such as "Yes, Socrates," or "No, Socrates." What is more, Socrates' main goal, Wittgenstein thought, "was to convict others or himself of some unclarity," but, as he pointed out, "we do not try to understand something simply in order to see that we still do not understand it."[14]

Even though Wittgenstein's teaching format in the 1930s was divided into Lecture (one hour) and Discussion (two hours) albeit on different days, the lecture "was itself of a very informal nature, liable to break off into discussion any time. He had no kind of system or technique but simply talked about problems that were on his mind. The discussions were not so dissimilar from the lectures [...] and he completely dominated any discussion he took part in, and these, associated with his lectures, were largely a "monologue," the problem being to find a question or problem to get him started and to provide the occasional interjection to keep him going."[15] Moore, who attended Wittgenstein's 1930 lectures, took notes and provided a good deal of help in the discussion classes by making comments that kept the ball rolling.

Do these reports of Wittgenstein teaching, if correct, not bring him closer, back to Socrates? Is there not a tension between inviting student participation in the discussion—the invitation to dialogue—on the one hand, and the subsequent behavior of a "dominatrix" on the other? We should recall that at the meetings of the Cambridge Moral Sciences Club, several students complained that Wittgenstein took all the oxygen out of the room through dominating the discussion to such an extent that others found it difficult to participate.[16] And do his occasional lecture "monologues" not remind us of Socrates occasionally reducing his interlocutors to "Yes, Socrates" or "No, Socrates"?

13 Reports on his style of teaching can be gleaned from student memoirs and friends' recollections. See, for instance, Theodore Redpath's *Ludwig Wittgenstein: A Student's Memoir*, Duckworth, London, 1990.

14 Wittgenstein, *Culture and Value*, p. 64e.

15 Wittgenstein, *Public and Private Occasions*, p. 341.

16 Ibid., pp. 333–34.

So, despite his attempt to distance himself from Socrates by negatively portraying his character and conversational style, we can see from his students' reports that he may have unwittingly shared some of them. Ironic? Yes. Embarrassing? For us, "Yes." For Wittgenstein, at least in retrospect.

Yet, there is a consensus among the student memoirists that both in his lectures and seminars, dialogue/discussion played an important part. In his classes, Wittgenstein encouraged students to speak their minds and contribute substantially to the discussion—to engage in dialogue. On one such occasion, Wittgenstein interrupted a student who had realized that he was about to say something clearly ridiculous and was trying to say something sensible instead: "No, don't do that. Say what you want to say. Be crude and then we shall get on."[17] A forthright and direct remark may elicit embarrassment on the part of the participant as well as other attendees, yet it gives expression to the gut reactions that are necessary to get to the root of a problem. Hence, a philosophical discussion always involves the risk of offending against the current social norms.

In this respect, we may note some similarities between the practice of teaching philosophy and Freudian psychoanalysis.[18] The blunt, awkward, or "socially incorrect" remarks remind us of the significance Freud ascribes to the slip of the tongue—the volcanic bubbling up of repressed material. If philosophical therapy is to be successful, then the socially "incorrect," the bizarre, the eccentric, the linguistically deviant, the inappropriate, like the slip of the tongue in Freudian therapy, need to be excavated and explored.

We can discern the new approach and style, as opposed to the dogmatic, didactive, anti-dialogue style in the characteristic gathering of a plurality of voices in the more or less brief paragraphs of the *Philosophical Investigations.* Wittgenstein's dialogues, roughly speaking, consist of the voice of a proponent for a position, a voice that critiques it, and a third voice which often points us in the right direction. This resonates with the Socratic dialogues, although now cast in modern form: crisp, to the point, and elegant. There seems to be a crucial difference, though: for Socrates, the dialectic conducted with others is a testing ground or experiment, while, for Wittgenstein, the conversations are essential for the struggle involved in philosophical activity: for coming to grips with and articulating the problem and the various possible resolutions to it.

17 Ibid., p. 365.
18 See Brian McGuinness, "Freud and Wittgenstein," in *Wittgenstein and His Times*, ed. Brian McGuinness, Basil Blackwell, Oxford, 1982, pp. 27–43.

So, Wittgenstein had become increasingly dissatisfied with the classic model of the teacher who knew a lot and transmitted this knowledge to students who knew little.[19] "The formulation of a philosophical problem that seemed most satisfying to him was: 'I am in a muddle, and I don't know my way about.'" On returning to Cambridge after the war, he started his lectures with a remark that prompted a second revolution in philosophy: "The nimbus of philosophy has been lost. For we now have a method of doing philosophy and can speak of skillful philosophers."[20] The fog surrounding philosophical problems has lifted, philosophy was demythologized, and teachers can teach the activity by example: getting a grip on the problem and applying the needed skills to resolve it. In most areas, the problem is staring us in the face and what preoccupies us is coming up with the solution. However, in philosophy, articulating the problem is already being halfway home to a solution or resolution.

The reference to skills may suggest a mechanical application of technique, but nothing could be further from the truth. The teacher and the student are engaged in the same struggle as they are trying to extricate themselves from the fly bottle. But even though the teacher shares the burden of the weight of the problems, does she not have the advantage of what moves to make in the right direction and what inclinations to avoid? Or is it that the problems themselves sometimes appear in a new guise, and then even that advantage disappears.

This was rarely a smooth journey. Often, he got stuck, asking his students to help him out, walking about muttering "I am a fool, I am a fool."[21] Occasionally he was heard to mutter: "Damn my bloody soul." Overly dramatic? Perhaps. "But such was the difficulty of the topics he discussed," recalled a former student, that "all this struggle did not seem to us to be in the least excessive."[22] Such gifted and good-natured students at Cambridge are rarely credited with making possible Wittgenstein's work, yet he could not have done without them. And Wittgenstein's self-recriminations belie the idea that dialogue is identical to mere brainstorming, since the harshness of the recriminations suggests that the teacher has a special responsibility to the students, to the problems and to himself, whereas in the free flow of brainstorming everyone seems to be on equal footing.

---

19 Wittgenstein, *Public and Private Occasions*, p. 358.

20 Wittgenstein's *Lectures: Cambridge 1930–1932*, p. 21.

21 Wittgenstein, *Public and Private Occasions*, p. 344.

22 Ibid.

However, both Socrates and Wittgenstein occasionally give this misleading impression: Socrates, with his "know-nothing" approach on the one hand, and Wittgenstein with his description of philosophical puzzlement: "I am in a muddle, and I don't know my way about." Yet they both lead the discussion, teaching in their own way a set of skills, whose proper application, they believe, enables us to relieve what troubles us and puts us on the right path.

Imagine, however, a student reacting entirely differently—who would feel embarrassed by a teacher asking those whom he is supposed to teach for help. Or feel embarrassed on behalf of such a teacher? Or indignant? The student may feel that the teacher shouldn't involve the audience in his struggle for clarity—that he should struggle solo first and then "feed" his students with the results of such a struggle. This sort of student failed to understand what Wittgenstein was doing, and Wittgenstein would discourage him from attending his seminars.

Wittgenstein's teaching style was, we have argued, dialogical, except for the occasional lapse into monologue. The dialogue, more engaging and more natural than the traditional discourse characterized by premises, argument, and conclusion, is also closer to how we proceed in our everyday interactions with one another. Aside from stating, arguing, and concluding, we perform many different speech acts in a dialogue such as describing, cautioning, objecting, protesting, avowing, imagining, swearing, praying, expressing, recriminating, scolding, and so on.

Now if the *Investigations* is a complex and "carefully crafted dialogue,"[23] then the question arises: Did Wittgenstein's dialogical form of teaching influence the dialogical structure of the *Investigations*? Was it its primitive ancestor? We believe that Wittgenstein's lectures and seminars were the workshop where the dialogue form was forged but not crafted. For it is well-nigh impossible to craft something as spontaneous as a philosophical discussion. The deliberate and careful crafting came after a long gestation period.

Integrity in Teaching: Fraudulence, Self, and Other Deception

In Wittgenstein's *Notebooks* and correspondence with his friend Ludwig Hänsel, we come across remarks not only critical of the conventional teaching of philosophy but positive suggestions as to how to teach it, as well as criticisms of his own shortcomings in teaching. Many of these remarks are motivated by

23 See Jane Heal's insightful "Wittgenstein and Dialogue," *Proceedings of the British Academy*, Vol. 85, 1995, pp. 63–83.

the quest for intellectual integrity. Let us consider first the critical remarks of the conventional teaching: "There are teachers of philosophy who pass off old bills now out of circulation and thus valueless."[24] The old "wisdom" is taught, Wittgenstein believed, even when it no longer has any relevance to our problems. This amounts to fraudulence in teaching. If someone is blunt enough to point this out, embarrassment and shame ensue. If the teacher has an ounce of integrity, he is embarrassed and ashamed. And the students may be embarrassed by the teacher or embarrassed on behalf of the teacher. Thus, embarrassment all around.

How could this happen? "A particular time and culture may deem something great but then there is a transvaluation of values because of some upheaval and then the old now worthless bills remain in circulation and people who are not quite honest pass them off as great and significant."[25] This, Wittgenstein suggests, is precisely our situation in our present culture, yet teachers of philosophy tend to teach as if it is business as usual. This sort of pretense is embarrassing for students in the know and should be for the teacher, once it dawns on him that what he has to say has become irrelevant.

What does it mean, however, to have a transvaluation of values? Is Wittgenstein not making a big mistake here in that he seems to believe that our values are turned upside down and that everything that was worthwhile in the past is suddenly worthless? This would amount to a rupture in our system of values. But does this ever happen? Even if such a "cultural revolution" occurs, certain things stand fast for us, and some continuity persists. Truth, truthfulness, honesty, intellectual integrity, courage still matters. Do we not still admire Socrates and recognize his virtues despite Wittgenstein's criticisms? So, our attention may be focused on hitherto neglected or new problems, but this shift need not exclude attention to the old problems too. For the latter may shed light on the new: how it emerged from the old and how some of the values of the "new culture" may be inflated because of their novelty.

It is here that Wittgenstein made a deep mistake in thinking that philosophy could be taught as a stand-alone study, as if it had no history. We have come across this error already in the early Wittgenstein as he dismissed the history of philosophy as of mere antiquarian interest.

Now to the question of how to teach philosophy honestly? Surprisingly, Wittgenstein takes G.E. Moore as an exemplar:

In his vocation as a teacher, he has been more useful than many others who had a decidedly greater talent than he. This is because Moore acknowledges

---

24 Wittgenstein, *Public and Private Occasions*, pp. 31–33.
25 Ibid.

that he himself is gnawing and is not yet clear. Even the least clever can learn from him: (1) how difficult it is to see the truth and (2) that one need not say that one understands what one does not understand. What is bad is not that you give them the "insufficiently digested," but that you give it to them as something digested. [...] Only through [...] your inner truth can you help the other to greater truth. There is no other means. Strangely, even in a lecture a person affects more through the example he gives than through the stated opinions.[26]

What does "inner truth" mean here and what role does it play in teaching? Could it be that it is the avoidance of self-deception in the teacher? If philosophy is, among other things, a kind of love, it must acknowledge that we all have our flaws and these can be brought to the surface if we practice it properly. This is hard slugging and the teacher, apart from teaching the skills, must teach them in the right spirit and set the example.

Finally, concerning Wittgenstein's assessment of his own teaching. Again, Moore is the standard of comparison: "This brings me to how little I have been following this example which I myself had in front of me. For countless times I kept from my audience how unclear the matter still was to me and acted as if it were clear already, when I was hoping it would yet become clear."[27] Other moments of shame or embarrassment concern situations where he "seeks to gain favour with his audience through a somewhat comic turn; to entertain them, so they willingly hear him out. That is certainly something bad."[28]

These sorts of embarrassment and shame, Wittgenstein thought, are essential for any honest teacher of philosophy. The unembarrassed life, it seems, is not worth living, even in the groves of academe.

26 Here we quote extensively from Ludwig Hänsel, "Wittgenstein: A Friendship, 1929–1940," in *Public and Private Occasions*, p. 301.
27 Ibid., p. 303.
28 Ibid.

Chapter VI

REFLECTIONS FROM AN EVOLUTIONARY POINT OF VIEW

> There's a blush for want, and a blush for shan't,
> And a blush for having done it;
> There's a blush for thought, and a blush for nought,
> And a blush for just begun it.
>
> J. Keats, "O Blush Not So!"

Preamble

Our main concerns, so far, have been conceptual analysis and the moral psychology of embarrassment. In this section, we turn to the science of embarrassment, and Charles Darwin's "Self-Attention, Shame, Shyness, Modesty; Blushing," the thirteenth chapter of his *The Expression of the Emotions in Man and Animals.*[1] Darwin's book is an exemplary contribution to what we now call "interdisciplinary research," and what was then called "natural philosophy." It is an amalgam of biology, physiology, anatomy, anthropology, social psychology, and philosophy.

Darwin assumed that if emotional expressions are the products of evolution, then individuals of the same species are likely to display the same emotional expressions. "Whenever the same movements of the features or body express the same emotions in several distinct races of man, we may infer with much probability, that such expressions are true ones—that is, are innate or instinctive."[2] That is, they are likely to have a biological basis. And since the expression of emotion is universal and innate, the emotions themselves are likely to be innate, too. His focus in this chapter is on the blush and its

1 See "Darwin Online," *The Expression of the Emotions in Man and Animals*, http://darwin-online.org.uk/content/frameset?itemID=F1142&viewtype=text&pageseq=1. Page references are to this text.

2 Ibid., p. 15.

etiology. Although he does not mention embarrassment directly, much of the discussion concerns the variety of causes of the blush, which includes embarrassment, and the discussion therefore sheds light on embarrassment itself.

Darwin and the Blush

One way Darwin collected evidence for the universality of human facial expressions of emotion was by distributing a questionnaire to "missionaries and protectors of the aborigines" who had contact with members of isolated non-European cultures throughout the world. Among the questions he asked were: Does shame excite a blush when the color of the skin allows it to be visible? and how low down the body does the blush extend? Inspired by his French contemporary, Duchenne de Boulogne, Darwin also devised a test for the recognition of emotions by reproducing a set of photographs of facial expressions and asking people to judge the emotional expression portrayed—no doubt an ancestral version of the Ekman/Friesen "pictures of facial affect" test.[3]

Blushing, Darwin thought, has the distinction of being a peculiarly ("strictly") human phenomenon, since nonhuman animals do not blush, while all humans regardless of race do, whether or not any change of color is visible in their skin.[4] He assembled an impressive range of cross-cultural evidence for this claim, limited only by the fact that his reporters all were Englishmen living in distant parts of the world. He rejected Humboldt's possible counterexample when he quoted, "without a protest," the Spaniard's sneer at the Indians of equatorial South America: "How can those be trusted, who know not how to blush?" The implication of a lack of capacity to blush was falsified, Darwin thought, by reports of blushing among the Brazilian aborigines from those more familiar with them.[5]

The observations Darwin adduced have a wide scope, ranging from the South and North American Indian tribes, through the tribes of Africa and the

---

3 For "the facial affect test", see P. Ekman and W. Friezen, "Constants Across Cultures in the Face and Emotion," *Journal of Personality and Social Psychology*, Vol. 17, pp. 124–29, 1971. For an argument that Darwin should get the credit for the discovery, see C. Izard and O. Haynes, "On the Form and Universality of Contempt Expression: A Challenge to Ekman and Friezen's Claim to Discovery," *Motivation and Emotion*, Vol. 11, pp. 1–15, 1987.

4 Charles Darwin, *The Expression of Emotion in Man and Animals*, 1872, p. 364. Darwin-online.org.uk.

5 Ibid., 319. See our discussion of the usefulness of expressions of emotion in understanding and assessing others and their cultures in Chapters 1, 3, and 5.

Indian subcontinent, to the aborigines of Australia. A blush, he reports, citing Mathews, has often been observed "on the faces of young squaws belonging to various wild Indian tribes of North America. At the opposite extremity of the continent [...] the natives, according to Mr. Bridges, 'blush much, but chiefly in regard to women; but [...] also at their own personal appearance.'"[6] Although the blush is not easily detected in very dark-skinned people, "still under such circumstances as would raise a blush in us, 'there can always be seen the same expression of modesty or confusion.'" He observes that "Most persons, whilst blushing intensely, have their mental powers confused [...] lose their presence of mind, and utter singularly inappropriate remarks."[7]

The universality of the blush, Darwin asserts, "affords a new argument in favour of the several races being descended from a single parent-stock, which must have been almost completely human in structure, and to a large extent in mind."[8] The study of expression, he goes on, "confirms [...] the conclusion that man is derived from some lower animal form, and supports the belief of the specific [...] unity of the several races," and then he adds: "as far as my judgement serves, such confirmation was hardly needed."[9]

Blush's Nature

Another issue addressed, which is especially important for our purposes, is that of the "nature of blushing." How did this peculiarly human phenomenon—"the most strictly human"[10] of all expressions—come about? Blushing, Darwin says, is an involuntary form of self-attention derivative from other people paying attention to our appearance and actions:

> The relaxation of the small arteries of the surface, on which blushing depends, seems to have primarily resulted from earnest attention directed to the appearance of our own persons, especially of our faces [...] and afterwards to have been extended [...] to moral conduct. [...] It does not seem possible that any animal, until its mental powers had been developed to an equal or nearly equal degree with those of man, would have closely considered and been sensitive about its own personal

6 Ibid., p. 318.
7 Ibid., p. 323.
8 Ibid., p. 361.
9 Ibid.
10 Ibid., p. 364.

appearance. Therefore, we may conclude that blushing originated at a very late period in the long line of our descent.[11]

What's true of the species—that its emotional life depends upon a complex intellectual capacity—is equally true of the individual: the human infant does not experience the self-conscious emotions; nor does the idiot.[12] This point addresses the discontinuity objection that the blush, because peculiar to humans, is a counterexample to the evolutionary doctrine of common descent. The discontinuity is explained by the vast evolution of the human mind required for some emotions.

Blushing, as opposed to the mere reddening of the face, is an expression that is different from others in that it cannot be elicited by any physical means such as laughing caused by tickling or frowning caused by receiving a blow. Rather, "it is the mind which must be affected."[13] The mental states that induce blushing "consist of shyness, shame, and modesty; the essential element in all being self-attention."[14] Indeed, the blush is not mere facial reddening; for the same reason that a smile is not a series of mere physiological events of nerve, muscle, and bone. The blush, like the smile, is internally related to its causes. All such expressions bring us face to face with a person and his intentionality.[15]

Self-attention, Darwin continues, is not merely "the simple act of reflecting on our own appearance, but the thinking what others think of us."[16] The desire to restrain or suppress the blush is counterproductive, since it just leads to more self-attention and hence more intense blushing. A little later, Darwin connects this up with child psychology and treatment of the young: "As shyness apparently depends on self-attention, we can perceive how right are those who maintain that reprehending children for shyness, instead of doing them any good, does much harm, as it calls their attention still more closely to themselves."[17] Shyness, we add, is an emotional response, or the disposition to respond, to one's recognition that he is judged to be modest, and ought, therefore, to behave accordingly: to be unassuming, humble, deferential, seen but not heard. Among its effects are apprehension over how one will be received,

---

11 Ibid.
12 Ibid., p. 311.
13 Ibid., p. 310.
14 Ibid., p. 326.
15 See the essay on Roger Scruton: "Dialogues in Scrutopia," by Daniel J. Mahoney, http://www.newcriterion.com/articles.cfm/dialogues-in-scrutopia-8674.
16 Darwin, *The Expression of Emotion in Man and Animals*, pp. 326–27.
17 Ibid., p. 333.

confusion, and increased awkwardness. Shyness, Darwin observes, is to be distinguished from humility.[18]

A Critique of the Design Theory of Blushing

It comes as no surprise that Darwin rejects the design theory of blushing—the view that blushing was specially designed by the Creator. The pressing question, then, is what evolutionary service does the blush perform for us? Dr. Burgess, an insightful design theorist, argued that the blush was created "to serve as a check on ourselves, and as a sign to others, that we were violating rules which ought to be held sacred."[19] Darwin works with this idea as he drops the element of design but retains the reference to norms and extends the role of others, suggesting that the blush has a communicative function. More generally, he holds that "the movements of expression in the face and the body, whatever their origins may have been, are in themselves of much importance for our welfare."[20]

The belief in design is obviously opposed to the general theory of evolution, and by the time Darwin's book on the expression of emotions appeared, the design theory had already lost credibility. The theory of evolution became so widely accepted that Darwin did not feel the need to argue for it and simply assumed it as he made his observations on the blush. Nevertheless, he claimed that proponents of the theory of design "will find it difficult to account for shyness being the most frequent and efficient of all the causes of blushing, as it makes the blusher to suffer and the beholder uncomfortable, without being of the least service to either of them."[21] This is Darwin's argument from the evils of shyness against the existence of God!

Shyness, however, because of its apparent uselessness, would seem to present a challenge not only for the theory of design but also for the theory of evolution. Likewise, embarrassment. Moreover, blushing, whatever its cause, would seem, prima facie, to constitute a rupture in evolutionary interconnectedness—in common descent—because it is uniquely ("strictly") human. The pressing question for Darwin and the evolutionists is: What is the evolutionary account of the origin of the blush and of at least some of its causes? We have said, above, that for Darwin the blush has a communicative function and is useful in our welfare. What are some of the details of this account?

18 Ibid., p. 336.
19 Ibid., pp. 337–38.
20 Ibid., p. 365.
21 Ibid., p. 338.

Is the Blush Merely a Physiological By-Product of Self-Attention?

To address these questions, consider a current contribution to the literature by the psychologists Cristiano Castelfranchi and Isabella Poggi.[22] They argue that on Darwin's account, the blush is a mere physiological by-product of self-attention caused by a concern for other people's opinions and hence it lacks causal efficacy and has no function and no meaning. In an effort to provide an account of blushing consistent with evolutionary theory, they claim that, on the contrary, blushing has a specific meaning and function: it is "a communicative signal of shame, functioning as an appeasement signal aiming at inhibiting aggression when the individual fears the group's blame for an actual or supposed fault with respect for some group value that the individual shares."[23] This is so, even if the blush is a non-intentional, even a counter-voluntary, communication.

Deep confusions lurk here in their account of the blush. A blush may appease, given that its etiology may include the belief that one has done something wrong. But that does not make the blush an appeasement signal—a sign of appeasement or apology. Appeasing and apologizing are (intentional) actions. The blush is a natural sign of its various causes, which are intentional, that is, meaningful mental states. But those states are not actions—not something one does. So, the blush is not a sign of appeasement or apology. Nor is the blush an action. It can be, therefore, neither apology nor appeasement.

A comparison between a blush and a slip of the tongue may shed light on this. When is a blush like a slip of the tongue? A slip of the tongue occurs when a person is saying or trying to say something: that is, when the person is en acte. What makes it a slip, in the Freudian sense, is that, in his endeavors, the speaker inadvertently reveals something about himself. Because inadvertent, we ought to say that he unintentionally reveals that thing; that the slip is unintentionally revealing.

Now a blush, like a slip, can be revealing, too. But unlike a slip, the blush may or may not be caused by something the person does. Its cause can be becoming aware of the gaze of another and may have nothing to do with what the blusher is doing or not doing. To mark this difference, we might say that, unlike the slip, where the person's behavior is unintentionally revealing of himself, the blush is something that happens to him. If so, it is

22 "Blushing as Discourse: Was Darwin Wrong?" in *Shyness and Embarrassment: Perspectives from Social Psychology*, ed. R. Crozier, Cambridge University Press, New York, 1990, pp. 230–54.

23 Ibid., p. 240.

non-intentional, where this distinction is meant to indicate that there is no agency in the etiology of the blush. There is, to be sure, something mental in that etiology. Likewise, we might say that he non-intentionally revealed something.

It may also be worth noting that slips are sometimes said to reveal something quite specific: they are often thought to be a kind of "gotcha moment," where something genuinely true of us is revealed, in contrast to what we merely say is true. If you are Freud, it's always something sexual—your lust for your mother or father or both, as the case may be. The blush, on the other hand, has any number of mothers, as it were, and is, by itself, inarticulate: its causes range from something as simple as the fact of observation by another, to a thought as complex as "I am not the person I think I should be."

In any event, Castelfranchi and Poggi claim that there is a radical difference between their account and Darwin's, since on their account the blush is a communicative signal while on Darwin's it has no meaning or function. This is a startling claim, for its general upshot, in contrast with the details, is precisely the same as that advocated by Darwin, who explicitly states that "expression in itself, or 'the language of the emotions,' as it has sometimes been called, is certainly of importance for the welfare of mankind."[24] Darwin reiterates this point, albeit in greater detail, when he says:

> the movements of expression in the face and the body, whatever their origins may have been, are in themselves of much importance for our welfare. They serve as the first means of communication [our emphasis] between the mother and her infant; she smiles approval, and thus encourages her child on the right path, or frowns disapproval.[25]

Thus, facial expressions are features of the child's training and socialization. What is more, they serve as communicative signals to others: "We readily perceive sympathy in others by their expression; our sufferings are thus mitigated, and our pleasures are increased; and mutual good feeling is thus strengthened."[26] So, the Darwinian blush is no mere physiological by-product or epiphenomenon—it does not idly dangle—but has a "communicative" function and pays evolutionary benefits in the sense that it enables us to cope with our social environment.

The expressions of emotion, together with gestures, are revelatory of our own and other minds. They

---

24 Darwin, *The Expression of Emotion in Man and Animals*, p. 367.
25 Ibid., p. 365.
26 Ibid., pp. 365–66.

> give vividness and energy to our spoken words. They reveal the thoughts and intentions of others more truly than do words, which may be falsified [...] The free expression, by outward signs of an emotion intensifies it. On the other hand, the repression, as far as this is possible, of all outward signs softens our emotions. He who gives way to violent gestures will increase his rage; he who does not control the signs of his fear will experience fear to a greater degree; and he who remains passive when overwhelmed with grief loses his best chance of recovering elasticity of mind. These results follow partly from the intimate relation which exists between almost all the emotions and their outward manifestations [...]. Even the simulation of an emotion tends to arouse it in our mind.[27]

The expression, then, is more reliable than the report because of the intimate relations between the expression and its cause. Those relations, unlike those of the verbal report, prevent falsity and deceit. No wonder, then, that Darwin commends the expression of emotions as a worthy study to physiologists and anthropologists because of its importance for the welfare of mankind.[28]

While Darwin rejected the theory of design, it is worth repeating that he did not reject the suggestion made by the design theorist, Dr. Burgess, that one of the functions of the blush is to remind us of the rules and norms that govern behavior. Rather, he put an evolutionary spin on it. Human beings do not simply follow rules but are also self-conscious in doing and not doing so. And blushing is an aid to self-knowledge and self-understanding as well as to the understanding of others. When perceived as breaking the norms of ethics or acceptable conduct, human beings are inclined to blush and to be ashamed or embarrassed.

In light of this textual evidence, we conclude that Castelfranchi and Poggi's criticism of Darwin is a straw man: he did not believe that the blush lacks efficacy, function, and meaning. Their own view of the blush simply echoes Darwin's general position: the blush is not devoid of meaning, and it has a communicative function. It thus pays evolutionary dividends.

Shame and Embarrassment

Darwin does not mention embarrassment specifically as a cause of blushing, perhaps because he regards it as more or less identical with shyness or shame. In any case, much of his discussion of the blush concerns its causes,

27 Ibid., p. 366.
28 Ibid., p. 367.

which include embarrassment, modesty, shyness, and shame. Moreover, some of what he says about shame may reasonably be understood to be true of embarrassment. He distinguishes between two sorts of shame: what we might call "shame proper," where what one does involves the violation of moral principles or ideals; and "superficial shame," where the objects of shame are relatively trivial, having to do with a real or merely perceived breach of etiquette or mere social convention. The latter

> have no necessary connection with the moral sense, and are often meaningless. Nevertheless, as they depend on the fixed custom of our equals and superiors, whose opinion we highly regard, they are considered almost as binding as are the laws of honour to a gentleman.[29]

Modesty, a common cause of embarrassment, is derived from the Latin modus, meaning "standard" of behavior and its origin makes it plain that it presupposes rule-governed norms and standards, as do embarrassment, shame, humiliation, and guilt.[30]

> Consequently, the breach of the laws of etiquette, that is, any impoliteness or guacherie, any impropriety, or an inappropriate remark, though quite accidental, will cause the most intense blushing of which a man is capable.[31]

In this case, embarrassment passes over into shame, and hence for Darwin, there is no sharp dichotomy between shame proper and embarrassment.

Can Animals Be Ashamed or Embarrassed?

Shame, for Darwin, whether its objects are deep or seemingly trivial, is a basic or universal human emotion and the blush is one of its natural expressions. Hence it plays an important role in the related language games of shame, embarrassment, humiliation, indignation, and guilt—concepts that presume a personal and social identity. The capacity to have these complex mental states is indicative of a complicated form of life that non-human animals do not have, and hence it makes no sense to speak of a blushing alligator or lion, even if they were to say, quite incredibly, "I am embarrassed." This brings to mind Wittgenstein's often misunderstood remark that "If a lion could speak,

29 Ibid., pp. 334–35.
30 From modestus: moderate, keeping due measure, sober, gentle, temperate.
31 Darwin, *The Expression of Emotion in Man and Animals*, p. 335.

we would not understand him."[32] The speaking lion obviously has the language but lacks the complicated "forms of life" presupposed by the language. Ditto for snakes, alligators, and, so it seems, for other animals. This suggests that the crucial difference does not exclusively hinge on language as such, but importantly, on the complicated forms of life with which language is bundled and of which it is expressive. This is why we easily understand cartoon animals: they are just like us but in animal form. Real animals eat, walk, and so on, but do not share our complicated forms of life, for example, shame, embarrassment, grief. Hence, if they were to speak of and express them, we would wonder what they could possibly mean.

Wittgenstein speaks in a strikingly Darwinian vocabulary in describing language games:

> This multiplicity of language games is not something fixed, given once and for all; but new types of language, new language games, as we may say, come into existence, and others become obsolete and get forgotten. Here the term "language game" is meant to bring into prominence the fact that the speaking of a language is part of an activity, or of a form of life.[33]

As our activities and practices change or evolve, so does our use of language. Yet, there is a big difference in perspectives between Darwin and Wittgenstein. Darwin regards the question of whether animals can blush as an empirical issue ("it would require an overwhelming amount of evidence to make us believe that any animal could blush"), to be decided by producing "evidence," while Wittgenstein sees the issue as conceptual.

The assumption here is that when we ask, "Do animals have minds?", we speak as if there were one answer to the question.[34] But not all animals are on equal footing. Obviously, what is true of lions may not be true of alligators, and only the reckless or the insane would share their home with them. Dogs, however, are very different, although even in their case we need to differentiate. Domesticated dogs are very different from their relatives like wolves and dingoes. We are willing to attribute to domestic dogs psychological predicates we are unwilling to ascribe to the others. Why? Again, the argument from analogy for other minds fails us. We respond to domestic dogs the way we do, not because we have hypotheses that they have minds and we have more

32 Wittgenstein, *Philosophical Investigations*, 3rd ed., p. 190.

33 Ibid., #23.

34 See Joseph J. Lynch, "Wittgenstein on Animal Minds," *Between the Species*, Winter and Spring 1996, pp. 47–52.

or less confirmed the hypothesis for some of them, that is, that we solved the other minds problem for some of them. If that were so, skepticism would always be present.

Rather than looking at the dog exclusively, we should look and see what our practices are and notice our interactions with them and our attitude. Our attitude to them is an attitude toward a soul, and thus we love them, look after them when they are sick, and grieve for them when they die.[35] This primacy of practice is a crucial first step before theorizing, for these interactions show that we are dealing with a minded creature. And this is so partly because we have trained them to participate in our forms of life and many of our practices. We share our home with them; have a long history and a relationship: recognition, greeting, and expectation. In general, there is empathetic response and reciprocity on their part. We play games with them and train them to carry out serious special tasks such as tracking criminals, sniffing out drugs, showing affection for the sick, and so on. We protect them and they protect us. Consider the family dog. Along he comes, wagging his tail and smiling. Its happiness-behavior, its pain-behavior, its fear-behavior and so on, is much like ours. Do we recognize his ensoulment, his person-like-hood, even if he is not a person like us? If so, we would respond to the look of shame on his puss similar to the look of shame on other persons as we would to any other person who is ashamed. It would be positively inhuman not to!

This is not to say that the dog feels shame, or embarrassment, or so forth, exactly like we do. And we are entitled to that skepticism based on how differently we and dogs are put together. We are conscious, practical, and self-conscious agents. They, well, something more primitive: conscious, definitely; but rational? Even that, but much less so. Whether they possess the self-consciousness required for the self-conscious emotions, including shame and embarrassment, is not so clear. They are agents, but more primitive than we. Might they not feel something like our emotions but without the intellectual content and connections of ours, a kind of simplified emotion, perhaps not unlike that of an infant? Fear, happiness, love, and anxiety, surely. But they don't have the mental horsepower of rationality required for, say, indignation.

Now what about those primates who are very close to us on the evolutionary scale—the great apes, say, chimpanzees or bonobos? Suppose you visit a zoo in the company of others and you encounter a chimp masturbating. You are embarrassed, blush, and turn away, but if the chimp's face reddens it is from effort and hardly from shame or embarrassment. And one reason for

35 See Wittgenstein, *Philosophical Investigations*, Part II, p. 152; and Ian Ground, *Listen to the Lion*, www.academia.edu/9298683/Listen_to_the_Lion.

saying this is that chimps are not possessed of the complicated weave of life in which the concepts of shame and embarrassment find their home. Consider instead a male chimp who executes a splendid leap, while his competitor fails at it and falls. Might the latter not be fully embarrassed? We are less certain about such cases, and we would rely on the sympathetic bottom-up approach of a Frans de Waal to come up with more evidence for such a possibility.[36]

But didn't the cynic Diogenes masturbate in public without blushing, saying: "If only it were as easy to banish hunger by rubbing my belly"? What, then, is the difference between a Diogenes and the masturbating chimp? The difference is that Diogenes was obviously socialized and deliberately rejected conventions that struck him as hypocritical and complacent, and valorized those he believed to be sincere and honest. He can be embarrassed and ashamed about lack of honesty but not about violating such "artificial convention" as table manners and social niceties.

So, where does this leave the paradoxical ideas of "I blush, therefore I am moral" and "I blush, therefore I have been properly socialized"? "Paradoxical," precisely because often when we blush, we blush for some faux pas or other violation of moral or social norms, while simultaneously endorsing them.[37] This is why Darwin thinks that the mere fact of turning red or crimson is not sufficient for shame, embarrassment, and their ilk.[38] It "would require," he says, "an overwhelming amount of evidence to make us believe that any animal could blush,"[39] because they do not possess the mental capacity for such complex cognitive states required by the paradox. So, again, when Humboldt echoes "without protest" that Brazilian aboriginals are untrustworthy since they cannot blush, he is mistaken, because, on careful observation, they do. We may also note that it is implied that creatures that lack the capacity to blush are said to be deficient in cognitive capacity and thus lack moral status.[40] The alleged absence of the blush was used as a rationalization to justify dehumanization and conquest.

Castelfranchi and Poggi bring up an important issue when they say that evolutionary explanations like Darwin's move from involuntary expression

36 Frans de Waal, *Are We Smart Enough to Know How Smart Animals Are?* W. W. Norton & Company, 2016. See also *Primates and Philosophers*, Princeton University Press, Princeton, 2006.

37 On the apparent paradoxical nature of embarrassment, see our discussion of Eliot, below.

38 See our discussion, above.

39 Darwin, *The Expression of Emotion in Man and Animals*, p. 310.

40 Those among us who cannot blush have some other impairment, perhaps some form of pathology.

(blushing) to emotional behavior (shame or embarrassment) and so leave out the cognitive mediation of biological and social facts. Such explanations, they rightly go on, deprive themselves of the cognitive processes and the analysis of relevant mental states which are useful in explaining goal-oriented behavior—the expressive devices underlying the language game of blushing and other behaviors. These factors enhance the power of evolutionary explanations of the blush and explain the gap between human and non-human animals in terms of cognitive capacities.

But does Darwin really leave out the cognitive mediation of relevant mental states? We see scant evidence that he does. On the contrary, he quotes with approval, as we have seen, the design theorist Dr. Burgess, that for the blush to happen "the mind must be affected" and then he lists shame (including embarrassment), modesty, shyness, and so on, as mental causes of the blush. We conclude, therefore, that Castlefranchi and Poggi's characterization of Darwin's evolutionary account of the emotions as leaving out the mediating roles played by thought is without merit: it is another straw man.

Throughout his book, Darwin makes insightful observations relevant to our investigations of the phenomenon of embarrassment and anticipates some of the counterexamples we produced to current theories of embarrassment. For instance, he is well aware that "in absolute solitude the most sensitive person would be quite indifferent about his appearance,"[41] and he claims that a necessary condition for shame and embarrassment is the regard for the opinion of others ("the thinking of what others think of us."[42] Yet he acknowledges the possibility of private shame and embarrassment when he remarks: "When it was suggested to [a young lady] that this might be due to her distress from the consciousness that her blushing was noticed (by others), she answered that this could not be the case, 'as she had sometimes felt quite as stupid when blushing at the thought in her own room.'"[43] Even though Darwin seems to be alive to the tension between the general account and this particular example, he simply notices it but does not feel the need to do anything to remove it. Perhaps his reason for not engaging this issue is that he thinks the young woman may have imagined or pictured to herself that certain well-regarded others have witnessed her faux pas.

Perhaps he would have proceeded much as we did and regarded private shame and embarrassment as derivative from the paradigm case of being embarrassed in front of others. Thus, he suggests that "when a blush is excited

41 Darwin, *The Expression of Emotion in Man and Animals*, p. 327.
42 Ibid.
43 Ibid., pp. 323–24.

in solitude, the cause almost always relates to the thoughts of others about us—to acts done in their presence or suspected by them; or again when we reflect what others would have thought of us had they known of the act."[44] There are exceptions, however: some "have blushed from shame at acts in no way relating to others," and even from "sympathy with another person who commits a flagrant breach of etiquette."[45]

Nor is it true, he says, that we blush only for our misdeeds:

> Even the thought [...] that others think that we have made an unkind or stupid remark, is amply sufficient to cause a blush, although we know all the time that we have been completely misunderstood. An action may be meritorious or of an indifferent nature, but a sensitive person, if he suspects that others take a different view of it, will blush. For instance, a lady by herself may give money to a beggar without a trace of a blush, but if others are present, and she doubts whether they approve, or suspects that they think her influenced by display, she will blush.[46]

Here the lady spontaneously donates, but when she becomes aware that someone else watches her act, the thought that her act might be seen as proceeding from a hypocritical motive—the desire to merely appear charitable—may cause her to be embarrassed. She is embarrassed to be ill-thought of, despite knowing it is undeserved.

This leads to another interesting observation which has to do with the little-noticed difference between the role of others and the role of the big other, God. "A man may feel thoroughly ashamed at having told a small falsehood, without blushing; but if he even suspects that he is detected he will instantly blush, especially if detected by one whom he reveres."[47] But do we (some of us, at least) not believe that God exists and hold him in high regard? And do we not also believe, at least as a grammatical remark, that God is a witness to all our actions? Yet, these beliefs notwithstanding, religious people generally do not blush in front of God. How come?

> The explanation of this difference between the knowledge by God and man of our actions lies, I presume, in man's disapprobation of immoral conduct being somewhat akin in nature to his depreciation of our personal appearance, so that through association both lead to

44 Ibid., p. 336.
45 Ibid., p. 337.
46 Ibid., p. 334.
47 Ibid., p. 333.

> similar results; whereas the disapprobation of God brings up no such association.[48]

There is nothing deviant about saying, "He looks like hell, but he is really a stand-up guy." God, we presume, is not interested in our appearance but concerned only with our spiritual and moral standing.

Finally, what of the differences between men, women, and children in their propensity to blush and thus to shame and embarrassment? There are scattered remarks in the text concerning this theme. "Children at a very early age," Darwin says, "do not blush; nor do they show those other signs of self-consciousness which generally accompany blushing."[49] He remarks, as do art historians about lions and tigers, on their detached gaze: "It is one of their chief charms that they think nothing about what others think of them. At this early age they will stare at a stranger with a fixed gaze and unblinking eyes, as on an inanimate object, in a manner which we elders cannot imitate."[50] Since blushing requires self-consciousness in the sense of normative self-identity, we would expect that blushing would kick in at a later stage of development, when ethical and social norms are internalized. And indeed, "The young of both sexes are much more sensitive on this head than the old, and they blush much more frequently than the old."[51] What is more, the young "are highly sensitive to the opinion of each other with reference to their personal appearance; and they blush incomparably more in the presence of the opposite sex than in that of their own."[52] Issues of sex and gender enter the fray when Darwin observes that "women are much more sensitive about their personal appearance than men are, especially elderly women in comparison with elderly men, and they blush more freely."[53] Since many young women, however, are also prone to blushing, Darwin's remark is perhaps more characteristic of Victorian times and manners. With different socialization and attitudes to women, this sort of gender difference may gradually be disappearing.

Darwin's evolutionary line of thinking about the blush as a communicative signal in the social and ethical sphere had resonance in the field of literature and moral psychology. In her novel Daniel Deronda, George Eliot engages with issues of embarrassment and blushing with remarkable insight and depth, and it is to this topic that we now turn.

48 Ibid., p. 334.
49 Ibid., p. 328.
50 Ibid.
51 Ibid.
52 Ibid.
53 Ibid.

Chapter VII

ELIOT'S DISSENT FROM DARWIN'S LANGUAGE OF THE EMOTIONS THESIS

A Blush Is No Language

Charles Darwin and George Eliot (pen name of Mary Anne Evans) were not only contemporaries but also friends who read and discussed each other's writings. All the same, judging by the remarks in her novel Daniel Deronda, she dissents from the language-of-the-emotions thesis. Here's what she says about the blush: "A blush is no language: only a dubious flag-signal which may mean either of two contradictories."[1]

This is a striking remark on several accounts. Notice first that she seems to give pride of place to language over non-voluntary reactions to self-conscious emotions like embarrassment and shame, in direct opposition to Darwin's claim that blushes are "expressions" which comprise the language of the emotions.

Second, why a "dubious flag signal"? Her argument, we believe, is that on Darwin's own account of the relationship between the blush and its emotional cause, the blush itself is more like a flag than a linguistic expression, since, as far as appearances go, all blushes are qualitatively alike, and therefore indistinguishable from one another by their appearance alone.[2] In contrast, there are, on Darwin's account, different blushes—the blush of shame, the blush of shyness, and so on—and they are unique, not in their appearances, but because of their causal origins in type-distinct emotional states. But because the different blushes are identical in their appearances, the blush-flag is a sign that cannot be read—or at least cannot be understood to mean more than that one is in the presence of some emotion or other. On this account, the blush is a "dubious flag signal"—a tell-tale—but with one or another tale to tell, and no indication as to which tale that

1 George Eliot, *Daniel Deronda*, Penguin Random House, Modern Library, New York, 2002, p. 250.

2 It's not as though there's a red blush for shame, a green one for envy, and so on.

is. The blush, like elements of a language, carries information alright, but what information—what it means—is at best ambiguous. It's a rather poor linguistic symbol in a language of the emotions that means, at most, that one is in the presence of a kind of creature equipped with the capacities of self-awareness and a range of emotional states—shame, shyness, modesty, and embarrassment. Eliot's first criticism of Darwin's language of emotions thesis is that the blush by itself is too resolutely inarticulate to be considered an expression in that language.

However, things are much worse, Eliot believes, than mere systematic ambiguity for Darwin's language of the emotions thesis. What's worse is that a blush "may mean either of two contradictories." The reason for this claim comes from Darwin himself. While discussing the emotion of modesty, Darwin is first careful to distinguish two forms of modesty, which he describes as "very different states of mind."[3] There is modesty in the sense of humility, and modesty as a reaction to a breach of etiquette. Thus, the blush of modesty means two "very different states of mind." Systematic ambiguity, again. But far worse for the language of emotions thesis is what arises within modesty as humility. By Darwin's reckoning, the blush of modesty-humility is an expression of "persons being greatly pleased and blushing at slight praise, or by being annoyed at praise which seems to them too high according to their own humble standard of themselves." The blush of modesty-humility, that is, means pleased or annoyed at being praised. Pleased or annoyed. Two contradictories. The language of emotions, then, would be like a language in which "yes" means "yes or no";[4] or a language in which "+" means "addition or subtraction." What good is a linguistic symbol that may mean "either of two contradictories"? A set of such symbols would not qualify as a language. This, we take it, is the strongest form of Eliot's criticism of Darwin's language of the emotions thesis.

Sympathetic Embarrassment and Weakness of Will

Similar problems arise with other emotions. The case of sympathetic embarrassment—embarrassment for the sake of another or on behalf of another—may produce the blush of embarrassment from mental states not including embarrassment. In sympathetic embarrassment, one "feels embarrassed" for

3 Darwin, *The Expression of Emotion in Man and Animals*, pp. 335–37.

4 As it does, so we've been told, in the language of varsity romance.

the sake of another, not for something one has done, and may blush for that reason. If sympathetic embarrassment is a kind of embarrassment, then its blush, presumably, is the blush of embarrassment, since there seems to be just one, even though in these cases, the blusher is not really embarrassed at all. The blush of embarrassment would mean, in this case, not embarrassment, but something like sympathy for the embarrassing plight of another, which, strangely, has the same effect as embarrassment itself. It would be another way in which the "flag signal" is dubious.

Consider now a case where one is wrongly thought guilty of some faux pas, is embarrassed by being ill thought of, even if falsely, and is resentful of the misattribution. The falsely accused may blush, but if it's the blush of embarrassment, it would convey the wrong information—one is not embarrassed for something one has done—and not the most interesting information about the complex emotional state that has arisen from being falsely accused. The blush would be silent about what is arguably the most salient feature of the agent's emotional state. As we shall see below, it is the inability of Darwin's language of emotions to convey what may be most salient about our emotional states that gives Eliot another, more general argument against his thesis.

Finally, consider an entirely ordinary case of embarrassment. Suppose I commit a faux pas and that I am embarrassed for it. For this to be so requires that I am committed to the rule (convention, or etc.) I have broken. Had I not believed myself obligated to comply, I'd have no reason to be embarrassed. To be committed to the rule is to intend to behave in accordance with it. Yet I have not. Thus, I am embarrassed for having violated a rule that I intend to comply with. If this is true, or something very like it, is true of central cases, then it's a logical problem at the heart of embarrassment. This seems like a familiar enough circumstance, but it smacks of the kind of logical problem—I intend to A, but I not-A instead—that gives rise to the well-known problem of *akrasia*" or weakness of will. Suppose as a general rule for rational agents such as ourselves that we act on our immediate intentions—our intentions to do something here and now. Suppose that I intend here and now to refrain from eating this second helping of chocolate cake, and yet, without changing my mind, I eat it nevertheless. My eating would still be deemed an action of mine—no one is feeding me the cake, after all, but to accommodate the deviation from the normal sort of thing, we would say that this eating was due to a weakness of my will that allowed me to act against my better judgment. It would count as an akratic action. Common enough, but how is it possible? How can it be both an action of mine, and therefore explainable by the general rule, and yet akratic, and so an action that precisely eludes explanation according to the general rule? We appear to have a contradiction at the heart of our understanding of action and akrasia.[5] Both embarrassment and akratic action suggest that we are much more liable to be involved in something like logical contradictions than we might otherwise like.

Psychological Complexity

Eliot's observations about the blush, that it is far too inarticulate to qualify as a symbol in the language of emotions, is an instance of her more general criticism of Darwin: that in arguing for his language of the emotions thesis, he relies upon an account of the psychology of persons that is far too simplistic to do us justice. We've encountered this, already, in Eliot's first criticism, where the case at issue required much more description to be understood than could be conveyed by a crude flag-signal blush. It is perhaps telling that Darwin's idea that there is a single blush of shame, for example, which is the sign of shame in the language of emotions, implies that there is a single, univocal emotion of shame—that all shames are the same. Likewise for the other self-conscious emotions. But surely it is not the case that shame, having been caused by a complex set of beliefs and desires, leaves the content of those causal states behind, to exist in isolation from them, as pure, undirected shame? Rather, the shame carries with it the salient content of its causes—it's shame for having done some specific thing, after all. And the emotion of shame will include other salient thoughts, such as how one came to do it, whether there were extenuating circumstances, what one must do to make amends, and so on. This suggests an account of the emotions radically different from the univocal thesis implied by Darwin that, given that the circumstances of each shame are unique, each shame is unique. Likewise, modesty, shyness, and embarrassment. It is not to be expected that these words have a unified employment. The way they look at us depends on their context and surroundings. So, shame or embarrassment is not some univocal emotion that exists in isolation from its causes and effects. It is, instead, one element in a rich, complex, contentful, psychological state that includes reference to its source and circumstance, including its effects. A language ought to be adequate to its task.

5 There is vast literature on this subject. For a first-rate treatment, see David Pears, *Motivated Irrationality*, Oxford University Press, Oxford, 1984.

Analysis of a Fragment from Daniel Deronda

Early in Daniel Deronda, Eliot makes an interesting remark about the psychology of persons that foreshadows her critique of the blush as language. In Chapter 4, she describes Gwendolen, one of the main characters. Eliot mentions her charm, her effect on others, the "iridescence of her character," which is "the play of various, nay, contrary tendencies."[6] She feels it is incumbent upon her to explain what she might mean and writes: "For Macbeth's rhetoric about the impossibility of being many opposite things in the same moment, referred to the clumsy necessities of action and not to subtler possibilities of feeling."[7] She elaborates: "We cannot speak a loyal word and be meanly silent; we cannot kill and not kill in the same moment; but a moment is wide enough for the loyal and the mean desire, for the outlash of a murderous thought and the sharp backward stroke of repentance."[8] Her observation seems to be that logical inconsistency is much more common to our psychology than might otherwise be believed, and that logical consistency is a necessity of action only, and therefore an imposition upon the mind from outside and at its interfaces with the world in which its actions occur. As Macbeth advises, the world is not hospitable to contradictions—she's a harsh mistress—but apart from the corrections imposed on the mind by the necessities of action, the mind unlike the world, is amenable to contraries and contradictories residing side by side, as it were, which may escape the "clumsy" strictures of rationality unless and until they are noticed and addressed. That is, commerce with the world imposes a rational discipline on the contents of the mind. But beyond its reach, one is free to want and abhor the same object in a single moment; to be both pleased and annoyed by a single compliment; to be ashamed and defiant, simultaneously modest and overconfident, shy and bold, indeed, all of the above, and more. The mind is far more complex, she argues, than the picture Darwin presented.

The context of the quote above, about the blush being not language, is a scene in chapter 25 that describes the emotional and intellectual complexity of a moment. It concerns Gwendolen and Deronda, the protagonist, and it has embarrassment at its core. The scene is The Abbey, the current residence of Deronda, which is being toured for the first time by Gwendolen and her newly acquired husband, Grandcourt, who has just inherited the property from its owner, his uncle Sir Hugo, and which therefore will become the couple's home. By this time, Gwendolen and Deronda have some history:

6 Eliot, *Daniel Deronda*, p. 26.

7 Ibid. Note: she is not talking here about feelings only.

8 Ibid.

they are attracted to one another, but she fears that Deronda, who has seen deeply into her character and judged her negatively for several things she has done, including her expedient marriage to Grandcourt. But at the same time, Gwendolen has reason to believe that Deronda has a standard by which he measures her and according to which she is not as guilty as she herself thinks. Deronda, she believes, may be her salvation.

Gwendolen's outburst about the stable:

> Oh, this is glorious!" Gwendolen burst forth, in forgetfulness of everything but the immediate impression: there had been a little intoxication for her in the grand spaces of courts and building, and the fact of her being an important person among them. "This is glorious! Only I wish there were a horse in every one of the boxes. I would ten times rather have these stables than those at Diplow."[9]

The following illustrates the complexity of Gwendolen's state of mind:

(1) There's the innocent, unguarded expression of her aesthetic experience ("Glorious"), and its attendant enthusiasm.
(2) There's the unguarded expression of her desires, prompted by her judgment of the object of that experience (a) "But I wish it were gloriouser"—that it had more horses; and (b) I'd rather have this stable than the one I now have. Oh, what's that you say? I do have it? Well, I really have married well, have I not?"
(3) There's the immediately subsequent fear that her incautious, unguarded expression of her desires will be interpreted to her disadvantage—that there is something unsavory in her character that her remarks have revealed: that she's materialistic, calculating, grasping, self-centered, inconsiderate of others, indifferent to the harm she caused to others by her actions in pursuit of her own advantage. (a) "I much prefer this new home that I will soon acquire, at Deronda's expense, to what I have now, and I don't mind saying so"; (b) "I will improve them by increasing the number of horses; (c) I'm very pleased with myself for having successfully married into them."
(4) This is doubly troubling, since she believes these interpretations of her remarks might be true of her, and that she desperately wants them to be false. And she would like others, especially Deronda, to believe they are false. So, she fears, and is probably angry at herself too, that she has confirmed Deronda's already poor assessment of her for having married

9 Ibid., p. 250.

for material wealth. She cares especially for Deronda's opinion because, despite her belief that he thinks ill of her, she thinks he may be her spiritual salvation.

(5) So, she's:
   (a) embarrassed for being so inconsiderate of Deronda as to have mentioned his pending removal from the Abbey. Note, she is nothing if not considerate of Deronda, yet acts, in this moment in a way inconsiderate of him;
   (b) ashamed for what she did—lied to Glasser; deprived her illegitimate children with Grandcourt of their inheritance in order to arrive at her position;
   (c) vexed for having inadvertently looked directly into Deronda's eyes, further revealing herself and thus confirming his poor judgment of her;
   (d) exaggerating the bad impression she has made on Sir Hugo and Deronda;
   (e) annoyed that her embarrassment has denied her the use of her repertoire of devices for disguising how she really feels, which repertoire she would have put to work to dissemble and distract, to feign indignation at any harsh judgment of her, has she not been barred from it by embarrassment;
   (f) frustrated, defeated, she wheels away, eyes heavenward.

Shame then is not some univocal emotion that exists in isolation from its causes and effects. It is, as we stated earlier, only one element in a rich, complex, and contentful psychological state that includes reference to its source and circumstance, including its effects.

The Blush Is No Language: It's a Natural Sign

A blush is a sign of an emotion. It is therefore meaningful, but it is not linguistic. What gives it meaning is not the blush's intentional content, for it has none—it is no artifact—but rather its cause, the emotional state that gives rise to it. Unlike words of a language, a blush is a natural sign, and its meaning is "natural."[10] Thus, "That blush means shame" is akin to "That smoke means fire," and "Those spots mean measles." As Grice points out, the test of whether a sign is natural is as follows: If X is a natural sign of Y, then you cannot say, without contradiction, that "X means Y, but there is no Y." The

10 See Paul Grice, "Meaning," *The Philosophical Review*, Vol. 66, pp. 377–88, 1957.

doctor cannot say without contradiction, "Those spots mean measles but you haven't got measles"; and one cannot say without contradiction, "This smoke means fire, but there is no fire." What makes this a test is that the natural sign is related to what it is a sign of by causation. Thus, you can't have the natural sign without the thing it's a sign of.

Darwin is aware of this very point when he observes that a blush is a more reliable indicator of one's psychology than one's own words, which may be misleading or false or "falsifiable."[11] "The movements of expression give vividness and energy to our spoken words. They reveal the thoughts and intentions of others more truly than do words, which may be falsified."[12] What makes the blush and other expressions of emotions unique among natural signs is that the causes of emotional expressions, unlike the cause of fire and measles, are themselves intentional.

What's true of the blush is true also of the other expressions of emotion—the smile, frown, grimace, and so forth—but with the following proviso: it is true of only those expressions that are caused by their emotion, and not true of, for example, the intentional smile or frown—where we turn a sign or expression into a gesture, a non-natural sign, which is the intentional forming of a facial expression for the purpose of conveying a message. In these cases, the smile or frown is no longer a natural sign, but is a non-natural sign, much more like gestures and other conventional signs than is the blush. So, we have to add this caveat to Darwin's observation: expressions of emotions are reliable if and only if they are natural signs, and not otherwise.

However, if the blush is a natural sign of emotion, on Darwin's account it is unlike other natural signs, since it is, as Eliot maintains, dubious: it may be caused by a range of very different emotions. Thus it is that the blush may mean either shame, or modesty, or shyness, or embarrassment in one of their infinitely many forms. The blush is a natural sign, but less articulate—less able to tell us what it means than is smoke or spots!

On the other hand: Isn't the blush akin to a word in a paragraph full of information? Rarely does the blush stand alone; and if it did, it would be almost meaningless to us—it would convey to us little information. But in ordinary circumstances, the blush is one element in an array of information about the subject gathered from a wide variety of sources.

---

11 Darwin, *The Expression of Emotion in Man and Animals*, p. 366.

12 Note, "more truly," perhaps, but not more completely. See how much text it takes Eliot to describe Gwendolen's emotional state when she blushes in the stables.

If the Blush Is a Language, Then Everything Is a Language

The blush, we have argued, is communicative without being linguistic. It is communicative because it is informational, but it lacks features of a language. However, there may be some temptation to say that informationality alone is sufficient for language. Unfortunately, that way lies incoherence. If we were to say that a blush is linguistic merely for being informational, we would be bound, by parity of reasoning, to say that other information-carrying states are likewise linguistic. Sensory states, like blue and solid, are informational. They tell us that we and the objects around us are constructed in some way that our causal interactions with them produce those states. Granted, this is not much information. Our sensory capacities are too crude to allow us to read further into our nature and the nature of the objects around us. They tell us little about that physics—no more than that there is a physical and biological story there to be discovered and told. But that story requires the full might of science for the telling. Likewise, pain and pleasure are information, as is every aspect of our consciousness. So, if the blush is linguistic for being informational, then, because we are surrounded by consciousness which is informational, then every aspect of our conscious lives is linguistic. And if everything is linguistic then nothing is.

There is a difference to be marked between our capacity to "read" objects and to read people. It takes science to understand why we are caused to have the informational states we have; why our informational sensory mental states have their contents. But it seems we have a much easier time with persons than with objects. A blush alone tells us little more than that we are in the presence of a certain kind of thing: a person and an emotion. But, at least for persons with whom we share some commonalities, we are very good at diagnosis: at recognizing their intentions in context and what else is on their minds. As compared to our capacity to understand the world, our ability to understand other persons is far superior. Is this a function of empathy? The capacity to understand others? Awareness of other minds? We adopt the other person's perspective for the purpose of understanding and assessing and predicting. We put ourselves in their place in order to understand what they are thinking, feeling, etc. This is a tried and proven strategy in law enforcement psychology, forensics, and profiling. And also, in empathetic embarrassment. We may say, with apologies to Descartes, that, as compared to our access to the world, we have something approaching privileged access to other minds.

Chapter VIII

WITTGENSTEIN ON SELF-DECEPTION IN SCIENCE, PSYCHOLOGY, AND PHILOSOPHY

> "The first principle is that you must not fool yourself—and you are the easiest person to fool."[1]

> "Let me hold on to this that I do not want to deceive myself. That is, a certain demand which I acknowledge as such I want to admit to myself again and again as a demand."[2]

Is Wittgenstein Still Relevant? Anti-Science or Anti-Scientism?

In Wittgenstein's notebooks, there are several extended remarks about science that may startle his admirers and arm his critics. In such remarks, observes Brian McGuinness, Wittgenstein seems to deny

> the central importance or paradigmatic role of science in our thought and life. Those who sought enlightenment from it, or who looked on it as the instrument or motor of progress, incurred his bitterest polemics.[3]

Today, science and technology are more influential than ever. Shall we therefore dismiss Wittgenstein as an embarrassment, as no longer relevant, as an anti-science and therefore backward thinker from whom there is little to learn? Or is McGuinness right when he says:

1 Richard Feynman, "Cargo Cult Science," Commencement address at the California Institute of Technology, 1974, p. 12.
2 Wittgenstein, *Public and Private Occasions*, p. 175.
3 McGuinness, *Approaches to Wittgenstein*, p. 124.

> To learn today from Wittgenstein's attitudes, we need to alter them—to mollify or to intensify or more probably to refocus them.[4]

It may be thought that McGuinness is suggesting a revisionary cleaning up of Wittgenstein's laundry. We believe it is better to gloss him as encouraging us to get at the roots of Wittgenstein's attitude to science, for there is something there for us to learn. This is the spirit in which we shall proceed: we will focus on Wittgenstein's remarks, with special attention to his critique of the idols of the age. Modernism has been successful in destroying idols and superstition, but in the process seems to have succumbed to the idolatry of science. "All that philosophy can do is to destroy idols. And that means not creating a new one."[5]

It is important to note that when McGuinness speaks of Wittgenstein's anti-science attitude, he is referring to the works of the later Wittgenstein, and not to the Wittgenstein of the *Tractatus*. The *Tractatus Logico-Philosophicus* embraces science by declaring that only the propositions of science have sense, and hence satisfy the Tractarian theory of meaning:

> The correct method in philosophy would really be the following: to say nothing except what can be said, i.e. propositions of natural science—i.e. something that has nothing to do with philosophy—and then, whenever someone else wanted to say something metaphysical, to demonstrate to him that he had failed to give a meaning to certain signs in his propositions.[6]

In this respect, Wittgenstein's early stance anticipates the Logical Positivists: they, like he, accorded meaning only to the propositions of the natural sciences. When Wittgenstein late in life said to Thouless, "And Hell, Blazes, I founded the Logical Positivists,"[7] he was no doubt referring to the influence of his *Tractatus* on, and his interaction with, the members of the Vienna Circle.

But the *Tractatus* is no Positivistic tract. It is Janus-faced in the following respects. On the one hand, Wittgenstein's "picture theory of meaning" allows only scientific propositions to be meaningful; only they may be true or false. On the other hand, our moral, aesthetic, and religious values are enshrined

---

4 Ibid.

5 Wittgenstein, "Philosophy," in *Philosophical Occasions*, p. 171.

6 *TLP* 6.53.

7 "Discussions between Wittgenstein, Waddington, and Thouless: Summer 1941," in *Public and Private Occasions*, pp. 381–96.

in their own transcendent realm,[8] insulated from the merely scientific, and thus a considerable counterweight to science and its effects. To the extent that the *Tractatus* so privileges science, it is, we claim, scientistic. To the extent that it acknowledges, protects, and reveres our values, it is explicitly anti-scientistic: science may have its place, but it is decidedly out of place in the matter of values. The Logical Positivists were more single-minded: they refused to accept transcendent values; they rejected Wittgenstein's distinction between "good nonsense," which points to insights that cannot be put into words, and plain nonsense that can be dismissed.[9] Nonsense, they averred, is merely nonsense. "If you can't say it, you can't whistle it either," Ramsey, no Positivist he, famously said in another context.

In later remarks, Wittgenstein signaled his reservations about the *Tractatus*, and his remarks foreshadowed the direction his later thinking would take. First, consider this diary entry from 1930:

> Aside from what is good & genuine, my book the *Tractatus* Log.-Phil. also contains kitsch, that is, passages with which I filled in the gaps and so-to-speak [...] in my own style.[10]

And Thouless reports that when he referred to the *Tractatus* at one point in their 1941 discussions, Wittgenstein said, "There is a lot that is very fishy about that book."[11] Finally, and more formally, in the "Preface" to *Philosophical Investigations*, Wittgenstein explicitly recognizes "grave mistakes in what [he] wrote in that first book."[12] We take these remarks to indicate that Wittgenstein had come to see the means he had earlier adopted of avoiding scientism—enshrining values in a transcendent realm—as not only ineffective, but fishy, and a bit of kitsch to boot.

---

8 In the *Tractatus* and the *Lecture on Ethics*, Wittgenstein adopts Moore's fact-value distinction. If you want to navigate the world successfully, you need to know what gets you where. However, absolute value, in contrast to relative or instrumental value, is placed in a transcendent realm and thus protected. Here are three quotes, all from 1929, when Wittgenstein had returned to Cambridge: "What is Good is Divine too. That, strangely enough, sums up my ethics."; "Only something supernatural can express the Supernatural"; "You cannot lead people to the good; you can only lead them to some place or other; the good lies outside the space of facts" (*Culture and Value*, p. 5e).

9 See David Pears, *Wittgenstein, Fontana Modern Masters*, Fontana/Collins, 1971, p. 57 and David Stern, *Wittgenstein on Mind and Language*, Oxford University Press, Oxford, 1995, p. 70.

10 Wittgenstein, *Public and Private Occasions*, p. 39.

11 Ibid., p. 396.

12 *Philosophical Investigations*, p. Xe.

Wittgenstein's criticisms of his early work suggest that he finds certain parts of it embarrassing. However, this should not be misconstrued as a wholesale condemnation. Consider the following remark in which he acknowledges that, flaws and all, it was a necessary part of his philosophical development:

I should not be where I am now if I had not passed through what is expressed in the *Tractatus*. When I wrote that, I had Plato's idea of finding the general idea lying behind all particular meanings of a word. Now I think of the meanings as like the fibers of a rope. One may run the whole way through, but none may.[13]

Perhaps Wittgenstein also recognized as another bit of Platonist kitsch his placement of inexpressible, absolute value in a separate transcendent domain.

On the matter of meaning, Wittgenstein's early work contrasts sharply with the later, where the theory of meaning as representation is rejected as too narrow, and the Tractarian domain of "good nonsense" fragments into the language games of ethics, aesthetics, and religion. But this is not to say that the language games of representation and reference are rejected. Representation and reference

> describe a system of communication, only not everything that we call language is this system. And one has to say this in many cases where the question arises "Is this an appropriate description or not?" The answer is: "Yes, it is appropriate, but only for this narrowly circumscribed region, not for the whole of what you were claiming to describe."[14]

Reference and representation, undeniably among our practices, have their own internal values and standards. Moreover, they and their practitioners are useful, although the extent of their usefulness may not measure up to what some, perhaps intoxicated by their usefulness, believe: "The real achievement of a Copernicus or a Darwin," he remarks, "was not the discovery of a true theory but of a fertile point of view."[15]

If this shift in attitude toward meaning is a correction of one of the "grave mistakes" Wittgenstein recognized in his *Tractatus*, then it constitutes one of the major discontinuities between the early and later philosophies. And if the conventional "anti-science" reception of the later Wittgenstein were right, it would constitute another important discontinuity. Orthodox Wittgensteinians accentuate the discontinuities; New-Wittgensteinians emphasize the continuities between the early and later works. We shall bypass this contest by

13 *Public and Private Occasions*, p. 387.
14 *Philosophical Investigations*, p. 3e.
15 *Culture and Value*, p. 26e.

aiming at a balanced view. If we are right, then both the *Tractatus* and the later works acknowledge the weight and importance of science in our culture. But the later work adds a clear diagnosis of the malaise of scientism, which the early work, in part, succumbed to. This is, of course, not to say that the disagreement about "nonsense" is not a telling difference between the early Wittgenstein and the Logical Positivists, for whom nonsense was just nonsense, while for Wittgenstein there was good nonsense—ethics, aesthetics, and religion, for example—that he "would not for his life ridicule."[16]

It is his remarks critical of science, scientists, and scientifically inclined psychology and philosophy that have been taken by some readers as evidence that Wittgenstein had become anti-science, as evidence of a strain of irrationalism in his later thinking, and thus a major departure from the scientistic elements present in the *Tractatus.* McGuinness does not quote or analyze these remarks but assumes that their anti-science import is evident. We will argue, via analysis of his remarks, that the anti-science reading of the later Wittgenstein is mistaken. What others have (mis)understood as anti-science, we claim, is really anti-scientism, a concern of his with its roots in the *Tractatus.* If we are right, his anti-scientism is a major, trackable thread that runs through the early and later work.[17] Furthermore, we will argue that not only is Wittgenstein not anti-science, but his critique of scientism also amounts to an acknowledgment that science has a rightful and valuable place among our practices. His diagnosis of scientism will reveal it as one manifestation of a more general tendency of ours to over-invest in theory, whether in science, psychology, or philosophy.

This takes us to another of Wittgenstein's abiding concerns. Our tendency to over-invest in theory is a manifestation of a general proclivity for self-deception. Wittgenstein saw self-deception as a general problem, one face of which is scientism. If so, his concerns over scientism and self-deception are two "fibres of a rope," a single, main, trackable thread that runs through his work. "Scientism" is the name we give to a particular strain of self-deception that infects our scientific theories and practices. It is a form of self-deception that would therefore also afflict overly scientific psychology and philosophy. What divides the early from the later work is the means he adopts to combat the affliction. We argue that he came to see that the early strategies of the

16 Wittgenstein, *Lecture on Ethics*, in *Philosophical Occasions*, p. 44.

17 For further textual evidence and treatment of the issue of scientism, see McGuinness, *Approaches to Wittgenstein*, chapters 7–9. We will show the less-noticed fact that the means, and their character, that Wittgenstein adopts to combat scientism in his earlier period are radically different from those he uses in his later philosophy.

Tractatus had actually played into the hands of the scientistic Logical Positivists by allowing them to accept what they found respectable in the *Tractatus*, while refusing the invitation to accept the "fishy kitsch" of its transcendent realm of values and attendant "good nonsense."

A new strategy against scientism was called for, and that became, in his later work, his conception of our various practices as "language games." Since language games, despite occasional overlap, are discrete and relatively autonomous, they provide less room for scientism to work its pernicious effects. Scientism would be confined to the domain of science if not for those misguided psychologists and philosophers who insist on making their subjects more scientific. However, even without such commingling, since scientism is only one strain of self-deception, and since self-deception is ours, all our practices, psychology and philosophy among them, inherit the risk.

Moreover, we shall show that Wittgenstein's reservations regarding overly scientific psychology and philosophy help illuminate what has become a classic problem in modern philosophical psychology: the nature of self-deception itself. Altogether we aim to show that his concerns with self-deception were intended to discipline our thinking, in all its forms.

Was Wittgenstein Anti-Science? The Evidence

In *Culture and Value*, Wittgenstein writes:

> It may be that science & industry, & their progress are the most enduring thing in the world today. That any guess at a coming collapse of science & industry were for now, & a long time to come, simply a dream, & that science & industry after & with infinite misery will unite the world, I mean integrate it into a single empire, in which to be sure peace is the last thing that will then find a home. For science & industry do decide wars, or so it seems.[18]
>
> The truly apocalyptic view of the world is that things do not repeat themselves. It is not, e.g. absurd to say that the scientific & technological age is the beginning of the end for humanity, that the idea of Great Progress is a bedazzlement, along with the idea that the truth will ultimately be known; that there is nothing good or desirable about scientific knowledge & that humanity, in seeking it, is falling into a trap. It is by no means clear that this is not how things are.[19]

---

18 *Culture and Value*, p. 72.
19 Ibid., p. 64.

As mentioned above, readers have been inclined to look on such remarks—a "coming collapse of science [...] is a dream"; "the scientific & technological age is the beginning of the end"; etc.—as anti-science. But a more compelling way to read them, we claim, is that their target is scientism, an approach that involves the application of science and its methods in areas to which they are ill-suited, as well as the abuse of science and technology for unjustifiable purposes. He dreams, not for the end of science, but for the end of its idolatry and attendant abuses. This reading is supported by another remark, even less temperate in tone:

> The hysterical fear of the atom bomb the public now has, or at least expresses, is almost a sign that here for once a really salutary discovery has been made. At least the fear gives the impression of being fear in the face of a really effective bitter medicine. I cannot rid myself of the thought: if there were not something good here, the philistines would not be making such an outcry. But perhaps this too is a childish idea. For all I can really mean is that the bomb creates the prospect of the end, the destruction of a ghastly evil, of disgusting soapy water science and certainly that is not an unpleasant thought; but who is to say what would come after such a destruction? The people now making speeches against the production of the bomb are undoubtedly the dregs of the intelligentsia, but even that does not prove beyond question that what they abominate is to be welcomed.[20]

What is "really salutary" about the bomb? For which illness is it a "really effective bitter medicine"? The illness, we believe, is the scientistic misconception of science, common among the "philistine" public, as a "soapy water" cure-all, an instrument of progress that can only improve our lives. The "ghastly evil" is the scientism inherent in the capture of science by what would become known as "the military-industrial complex." What's "really salutary" is the prospect, thanks to the fact of the bomb, of exposing as scientistic propaganda such a naïve and manipulative conception of science. He dreams of the destruction of a collective illusion, a product of self-deception that had made science an idol of the age.

Here, then, is a theme that runs through this chapter. It is Wittgenstein in a Socratic mood, warning us of certain bad habits of thought which, if left unrecognized and unchecked, will lead to error, misunderstanding, and worse. Science, psychology and philosophy, despite their achievements, inherit these habits—how could they not? Unless we are alive to our bad

20 Ibid., pp. 55e–56e.

habits and vigilant against them, science, psychology and philosophy, like their ancestors, myth and superstition, will lead us astray. And astray we do not want to go, more so now than ever before, perhaps, now that science has unlocked some of nature's powerful secrets.

The complexity of Wittgenstein's attitude toward science is further revealed by this telling remark:

> Science: enrichment & impoverishment. The one method elbows all others aside. Compared with this they all seem paltry, preliminary stages at best. You must climb down to the sources to see them all side by side, the disregarded & the preferred.[21]

Science is enriching. But bedazzled by its success, we are blind to its limitations. One source of the attendant impoverishment is the strong tendency to recognize as real only "preferred" phenomena—those with a scientific pedigree. The remedy for such impoverishing scientism is to recognize that the scientifically "disregarded" are no less real for being left out of scientific accounts. Moreover, there is more to knowledge than what is produced by applications of the scientific method. To think otherwise is to minimize or ignore tacit knowledge, the know-how learned at one's parents' knees, in coping with the everyday, in apprenticing, in ordinary skills, in knowing how to act, how to conduct oneself, how to be tactful, and so on. This "back to the rough ground" attitude is brought to bear on naturalizing science as well:

> In the course of a scientific investigation we say all kinds of things; we make many utterances the role of which in our investigation we do not understand. For of course not everything we say has a conscious purpose, but our tongues just keep going. Our thoughts run in established routines, we make, automatically, transitions according to <u>techniques</u> we have learned. And now comes the time for us to survey what we have said. We have made a whole lot of movements that do not further our purpose, even impede it, and now we have to clarify our thought processes philosophically.[22]

There is no textbook-like, crystalline purity to scientific investigations. Rather, its methods and procedures are shot through with knowledge and abilities that are beneath the notice of science.

---

21 Ibid., p. 69e.

22 Ibid., pp. 73e–74e.

However compelling this reading may be, it seems inconsistent with Wittgenstein's remarks about our need for wonder:

> As though today lightning were more commonplace or less astounding than 2000 years ago. In order to wonder, human beings—and perhaps peoples—have to wake up. Science is a way of sending them off to sleep again [...] Scientific explanation cannot intensify wonderment and the spirit in which science is carried on nowadays is not compatible with wonder of this kind.[23]

Is this a recommendation that we replace science with an anti-scientific, enchanted picture of the world? There are remarks that suggest otherwise:

> Compare the solution of a philosophical problem with the fairy tale gift that seems magical in the enchanted castle and when it is looked at in the daylight is nothing but an ordinary bit of iron (or something of the sort).[24]

When we feel a philosophical problem weighing on us, Wittgenstein suggests, we are enchanted by pictures embedded in our grammar, by surface grammar. The way to resolve the problem is through disenchantment, by looking to see how the "ordinary bit of iron" is used.

We presume this advice carries over to science. But if the previous remark is not to be understood as an expression of a preference for fairy tales over science, then what does it mean? What is the soporific effect of "the spirit in which science is carried on nowadays"? We suggest that the "sleep" he has in mind is another symptom of scientism; that among the effects of the possession of powerful, well-confirmed theories, and the overconfidence that success breeds, is our tendency to overreach: to apply scientific theories uncritically and mechanically, and in areas to which it is ill-suited. This is a warning about the general dangers of theory: that theories, scientific and otherwise, can deceive us into thinking that matters are settled, as though no open questions remain. So deceived, we fail to acknowledge phenomena not captured by a theory; fail to "wonder" about phenomena that fall outside its categories, and which may elude study by its methods. How unscientific; how irrational! One of Wittgenstein's points here is that to be aware of everyday occurrences is one thing, but to wonder at them requires noticing and attending to them, and there is nothing "primitive" about that. Rather, the unexamined life is "primitive" in the pejorative sense.

---

23 Ibid., pp. 7e–8e.
24 Ibid., pp. 13e–14e.

Ten years later, Wittgenstein returns to the theme of wonder:

> The mathematician too can of course marvel at the miracles (the crystal) of nature; but can he do it, once a problem has arisen about what he sees? Is it really possible as long as the object he finds awe inspiring or gazes at with awe is shrouded in a philosophical fog? I could imagine someone admiring trees, & also the shadows, or reflection of trees, which he mistakes for trees. But if he should once tell himself that these are not after all trees & if it becomes a problem for him what they are, or what relation they have to trees, then his admiration will have suffered a rupture, that will now need heeling.[25]

The concern here, as above, is for the proper functioning of science. But unlike his previous remarks, here Wittgenstein is concerned about the effects of too much wonder, not of too little. It is about the harmful effects that skeptical philosophical arguments can have on the very possibility of science. Philosophical doubts induced in the scientist shroud the objects of scientific inquiry in a philosophical fog, so that the "admiration" that motivates scientific inquiry is "ruptured" and needs "healing" from too much philosophy. These are not the concerns of a man dismissive of science.

The cognitive core of Wittgenstein's remarks is that science is a powerful instrument whose value depends on its uses and applications. It is not intrinsically valuable and certainly not redemptive in itself.

It is noteworthy that Wittgenstein's old teacher and mentor, and later bête noire, Bertrand Russell, was one of those arguing against nuclear proliferation and may well have been one of Wittgenstein's targets. Recall that Russell said:

> The later Wittgenstein [...] seems to have grown tired of serious thinking and to have invented a doctrine which would make such an activity unnecessary.[26]

And recall that Wittgenstein said of Russell's works that they should be divided into two sorts: one bound in blue—the logical/mathematical works—that everyone should study, and another bound in red—the popular books on ethics and politics, on Bolshevism, morals and marriage, and so on—that should be placed on the index prohibitorum.

If Wittgenstein had Russell in mind, is his critique fair? Russell had argued for a scientific philosophy, but surely not for a "soapy water science." And if

25 Ibid., p. 65e.

26 Monk, *Ludwig Wittgenstein, The Duty of Genius*, p. 472.

he had any such illusions, he woke up when confronted with Leo Szilard's proposal for the production of the bomb.

The conclusion we derive from revisiting these allegedly "anti-science" passages would be surprising only to those who have accepted the received view of Wittgenstein as an irrationalist who is hostile to science. Wittgenstein's appraisal of science is realistic: science is a powerful instrument; it has a bad rap insofar as it is overblown; and it can be used for good and bad purposes. Those who focus only on its possible benign and redemptive uses are as self-deceived as those who focus only on its possible harms.

Wittgenstein on Scientism in Psychology and Philosophy

While we find no compelling evidence of an anti-science attitude in any of the above remarks, there are others which seem to express Wittgenstein's profound misgivings about the "culture" of science, and about the effect of science on the way "modern philosophy" was done. These twin concerns relate to what he sees as the cultural malaise of the West:

> It is all one to me whether the typical western scientist understands or appreciates my work since in any case he does not understand the spirit in which I write. Our civilization is characterized by the word "progress". Progress is its form, it is not one of its properties that it makes progress. Typically, it constructs. Its activity is to construct a more and more complicated structure. And even clarity is only a means to this end & not an end in itself. For me on the contrary clarity, transparency, is an end in itself. I am not interested in erecting a building but in having the foundations of possible buildings transparently before me. So, I am aiming at something different than are the scientists & my thoughts move differently than do theirs.[27]

This passage, we claim, is neither anti-science nor anti-scientist. It is about how the later Wittgenstein's conception of philosophy differs from science and from that of scientifically oriented philosophers. Furthermore:

> Some philosophers (or whatever you like to call them) suffer from what may be called "loss of problems". Then everything seems quite simple to them, no deep problems seem to exist any more, the world becomes

27 Wittgenstein, *Culture and Value*, p. 9e.

> broad and flat and loses all depth, and what they write becomes immeasurably shallow and trivial.[28]

Who are these philosophers "put to sleep" by philosophy so that no deep problems remain? We may be surprised by the two names mentioned: "Russell and H. G. Wells suffer from this."[29] The remark that follows immediately sheds light on why Russell is mentioned:

> Philosophical investigations: conceptual investigations. The essential thing about metaphysics: it obliterates the distinction between factual and conceptual investigations.[30]

In this sense, Russell's advocacy of a scientific approach to philosophy is really a kind of metaphysics that does not leave room for philosophy, since it conceives of philosophy as continuous with science: "Philosophy was defined as all those primitive propositions which are assumed as true without proof by the various sciences."[31] The later Wittgenstein says in a fragment: "In a certain sense one cannot take too much care in handling philosophical mistakes, they contain so much truth."[32] There is no better expression, we believe, of the distance between the early and the later Wittgenstein's conceptions of philosophy than this contrast.

There seem to be three strands of thought discernible in the above quotations. One objects to scientism, and by implication defends science into the bargain. Another brings to the fore the differences between science and Wittgenstein's conception of philosophy as the clarification of concepts connected to our ways of life, including scientific practices, which must therefore include clarifying scientific concepts too. A third strand of thought, conversational in form, attempts to understand a hard-boiled skeptic about science and technology. The conventional view is that these skeptics are irrational luddites, beyond the pale of rational discourse. But Wittgenstein attempts to understand them, to clarify the extreme skeptical position and the arguments behind it. This conversational form is characteristic of the later Wittgenstein.[33]

---

28 Ludwig Wittgenstein, *Zettel*, edited by G.E.M. Anscombe and G.H. von Wright, Blackwell, Oxford, 1967, #456.

29 Ibid.

30 Ibid., #458.

31 Talk to the Cambridge Moral Club on "What is Philosophy?" in *Public and Private Occasions*, p. 332.

32 *Zettel*, #460.

33 See David Stern's "Introduction" to *Wittgenstein in the 30s: Between the Tractatus and the Investigations.*

Another interesting aspect of these quotations is that Wittgenstein employs the then current conception of science to show how his conception of a philosophical investigation differs from a scientific investigation. A broad-brushed picture of science emerges: that science is much the same thing—hypothesis testing and confirmation, according to the scientific method. This view of science as uniform is rather un-Wittgensteinian, and, as McGuinness suggests, it is possible to mount a Wittgensteinian critique of it.[34] Such a critique would show that science is a family resemblance concept, with the different sciences as members of the same family, using a family of related but different methods. What is more, the remarks suggest not only a narrow picture of science, but also a theory of science. But the later Wittgenstein is an anti-theorist, and surely this has to be extended to his remarks in the philosophy of science too. Still, we should take him at his word. When we do, we can use his anti-theory stance for a critique of his own remarks about science itself. However, a better way of reading him, one that is consistent with his perspective, is that he is interested in making critical remarks about misguided pictures of science and philosophy.

Was Wittgenstein Anti-Psychology? The Evidence

The dominant approach of recent philosophical psychologists tends toward the search for general theories continuous with science.[35] Wittgenstein thought that such philosophers are inclined to see only the method of science before their eyes and to question and answer in the way science does. This scientism results in a loss of conceptual sensitivity; a rigidity sets in, and we can no longer imagine what it would be like to look at things differently. Such a one-sided approach does not give its due to ordinary knowledge and common sense, which are required to undertake scientific investigation in the first place. The point is similar to the point about the logico-philosophical disparagement of ordinary language:

> When I talk about language (words, sentences, etc.) I must speak the language of every day. Is this language somehow too coarse and material for what we want to say? Then how is another one to be constructed?—And how strange that we should be able to do anything at all with the one we have![36]

34 McGuinness, *Approaches to Wittgenstein*, p. 129.
35 Mind–brain identity theorists and eliminative materialists come to mind.
36 *Philosophical Investigations*, #120.

These general remarks have direct application to philosophical psychology. According to the modern philosophical tradition, it is the science of psychology that provides the foundation for the philosophical study of psychology. Hence scientifically minded philosophers in the twentieth and twenty-first centuries have based their philosophical psychology on the foundations of the best available science.[37] This involves a scientistic perspective, in that on this view philosophical psychology is on the same footing as science; in fact, it is simply a continuation or extension of science.

In contrast, Wittgenstein thinks it is a ground-floor mistake to think that clarity is based on scientific foundations. People did not wait for science to have a philosophical psychology—a cluster of concepts they used for describing and understanding one another. Rather, these ordinary, folk-psychological concepts have persisted like a riverbed while the fresh waters of science flow over them. Likewise, the ordinary "folk-physical" concepts that allowed our pre-scientific ancestors to think, do, struggle, and take care of the essential things in life. The clarity Wittgenstein seeks is a clear overview and description of our use of concepts. What is more, even scientific work starts with our everyday concepts. If they were so crude and useless, how could we get such splendid work done with them?

> If anyone should think that he has solved the problem of life & feels like telling himself everything is quite easy now, he need only tell himself, in order to <u>see that he is wrong</u>, that there was a time when this "solution" had not been discovered; but it must have been possible to live then too & the solution which has now been discovered appears <u>in relation to how things were then</u> like an accident. And it is the same for us in logic too. If there were a "solution to the problems of logic (philosophy)", we should only have to caution ourselves that there was a time when they had not been solved (and then too it must have been possible to live and think).[38]

The assumption that without the best of now-available science it would be a miracle how human beings got things done at all is a form of scientism that the early Wittgenstein succumbed to. His attitude in the *Tractatus* was that, while unable at the time to specify the elementary propositions, he would be able to do so later. However, he would come to mock the very idea that every unsolved problem will be solved by the progress of science:

---

37 See the work of Smart, Quine, and the Churchlands, for example.

38 *Culture and Value*, p. 6e.

> "We still don't know that; but it is knowable & it is only a question of time till we know it!" As if that went without saying.[39]

We want to connect and elaborate this theme of anti-scientism with the question about the practice of philosophical psychology. Does Wittgenstein see any room for it? If by "philosophical psychology" is meant the traditional enterprise of constructing a theory about the nature of the mind and its place in nature, then Wittgenstein is nihilistic about philosophical psychology. In that old sense, Wittgenstein hasn't one.

If there were room for philosophical psychology, then for Wittgenstein it would consist in an activity. What would such an activity be like? There are remarks scattered throughout the Wittgenstein corpus that indicate that such an activity cannot be equated with psychoanalysis, experimental psychology, neurology, or introspective psychology. In brief, Wittgenstein saw introspective methods as implying confusion between the objects and processes that are described in our language and philosophically pernicious inner objects and processes. Introspective methods assume that the essence of the mental lies within and is seen when we look into ourselves, as it were:

> We feel as if we had to penetrate phenomena: our investigation, however, is directed not towards phenomena, but [...] towards the "possibilities" of phenomena. We remind ourselves [...] of the kind of statement that we make about phenomena.[40]

"For what is hidden, for example, is of no interest to us."[41] Such introspective methods also lead to the dangerous idea that there is a purely subjective means of gaining self-knowledge, and thus knowledge in psychology. The resonance is Cartesian, as if there is nothing that I am in a better position to know than my own mind. So, if I understand the meaning of a word, then, according to this picture, I know that I understand it through introspection. But Wittgenstein repudiates this picture:

> Introspection can never lead to a definition. It can only lead to a psychological statement about the introspector. If, e.g., someone says: "I believe that when I hear a word that I understand, I always feel something that I don't feel when I don't understand the word"—that is a statement about his peculiar experiences. Someone else perhaps feels something quite different; and if both of them make correct use of the

39 Ibid., p. 46e.
40 *Philosophical Investigations*, #90.
41 Ibid., #126.

> word "understand", the essence of understanding lies in this use and not in what they may say about what they experience.[42]

Nor can philosophical psychology be equated with experimental psychology and its modes of explanation and theory construction. Recall a remark placed by the editors at the end of the *Philosophical Investigations*:

> The confusion and barrenness of psychology is not to be explained by calling it a "young science" [...] The existence of the experimental method makes us think we have the means of solving the problems which trouble us, though problem and method pass one another by.[43]

Experimental psychology, Wittgenstein thought, is vitiated by the failure of measurement and localization to address the puzzling features of our mental lives that have the backdrop of "the problems that trouble us." Since experimental psychology is concerned with other matters, we get nonsense when we bring its methods to bear upon psychological problems. What troubles us must be in the language of trouble.

Finally, Wittgenstein saw psychoanalysis as a form of storytelling, which, whatever the discursive genius of its practitioner and its efficaciousness—indeed because of these features—could not produce philosophical understanding: "But the dream story all the same has its own charm, like a painting that attracts & inspires us," yet

> Freud's fanciful pseudo-explanations (just because they are so brilliant) performed a disservice. (Now every ass has them within reach for "explaining" symptoms of illness with their help.)[44]

This is not to deny that Wittgenstein had a complex and ambivalent attitude to Freud and psychoanalysis, accepting and rejecting him in equal measure. In the early 1930s, Wittgenstein thought that dissolving a philosophical problem is like resolving a problem in psychoanalysis, in that the difficulty in both was primarily emotional, where resistance of the will has to be overcome, and not so much intellectual as in the sciences. It can be as hard not to use an expression as it is to hold back tears or an outburst of anger. Another shared theme in Freud and Wittgenstein is that meaning is not there all at once but

42 Ludwig Wittgenstein, *Remarks on the Philosophy of Psychology*, Vol. 1, edited by G.H. von Wright and Heikki Niemann, translated by C.G. Luckhardt and M.A. Aue, The University of Chicago Press, Chicago, 1988, #212.

43 *Philosophical Investigations*, p. 197e.

44 *Culture and Value*, pp. 62e–63e.

emerges through discussion and consideration of context and what is said where and when.[45]

On the other hand, Wittgenstein was sharply critical of Freud's specific claims as well as his attempt to pass off the "mythology" embedded in his thought as science. Also, he complained that Freud's seductive means of expression obscured the original facts:

> It is as if he draws a typical face like this (drawing a diagrammatic face). Then when he sees a new face he draws it always the same way [...] what is necessary is to get right away from Freud's drawing a face.[46]

Wittgenstein's ambivalent attitude to Freud is strikingly expressed in the 1930 remark:

> Freud surely errs very frequently & as far as his character is concerned he is probably a swine or something similar, but in what he says there is a great deal. And the same is true of me. There is a lot in what I say.[47]

We are tempted to say: With a follower and disciple like Wittgenstein, does Freud need any critics?[48]

So, philosophical psychology cannot be a descendant of psychoanalysis or its variant forms. However, such approaches, current in the mid-twentieth century, do not exhaust psychology. We might well ask what Wittgenstein's attitude would have been toward cognitive science, the attempt to model human thought processes by considering the flow and treatment of information through a system. Wittgenstein's anti-scientism, and his critique of the idea that experimental psychology can take care of the conceptual/philosophical problems that trouble us, presumably would have carried over to these efforts as well. Would this simply have signaled his irrelevance, backwardness, and hidden a priorism? Or are there any lessons to be learned from his claim that certain mental phenomena cannot be studied either by examining physical processes or by being treated on analogy with physical processes, but only understood by a kind of narration?

A case in point. Scientistic philosophical theories, when applied to questions of meaning concerning our psychological concepts and phenomena, are reductionist: they are after the essence underlying such phenomena, and thus

---

45 Here we are building on a remark by McGuinness in *Approaches to Wittgenstein*, p. 233.

46 *Public and Private Occasions*, p. 395.

47 Ibid., p. 17.

48 For Wittgenstein's relation to Freud, interested readers should see McGuinness' essay "Freud and Wittgenstein," in *Wittgenstein and His Times*, pp. 27–43.

they tend to narrow down and distort the complex and rich terrain of our everyday "folk-psychology," as if it were merely a primitive, preliminary stage that is to be overcome, like "baby talk."[49] This anti-reductionism is a central theme that runs through the later Wittgenstein's critique of psychologism—a common form of scientism in Wittgenstein's times—in all its forms, whether in logic, philosophy of language and mind, or aesthetics. This attitude of anti-scientism questions the widely shared assumption in our culture, made precisely because of the acknowledged success of the sciences, that there is only one method and one way of knowing. The idea that human beings knew little or nothing before the advent of modern science comes in for critical assessment. What is argued in particular is that scientistic philosophical theories about the mind, including their Cartesian introspectionist offspring, psychoanalysis, experimental psychology, and information theory, involve an ideology of science when it comes to their attempts to treat conceptual issues.

These snapshots of Wittgenstein's attitude toward then current scientific candidates for psychology show that he read and reflected on the works of their practitioners and on what the implications of such works might be for a philosophical psychology. Hardly the attitude of an "anti-science" person. If so, then we can imagine Wittgenstein discussing recent advances in neuroscience more constructively than most Wittgenstein scholars would allow, because they tend to think of Wittgenstein as "anti-science." The fact that his conclusions were mostly negative—that whatever knowledge we acquire through these "sciences" sets us "(new) ethical and philosophical problems; but contributes nothing to their solution"[50]—is neither here nor there, since Wittgenstein was performing the philosophical service of clarification—of destroying the idols and self-deceptive illusions of the age. The "philosophical scientists," as it were, claimed to be selling sausages when in fact they were selling cheese.

Self-Deception: What Wittgenstein Said and Might Have Said

Self-deception, we have seen, plays an important role in Wittgenstein's reflections on science, psychology and philosophy, as well as in his reflections on self-knowledge and self-understanding. Since scientistic theorizing, in its attempts at reduction, often feeds on a steady diet of one-sided examples, it tends to oversimplify, and thus constrain our view of things. The formulaic theory

49 In this connection, see Austin's remarks on ordinary language in "A Plea for Excuses," Austin, *How to Do Things with Words*, p. 130.

50 Wittgenstein, *Culture and Value*, p. 40e.

renders some things salient—the "preferred phenomena"—and ignores or neglects others. This shows how in Wittgenstein's view philosophical understanding and self-understanding are internally connected, for the fault lines of philosophical error and self-deception are strikingly similar. In both cases, we as agents and participants know our practices, yet when we think about them to give an account, we go astray.

In his diaries, Wittgenstein again takes up the difference between science and philosophy. The following remark shows that he was acutely aware of the elusive nature of philosophical problems and how difficult it is to cultivate a nose for their discernment:

> People have sometimes said to me that they cannot make any judgement about this or that because they have never learned philosophy. This is irritating nonsense, it being assumed that philosophy is some sort of science. And people speak of it as they might speak of medicine.[51]

Having repudiated the picture of philosophy as a species of science, Wittgenstein glosses this "modest" reaction as follows:

> What one can say, however, is that people who have never carried out an investigation of a philosophical sort, like most mathematicians for instance, are not equipped with the right optical instruments for that sort of investigation or scrutiny. Almost, as someone who is not used to searching in the forest for berries will not find any because his eye has not been sharpened for such things & he does not know where you have to be particularly on the lookout for them. Similarly, someone unpracticed in philosophy passes by all the spots where difficulties lie hidden in the grass, while someone with practice pauses & senses that there is a difficulty here, even though he does not yet see it. And no wonder, if one knows how long even the practiced investigator, who realizes there is a difficulty, has to search in order to find it. If something is well hidden it is hard to find.[52]

In light of this passage, it is strange that Wittgenstein seems to neglect the problems involved in self-deception, and he bypasses the salient spots where difficulties lie hidden. There is little indication that he pauses, senses, or searches for conceptual difficulties. He brings up the issue in a few scattered remarks, employing the concept of self-deception as if it needs no clarification or justification, despite its conceptually or grammatically puzzling nature.

51 Ibid., p. 33e.
52 Ibid.

The trouble with Wittgenstein, then, is that he says little concerning such questions, despite the fact that the problem of self-deception is an instructive philosophical problem on Wittgenstein's conception of what a philosophical problem is: confusion in the form of paradox and tension conjured up by a misleading grammatical picture.

Having said this, we point out that Wittgenstein acknowledges self-deception as an existential and ethical problem, and he remarks on the moral difficulties involved in the struggle to avoid it, connecting self-deception with one's creative endeavors, work, style, and artistic integrity. "Nothing is so difficult as not deceiving yourself."[53] Notice he does not say that the concept is so problematic and riddled with difficulties that it is useless. There are other penetrating observations:

> When you bump up against the limits of your own honesty, it is as though a whirlpool of thoughts is generated, & an endless regress: you may say what you like, it gets you no further.[54]

Again, the context is moral and spiritual, and the sense of the remark has to do with the confusion we encounter when the dim realization sets in that we may be self-deceived: we do not know how to extricate ourselves, and until we learn, anything we say is suspected as motivated rationalization. This is followed by: "If you use a trick in logic, whom can you be tricking but yourself?"[55]

If we place this much weight on a concept that sits uncomfortably in our critical vocabulary, then we had better look at it more closely. Wittgenstein, we might say, supplied the general resources to tackle the conceptual problem and shifted the problem to a moral level. We are made aware that self-deception is irreducible to a problem in "the science of the mind," and involves a language game other than simply information and description. In the spirit of McGuinness's recommendation, we deploy the tools and attitudes that Wittgenstein provided to see what he might have said had he squarely faced the problem of self-deception. We will look at the issue through a lens on psychological concepts that Wittgenstein himself provides, but does little with, perhaps because the classifications strike him as narrowing things down:

53 Ibid., p. 39e.
54 Ibid., p. 11e.
55 Ibid., p. 28e.

> Psychological verbs characterized by the fact that [...] sentences in the third person of the present: information. In the first person present: expression. (Not quite right.)[56]

If we apply this asymmetry—first person present: expression; third person present: description—then self-deception, despite including beliefs, motives, and so on, exceeds the proposed criteria for psychological concepts, since "I am self-deceived" is not simply an expression as such, and "He is self-deceived" is not merely a description or a report. Both include assessment and appraisal which are done with norms, values, and a personal history as backdrop.

This is in sharp contrast to the recent history of the treatment of self-deception by analytical philosophers who have regarded it as a problem in epistemology and the philosophy of mind. The upshot is that self-deception is difficult because the concept is so paradoxical as to verge on incoherence. Therefore, before we talk about self-deception in moral contexts, we should send the concept to the laundry to have its murkiness removed. The fact that issues of responsibility and blame enter the picture makes the identification and description of the concept even more crucial. The trouble is that when we get it back from the philosophical cleaners, the concept is so misshapen that it no longer fits or it fails to distinguish self-deception from its close neighbors, which may call for quite different assessments of the person-agent, and correspondingly different treatment.

To illustrate, consider a woman with lots of evidence that her husband is unfaithful, but she nevertheless believes he is faithful. One possible explanation is that she is the victim of confirmation bias which favors evidence that supports her commitments and discounts what would undermine them. Her desire for her husband's fidelity tends to enhance the salience of the data apparently supporting the proposition that her husband is faithful. The more vivid the data, the more they dominate her attention and the more they become available for confirmation and inference. The bouquet of red roses for their anniversary has much more weight than his frequent and unexplained absences. His gifts are taken as testimonials to his love rather than as attempts at appeasement, and so on.

This explanation, however, runs together related but somewhat different concepts. For instance, willful ignorance and wishful thinking bear some

---

56 *Zettel*, #472. For an original and illuminating discussion of Wittgenstein's philosophical psychology, see Joachim Schulte, *Experience and Expression*, Clarendon Press, Oxford, 1993.

of the marks of self-deception, but paradigm cases would seem to include more.[57]

So suppose that the woman knows that her husband is unfaithful but does not believe it; that she believes instead that he is faithful. Suppose further that her knowledge that her husband is unfaithful is causally active in forming her belief that he is not. On the assumption that knowing that p implies believing that p, we need to ascribe to her the belief that he is unfaithful and the belief that he is not, and that the belief that he is unfaithful is involved in the generation of the belief that he is faithful.

To account for this possibility, it may be tempting to regard self-deception as posing a problem in mental engineering where the initially puzzling capacity is rendered intelligible through a description of the inner mechanism that generates it.[58] Imagine the brain split into two parts. Inscribed in one part is the physical equivalent of the sentence "My husband is faithful"; in the other, "My husband is unfaithful." The dynamics of self-deception is then explained by physical communication between them, so that the belief in one part causes the disbelief in the other. Since evasions, avoidances, and filtering can be useful in protecting our important interests—such as knowing that one's spouse is unfaithful—our cognitive apparatus is designed to contain filtering devices that recognize anxiety-causing information as well as reduce its impact in case of overload.

Such a picture is tempting because it seems to underlie a variety of cases of what we might call aberrant mental functioning: oversight, weakness of the will, as well as self-deception. In weakness of the will, for example, it is tempting to say that a belief that it would be best to desist from eating pie—is resident in one part of the brain but is prevented from exercising any causal influence on the part of the brain controlling action, so that the subject eats the pie anyway. There are cases of oversight in which we become aware that we have repressed a stimulus that was important to our interests: finding one's

57 See Catherine Wilson, "Self-Deception and Psychological Realism," *Philosophical Investigations*, Vol. 3, 1980, pp. 47–60; Béla Szabados, "Wishful Thinking and Self-Deception," *Analysis*, Vol. 33, 1973, pp. 201–05; Alfred Mele, *Irrationality: An Essay on Akrasia, Self-Deception and Self-Control*, Oxford University Press, Oxford, 1987. For an exhaustive and exhausting overview of self-deception, see the Stanford Encyclopedia of Philosophy. https:/plato.stanford.edu.

58 Donald Davidson, "Paradoxes of Irrationality," in *Philosophical Essays on Freud*, edited by Richard Wollheim and J. Hopkins, Cambridge University Press, Cambridge, 1982, pp. 289–305; and his "Deception and Division," in *The Multiple Self*, edited by Jon Elster, Cambridge University Press, Cambridge, pp. 79–92. See also Jon Elster, *Ulysses and the Sirens*, Cambridge University Press, Cambridge, 1979. We are indebted to Catherine Wilson for discussion of Davidson's ideas.

oven in flames, one realizes that one had been aware of the smell of smoke but repressed this knowledge as too improbable, as not fitting with one's desire not to be disturbed and general knowledge to the effect that there is no fire there.

It is beyond question, then, that our cognitive apparatus contains many filtering devices which, to serve as filters, must both recognize information for what it is and neutralize its impact. There is nothing contradictory in this, even if one may wonder initially how it serves its function. An ostrich that sticks its head in the sand when an enemy approaches would not last long. When vitally important information is about, it is important to get it. As creatures produced by a long line of evolution, we are constructed so as to get the maximum of information from the environment, and to ensure that our beliefs form a maximally consistent set, so that we know which beliefs to operate on.

There are reasons, however, to suppose that evasions, avoidances, and filtering can have an overall utility. Some people are overcome by profound sleepiness during domestic arguments. From a subjective, culturally determined point of view, they are missing a lot of allegedly important information by falling asleep: a recitation of their faults, for example. They are not too sleepy, however, to notice that their faults are being catalogued. Again, we see this pattern of knowing and not knowing. However, the quality of this information is not, in evolutionary terms, necessarily very high, while the advantage of avoiding stress is. We can easily imagine a mechanism that registers information to the point where it reaches overload, measured by feelings of stress or discomfort, and then takes steps to annihilate the information or to avoid receiving more.

However, such evasion, avoidance, and filtering can be problematic if, as in the ostrich case, vital interests are hindered. We presume that it is in one's vital interest to know that one's child is a drug addict or one's spouse unfaithful. We presume this because of the profound personal and cultural significance these facts have and because, when a person knows them to obtain and frankly acknowledges them, they are likely to result in lots of overt behavior. For all that, we should not identify them with a person's vital interests in any biological sense; and it is biology, after all, which has allegedly designed these filtering mechanisms.

This much, then, can be said against nihilism regarding philosophical psychology: we can imagine a mechanism of self-deception, involving a host of perceptual and cognitive phenomena, which shows that information is actively processed, not simply reflected into the mind from the environment. There are, however, limitations to this approach.

First, if one were interested in modeling the mind, one would have to incorporate a mechanism for self-deception of the sort we have described: a filtering mechanism for stress-inducing beliefs. But one would also have to incorporate mechanisms that would behave in precisely the opposite fashion: that would, when supplied with information engendering stress, be extra vigilant in seeking out confirming information. Pathological jealousy, of the sort displayed by Proust's narrator, seems to call for such a mechanism. Rather than suppressing mild evidence of his girlfriend's infidelity to lower his stress, the narrator works himself into a frenzy seeking further confirmation and attempting to construct a coherent system from unrelated facts, just as the self-deceiver seeks to dismantle systematic interpretations of facts—refuses to put 2 and 2 together.[59]

The problem now is that this operation of an advanced truth-seeking mechanism may itself be considered a form of self-deception.[60] The pathologically jealous man can be said to know that his girlfriend is not unfaithful but to believe that she is. Stress is apparently caused in him by appearances of her fidelity, and relieved momentarily by the discovery, even manufacture, of counterevidence. The upshot is that, if we want to model the mind by building into it devices that either filter information or generate excessive amounts of information, we cannot model the mind in general. To ascribe self-deception then to a particular mechanism becomes impossible. The same mechanism may be rational in one case, irrational in another. We can model the self-deceiving and pathologically jealous mind, and we can model the self-deceiving, evidence-overlooking mind. But these are different minds. We can find some regularities at the perceptual level: most people appear to have, for example, some blocking mechanism which affects their cognitive processing of obscene words. But when we reach the level of self-deception, the details of the particular cases may become so important that both information-filtering and information-generating become aspects of self-deception.

We can see this more clearly, perhaps, by considering cases in which we describe, not a particular episode, but a protracted period of a life. The loss of faith in a way of life which Wittgenstein occasionally describes as occurring, suddenly or gradually, may entail the realization that one has been living a lie. One comes to identify one's own cognitive relation to the world as aberrant: there was too much filtering, or too much wishful thinking, or both.

---

59 This is a case of what Mele calls "twisted self-deception." See Alfred Mele, "Twisted Self-Deception," *Philosophical Psychology*, Vol. 12, 1999, pp. 117–37.

60 See Donald Davidson's influential essay "Deception and Division," pp. 79–92. See also Elster, *Ulysses and the Sirens*.

Such realizations, according to Wittgenstein, have no truth conditions—it is not the case that, objectively speaking, one was living a lie or not. One comes to see it that way; it takes on that aspect; that is how one interprets it. The businessman who gives up money-making for participation in a religious cult is apt to describe himself as having been self-deceived during the period of his financial success. But here it is less than tempting to speak of the operations of a particular mechanism. The statement "I was deceiving myself about p" need not be true in virtue of the existence and normal operation of some filtering mechanism. More likely, such an avowal reflects a profound change in one's values and goals, and one's ways of living, together with the belief that these newfound ideals, unlike their predecessors, are the real McCoy.

Our perspective on the above case resonates with Wittgenstein's remark:

> My attitude towards him is an attitude towards a soul. I am not of the opinion that he has a soul.[61]

The man who now looks on his former life as a stockbroker and says "I was self-deceived" is like the religious convert. Standing on a new ethical/religious plane, he is not of the opinion that his former self was self-deceived, as he would be if he had merely discerned some cognitive dissonance or conflicting mechanisms in another. This is not a case of "third-person description." It need not be that he sees something in his past self that he did not see before. Rather, there is a change of aspect: he sees his past self in a different way. The difference is like the difference between playing Frère Jacques as a lullaby and as a funeral march: the notes are the same, but the tone and attitude are different.

If an old friend were to attempt to correct him, by mentioning his former life of contentment and ease, he would be missing the point. The born-again man registers the way he now perceives his past life from his newfound spiritual/ethical perspective. He is making a confession, and "a confession," Wittgenstein tells us, "has to be part of your new life."[62] If the man speaks the truth, that is, if he is truthful, then he is already at home in his new ethical/spiritual way of life. It is noteworthy that the object of the born-again man's claims of self-deception was his former "self"—his moral identity—and not simply a particular belief or emotion. Even if there were, as in similar but somewhat different cases, evidence of moments of past discontentment and ambivalence, that evidence is now salient and perceived from his new spiritual perspective as revelatory of his having lived a lie. While the convert's

61 *Philosophical Investigations*, p. 152e.
62 *Culture and Value*, p. 16e.

ostensible attribution of self-deception has his former self as its grammatical subject, its logical subject is himself, and instead of a simple ascription, it is an expression of his commitment to his newfound values and beliefs. "First-person—expression."

One moral is that although pictures and analogies with physical processes may help us to relate classes of psychological phenomena—to picture them for ourselves, as well as to remove the superficial paradox associated with believing p and not-p—they have their limitations. Our description of our mental lives, as Wittgenstein stressed, is learned through conversation, reading, comparison, and reflection. It is not simply produced as the epiphenomenon of processes of which we are unconscious. Another and related lesson is that self-deception is part of our critical normative vocabulary, and it is best thought of as a family resemblance concept: the varied and diverse cases previously mentioned have striking affinities as well as interesting differences from one another and are more or less distant from what we might regard as an essentialist paradigm. Finally, the sorts of inclination to self-deception that we encounter in the course of our philosophical activity and theorizing track the inclinations to self-deception we struggle with in our everyday lives. Philosophy offers no way of escape and no privileged higher ground.

Earlier we noted Wittgenstein's concerns over the "culture of science" in particular, and the cultural malaise of the West, in general. We argued that the culture of science that concerned him was a form of scientism, rooted in self-deception. But self-deception amounts to a cultural malaise only if it rises to the level of a collective illusion. However, collective self-deception seems to differ in its contours from the self-deception that troubles our personal lives, where we are its responsible agents, as well as its cure. Its cultural or collective form, on the other hand, resides in our institutions, practices, and language games, where self-deception may be "baked into" their very structures. Once initiated into them, we may find ourselves in the midst of deceptions embedded in the grammar of the very language we have learned to use. In these cases, we are more like patients than agents, yet self-deceived, nonetheless.

Apart from their origins, both manifestations of self-deception are alike enough: they are motivated by self-interest and identity; they persist via failures of reason, including oversight and confirmation bias. As rational agents, we are as obligated to be critically self-conscious of imposed cultural/social illusions as we are of our own self-deceptions, and to make use of our moral and critical resources to see through and emerge from them. This way of looking at the matter resonates with Wittgenstein's remark about philosophy: "We are struggling with language. We are engaged in a struggle with language."[63] And the struggle is internal: we need to use the resources of language against language—against the pictures and false analogies language sometimes foists on us.

Concluding Remarks

Taking Wittgenstein at his word, we have found him with a warning: deception is a recurrent threat to our inquiries, including science, psychology, and philosophy. Deception arises in our theoretical practices, aided and abetted by our tendency to over-invest in theories. We feed our theories on a steady diet of one-sided examples, and once they are established, we tend to overlook phenomena beyond their purview. Our thought is coarsened and our lives correspondingly diminished. If we are to avoid these outcomes, we must be clear about the sources of deception and its family of mechanisms. At least, so we think. We could be deceived about this.

63 Ibid., p. 13e.

Chapter IX

EMBARRASSMENT: AN OVERVIEW

Introduction

Our concern here is the nature of embarrassment. We endeavor to formulate and argue for an account—a perspicuous overview—to the effect that embarrassment is a complex mental state, a complex of cognitive content, phenomenology—embarrassment's distinctive feel—and causal relations.[1] To be or feel embarrassed is to understand oneself in a certain way, and which way one understands oneself will be, in part, what distinguishes embarrassment from its close conceptual neighbors, such as shame and guilt. The task of identifying embarrassment's cognitive properties leads immediately to an investigation of its relational features, not only because they contribute to what makes embarrassment the emotion it is, but also because they throw light on the cognitive and causal nature of those creatures that experience it.

Our larger concern is to discern what embarrassment reveals about the nature of creatures that are capable of embarrassment. On the standard conception, embarrassment is conceived as an essentially public or social emotion, and this raises a central issue: whether private embarrassment is conceptually coherent. We claim that the nature of embarrassment, together with the nature of those that experience it, will determine its scope, and with that, the extent to which embarrassment may be private. So we proceed, then, with a lively sense that the standard view unduly limits our mental lives, and one of our foci is to test embarrassment's alleged essential publicity. However, even if we succeed in showing the standard view to be too narrow, we maintain an equally lively sense that although the account that will emerge may move embarrassment into the private, it may at best only asymptote to solipsistic embarrassment.

1 For a canvass of various views in the literature and an alternative account, see Luke Purshouse, "Embarrassment: A Philosophical Analysis," *Philosophy, The Journal of the Royal Institute of Philosophy*, Vol. 76, Issue 4, 2001, pp. 515–40.

The Standard View

We have seen that, while there are differences over the precise nature of embarrassment, there is also some common ground, and it is with that common ground that we begin. To take an uncontroversial case, suppose that Jones is embarrassed by his public faux pas. That the standard view of embarrassment conceives of it as a social emotion means that Jones—the embarrassee—must see himself as having lost esteem in the eyes of others. As the social psychologist, André Modigliani put it:

> Loss of situational-public-esteem is a necessary condition for embarrassment. Unless a person believes that his inept performance is being negatively evaluated by others, he will not experience embarrassment.[2]

Robert Solomon agrees: he claims that embarrassment is interpersonal, that "it is the negative opinion of others or what one takes to be the opinion of others that embarrass us."[3]

William Lyons not only agrees but gives reasons for doing so:

> We cannot evaluate ourselves as having made fools of ourselves or evaluate ourselves as having lost face in front of ourselves. You cannot make a fool of yourself in solitary confinement.[4]

And finally, Ronald de Sousa implicitly endorses the social conception of embarrassment by identifying what is sufficient to cancel it:

> Of the emotions that involve characteristic thoughts, some emotions appear to be founded entirely upon belief. To change them, all one needs to do is change the relevant belief. Embarrassment is of this sort. For my embarrassment to vanish, it is sufficient that I should find out either that no one was watching my faux pas or that I did not in fact commit one.[5]

These passages argue for the necessity of embarrassment over the perceived negative judgment of others. Thus, for Jones to be embarrassed, on the standard view, requires that he believe that his faux pas was observed, and that it was observed as such, so that he lost "situational-subjective-public esteem,"

---

2 Andre Modigliani, "Embarrassment, Face work and Eye Contact," *Journal of Personality and Social Psychology*, Vol. 17, 1971, pp. 15–24.

3 Robert Solomon, *The Passions*, Anchor/Doubleday, 1976, p. 306.

4 William Lyons, *Emotion*, Cambridge University Press, 1980, p. 114.

5 Ronald de Sousa, *The Rationality of Emotion*, MIT Press, Cambridge, MA, 1987, p. 137.

has incurred the "negative opinion of others," "made a [public] fool of himself," "lost [public] face."

As a first step toward a finer-grained account of embarrassment, we offer the following analysis of what is both implicit and explicit in the standard view. What we called embarrassment's cognitive content would seem to include Jones's belief that he is judged negatively and his desire not to be judged negatively, or perhaps to be judged positively. Notice, there seems to be nothing in the standard view to restrict "performance" to overt action, and so nothing to prevent one from being embarrassed by one's omissions and inabilities. Think of the embarrassment from "missing one's cue" or from being unable to perform altogether, or by one's actions, mistakes, accidents, and inadvertencies. All that is required is some index of agency, and performance may serve as the object which, when written to one's account, as it were, one is the less for it.

The characteristic feel of embarrassment, the discomfort, unpleasantness, perhaps even pain that in part comprises embarrassment, is plausibly regarded as an upshot of the belief that one has been judged negatively. We suggest that this is an effect of an awareness of the dissatisfaction or frustration of the desire not to be judged negatively, or perhaps of the desire to be judged positively. Just as pleasure often accompanies desire satisfaction, displeasure often accompanies desire frustration. We are inclined to think that the red-facedness that accompanies embarrassment is a "natural sign" of the perception of one's relative inferiority.

That this much at least is true of embarrassment indicates that the standard view carries with it a rich set of presuppositions about the nature of embarrassable creatures. Among these presuppositions are: An embarrassee must have a conception of the self as an enduring item with interests affected by negative estimation, his own as well as others. That conception presupposes self-awareness and self-consciousness—beliefs about the self that are grounds of first-person reports—and certain desires about the self—specifically, the desire to be well thought of, not only by oneself, but also by others: the desire for high public esteem. A further presupposition of the standard view is that the embarrassee has a conception of others that allows them to play their role in embarrassment. He must believe that others have a conception of him and evaluate him based on his performance. This point highlights the presupposed shared belief that agents are in some respects and to some extent transparent to themselves and to one another, especially in their actions. And this fact points to our shared conception of action as a revelatory, diagnostic concept.

To this standard view of embarrassment, we add a feature it shares with other emotions. Like fear, for example, embarrassment has the power to disrupt agency, perhaps even thwart it altogether. We offer an account and an explanation of this feature later, where we suggest that, while their upshots may be similar, fear and embarrassment differ importantly in the mechanisms by which they disrupt agency. We sense in these features of embarrassment and embarrassable agents the promise of an account that would move this emotion further into the private than the standard view would permit.

Epistemic and Normative Conditions of Embarrassment

The standard view of embarrassment as a social emotion requires that its participants satisfy certain epistemic and normative conditions. The publicity condition requires not only the presence of a public but a public of a certain sort, and requires of that public a certain role. Thus, if Jones is embarrassed by his public faux pas, his audience must satisfy the following conditions: (1) It is aware of Jones's performance, (2) It assesses that performance negatively, and (3) It assesses Jones negatively on the basis of his performance.

This much alone is insufficient for Jones to be embarrassed, except in the elliptical use of "is embarrassed" in which one is said to embarrass oneself without knowing it. To experience the emotion, Jones himself must satisfy certain epistemic and normative conditions, what we are calling embarrassment's cognitive content. Jones will be embarrassed, then, just in case he: (4) Believes that the publicity condition is satisfied, and (5) Desires not to be judged negatively. With these conditions satisfied, we would expect Jones to experience the feel and effects that characterize embarrassment.

Testing the Standard View

Now we marshal a set of examples, each of which challenges various aspects of the standard conception of embarrassment. To begin, consider a case that only seems to challenge that view. There is a sense in which an agent may embarrass himself without knowing it. So, suppose that Jones presses on, blissfully unaware that he has embarrassed himself. Presumably, such a description means not that Jones is experiencing the emotion of embarrassment without knowing it, but that Jones has unknowingly satisfied some criteria of embarrassment. So, while he isn't embarrassed, Jones has done what would be sufficient for embarrassment should he become aware of that fact: then he would be or feel embarrassed. Such a case might provoke a sympathetic audience to enlighten Jones with a remark such as "Say, why don't you stop embarrassing yourself." Nothing in this makes trouble for the standard view.

From Awareness to Embarrassment

However, consider a more troublesome case. Suppose I know I have nothing to be embarrassed about, but I am. This may sound paradoxical, especially on the assumption that a necessary condition for embarrassment is the belief or recognition that something negative about the self has been revealed. But there is an analysis of this that does not threaten the standard view. Suppose that in the midst of his lecture on Post-Modernism, Jones notices that he has just contradicted himself, feels embarrassed for it, and utters "I know I have nothing to be embarrassed about, but I am." Jones, aware that at least some in his audience embrace self-contradiction, is ironic, but embarrassed in the straightforward sense.

Now suppose that Jones is not ironic. Can he be embarrassed while believing that he has nothing to be embarrassed about? Well, suppose that, in the first instance, Jones, perhaps because of some theory he embraces, has what he takes to be good and sufficient reasons for believing that self-contradiction is not undesirable. Imagine however, that his theoretical attachments have failed to have their effects felt at the level of his actual beliefs. This may be due to akrasia, self-deception or the like, so that he believes that self-contradiction is something to be embarrassed about despite his theoretical commitments. In that case "I know I have nothing to be embarrassed about, but I am" may non-ironically report his conflicted state of mind.

An alternative interpretation resembles the first in that, again, Jones is theoretically committed to there being nothing objectionable about self-contradiction, but now his practical beliefs do align with his theoretical commitments. If he nevertheless desires to avoid self-contradiction, again perhaps due to some cognitive dissonance, self-deception or akrasia, he may be embarrassed by it, and we would again have an accurate report of his predicament.

Finally, suppose that Jones' practical beliefs and desires have aligned with his theoretical views; that he finds nothing objectionable about self-contradiction, does not desire to avoid it, even embraces it wherever he finds it. May he still be embarrassed? If so, he would be embarrassed despite the lack of sufficient cognitive conditions of embarrassment: a case of non-cognitive embarrassment, where Jones is merely caused to be embarrassed, perhaps due to some habit of mind. If this is plausible, it suggests that, while one can be embarrassed through cognitivity, as it were, when the requisite beliefs and desires are in place, one can also be embarrassed despite cognitivity. This analysis recognizes a merely causal route to embarrassment which bypasses cognitivity, unaffected by the lack of cognitive content thought essential to embarrassment, say, habitual embarrassment, where a habit of mind is unaffected by one's beliefs.

There may be some reluctance to consider this last reading as a case of real embarrassment, lacking as it does so much of embarrassment's alleged cognitive content. Perhaps it is better treated as an aberrant mental state that shares only some of the properties of embarrassment. This view is supported, we believe, by the different strategies such a state would prompt in us. Such a state may still disrupt agency and have the characteristic feel of genuine embarrassment, and so on, but it would provide no reason to adopt the kinds of strategies that genuine embarrassment engenders, such as revising one's beliefs and desires, taking steps to avoid embarrassing situations, and so on. Perhaps all one could do in the face of habitual "embarrassment" is lament being a victim of one's deep causal nature.

Consider another troublesome case for the standard view: "I realize I ought to be embarrassed about this, but I am not." This is, in some respects, similar to "I know I have nothing to be embarrassed about, but I am," since there is an ironic reading of it: Jones is aware that his audience finds self-contradiction objectionable, but he does not. So, he is not embarrassed by it. Suppose, however, that he is not ironic. Can he fail to be embarrassed despite his awareness that the normative conditions of embarrassment have been satisfied? Suppose, as above, that Jones has what he takes to be good and sufficient reasons for believing that self-contradiction is undesirable. Then again, perhaps due to some cognitive dissonance, self-deception or akrasia, he believes that it is not undesirable. If so, it is plausible that Jones would not feel embarrassed by his performance.

Finally, suppose again that Jones's practical beliefs and desires have aligned with his theoretical views so that he finds self-contradiction objectionable and does desire to avoid it. May he yet fail to be embarrassed? If so, he would fail despite the presence of what ought to be sufficient cognitive conditions of embarrassment: a case in which cognitivity would fail to have its standard effects. If this is plausible, it would indicate another point along the informational pathways of agency where aberration may occur.

The Publicity Condition

The standard conception of embarrassment as a social or public emotion means that an embarrassee must believe that an audience has judged him negatively on the basis of his performance. The performance and the negative assessment of others comprise the "publicity condition" of embarrassment. Let us now look at cases that raise questions about the necessity and sufficiency, ceteris paribus, of this component of the standard view. Suppose that Smith, anticipating his imminent failure to make the free throw, is embarrassed. This may be a case of premature embarrassment, but embarrassment, nonetheless. Where it departs from the standard view is in the absence of an index of Smith's deficient agency and the subsequent loss of public esteem. Smith has yet to perform, has yet to "embarrass himself," but his expectations are sufficient to produce in him all the characteristics of embarrassment. He feels badly for what he takes will be his imminent loss of esteem and endures the distraction that it characteristically brings.

Consider now a different case. Suppose Smith is alone on the practice court, misses what should have been an easy shot, and is embarrassed wondering whether anyone has noticed. Here Smith has done what he feels is embarrassing, and without believing that he has lost public esteem, is embarrassed in merely wondering whether he has.

Another scenario: Smith imagines himself missing the crucial shot and is embarrassed at the prospect. This case departs from the standard view by allowing that Smith is embarrassed despite the absence of some performance, and, as well, without the subsequent loss of public esteem. The difference of this case from the two previous ones is that in this instance there is no damaging performance imminent. Suppose that Smith is alive to just how important his performance is: it is his esteem, after all, that is at stake. That may be sufficient to prompt him to envisage the worst case, among others. If so, he may endure all that characterizes embarrassment. What would be doing the work in Smith is his vivid imagination. But clearly, he doesn't imagine that he is embarrassed; he is embarrassed because of what he imagines.

Now consider yet another scenario. With nothing on his agenda, Fred is embarrassed merely at being seen. This differs from the three previous examples in that there is neither an anticipated, suspected, nor an imagined performance to serve as an index of Fred qua agent. For Fred to be embarrassed by the mere gaze of another would suggest that he believes he is, at least partially, transparent to his audience even without some performance. With this belief in place, Fred has to wonder how much of the self has been revealed, how much more his audience may know about Fred than he himself knows. The mere gaze of another is an epistemic invasion that threatens Fred's presumption of privacy and privileged access to his own mind. That Fred's audience may know more about him than he knows himself is a challenge to Fred's conception of himself as an autonomous agent. If there are reasons for Fred's behavior of which he is ignorant, how autonomous can he be? Each of these thoughts may be acutely embarrassing for Fred. We suggest that shyness may be a dispositional embarrassment of just this sort.

These cases are suggestive of a way to understand the phenomenon that in sports is sometimes referred to as "choking." Athletes sometimes fail where they would otherwise succeed because of the pressure to succeed. An athlete who anticipates or imagines failure, or who merely appreciates what is at stake, may be embarrassed and so suffer one of embarrassment's salient effects—its power to disrupt or derail agency. The unfortunate upshot of embarrassment's distraction is an increased likelihood of failure.

The Normative Condition

According to the standard view of embarrassment, an embarrassee must be aware that his audience has judged him negatively in light of his performance and that he desires not to be so judged. We refer to this complex of normative content as the "normative condition" of embarrassment. We now proceed to examine a set of cases intended to question the standard view's conception of the normative component of embarrassment. Suppose that Tom is embarrassed at being praised. This seems common enough. But how can praise embarrass Tom, if it is loss of public esteem that embarrasses one? Perhaps, but we suggest alternatives. If Tom recognizes the importance of what's at stake in this assessment of him, he may be embarrassed. Or he may find the fact that he is assessed at all, irrespective of the outcome, sufficient to produce embarrassment. This would be especially true of a person who judges the praise to be inappropriate, in either its source or its content. If I am praised by a person I judge to be in no position to judge me, I may be embarrassed. And if they get it wrong, if they misperceive and/or misjudge me, I may be even more embarrassed at their mistake. Finally, I may be embarrassed at the thought that I have been unwittingly complicit in their false assessment of me.

Now imagine that Tom commits what both he and his audience would agree is a faux pas and he feels embarrassed about it even though his sympathetic audience does not judge him negatively. This case lacks the normative component of the standard view that would require the embarrassee to be judged negatively and so lose public esteem. If Tom is embarrassed here, it is his own negative assessment of himself for having done what he believes ought to lose him public esteem. Whether it does or not, or even in spite of not losing public esteem, it is sufficient to produce embarrassment.

If we all agree, however, that Tom's mistake was justified, then it is not something that ought to be written on Tom's account under a negative description. If it is not, then Tom loses neither public nor self-esteem. How then can he be embarrassed? One suggestion is that Tom is embarrassed, not for the faux pas itself, but for his epistemic shortcomings in not knowing better than to have committed it. He might agree that by the standards embodied in a reasonable person, he is not to be blamed. But if his standards for himself exceed those required of a reasonable person, he may be embarrassed by an epistemic performance he judges not quite up to snuff.

Now suppose my host, who is not in the know, misperceives my behavior as socially inept, and I am embarrassed for it. Here I am embarrassed for the loss of public esteem despite my belief that I do not deserve it. The discomfort and temporary paralysis I feel may produce that awkwardness we associate with embarrassment, and this may be further compounded by my not knowing how to gracefully extricate myself from my predicament.

Another case, where it would seem that I am embarrassed about having done something despite my belief that it was nothing to be embarrassed about, goes like this: A visitor in a foreign country, I kiss my wife in public, ignorant of the fact that this is considered taboo by my hosts. To unravel this case, a distinction is needed between what I intended and the unforeseen consequences of what I intended. So, while I may be embarrassed for having given offense, and for my action, as it was considered a violation of a social convention, I am not embarrassed by what I intended, which was an act of affection for my wife. Suppose, however, that despite my audience's reaction to my performance, I am resolutely unembarrassed. Others, but not I, think that I committed a faux pas. Despite their negative assessment of me, I am steadfast in my view that I have nothing to be embarrassed about, and I am not. Such a case suggests that an awareness of loss of public esteem may be insufficient for embarrassment.

Embarrassment then requires neither that the embarrassee be judged negatively by others, nor that the embarrassee concur with others' negative assessment of him. An agent's sense of self-esteem may cancel or prevent embarrassment altogether despite such a negative assessment. This suggests that we can move our conception of embarrassment further into the private than the standard view would allow. The question is how far into the private it may go.

Private Embarrassment and Private Language

I happen upon my diary and read with acute embarrassment my adolescent musings. Suppose I identify with my youthful self, perceive myself now as that former self, and believe that what I have written is embarrassing. I feel embarrassed at what I have done even though at the time of writing I thought it witty, insightful, or the like. If I literally identify with my former self, I should not now be embarrassed, since he was not. But if his reasons and now my reasons demand a different appraisal, they may cause embarrassment. This is empathetic embarrassment: I am embarrassed as my former self. Notice that in such a case, there need be no other, no public, to witness the embarrassing behavior and to assess it negatively. Nor need there be any anticipation or threat of exposure, nor imagined exposure. There is no observer–observee distinction, no distinction between the judge and the embarrassee: a case of private embarrassment.

Alternatively, suppose that I do not identify with my former self, care about him as I would about my son or other loved one, and believe that what he has written is embarrassing to him. I may feel embarrassed for him on his behalf. I am embarrassed for my former self, but not as him: a case of sympathetic embarrassment. Notice here that there is a distinction between observer–judge and observee–embarrassee, but that I, in two incarnations, play both roles. As such, it is a case of private embarrassment that does not challenge as directly as the previous case did, the role of the other that we find in the standard view.

Now imagine that I come across my son's diary and read with embarrassment his adolescent musings. Suppose that I identify with my son—I see myself in him—and I judge that he has embarrassed himself. If it is now for me as though I have done the embarrassing deed, I am empathetically embarrassed: I am embarrassed as my son. In this case I perform two roles: I am both observer/judge of my son's behavior and, by virtue of empathy, I am the one observed and judged. But because I—observer–judge—identify with the one who embarrassed himself, there is no distinction between me as judge-observer and the one who is embarrassed. This is a sort of hybrid case of private-public embarrassment.

Alternatively, suppose I do not identify with my son, but care about him so that his well-being, esteem, and so on, are as much a concern of mine as are my own, and believe that what he has written embarrasses him. Then I may feel embarrassed for him, on his behalf, in his stead, since he was not. In such a case, I am embarrassed for another, and this is another case of sympathetic embarrassment.

Each of the foregoing cases of empathetic and sympathetic embarrassment ought to be distinguished from the case in which I am embarrassed by my former self's behavior or by that of my son. These seem to be cases which require that I believe that another, my former self or my son, behaves in a manner that reflects badly on me, that I lose esteem by virtue of their intimate relation to me.

There is a scene in Carol Shields's *Stone Diaries,* which is as good an example of private embarrassment as one might hope to find. Barker Flett harbors deep affection for Daisy, his much younger niece, a fact he finds painfully embarrassing. Flett is so troubled by his love for Daisy that he takes extreme precautions and undergoes elaborate rituals intended to keep these facts private, not only to himself but also from himself—out of his consciousness. There is no threat of exposure, no anticipated nor imagined audience for his feelings, but when his suppressed desires leak back into consciousness, his mind is "aerated by acts of private embarrassment." At these moments, he is transparent to himself and what he sees privately embarrasses him.

We have argued for the possibility of private embarrassment. At this point, it might be asked how the privacy of private embarrassment is different, if at all, from the privacy of private language? Avoiding the intricacies of Wittgenstein's private language argument, we might say that its aim, roughly speaking, is to show that I cannot give meaning to terms that I want to use for my sensations if I intend this meaning to be private.[6] Having a sensation is not sufficient for establishing meaning. But once the meaning of a sensation has been established properly, that is publicly, then I can use it to talk about my sensations. "Embarrassment" is a term we can use for "a feeling" because its meaning has been established publicly. So, we can talk about this feeling in ways that others can understand. There is no question of meaning here. Still, I can try to keep the feeling private; that is, hide it from others or even from myself.

This is "privacy" in a quite different sense than is privacy in private language. In the case of private embarrassment, the issue is not that I can't intelligibly talk about it. The issue is, rather, that I don't want to. In the case of Barker Flett, things are more complicated. He not only wants to hide his embarrassment from others, but also from himself. And this requires not only deception but self-deception or repression, which may be punctured at any moment by the stubborn arousal of desire for his niece. So, the private linguist has the problem of expression—of how to communicate what he means to others. In contrast, the problem of private embarrassment is one of suppression—of how to hide the public signs of embarrassment from others or oneself.

Finally, consider a philosopher, working on the complexities of embarrassment, who is embarrassed to discover a howler in his analysis. This may be a case in which anticipated or imagined counterfactual exposure causes the embarrassment: "Just imagine how I would feel were this to get out!" Or our philosopher may be embarrassed simply to discover that he fails to meet his own standards of conduct. Or he may be embarrassed to learn that what he has professed to be is false. No one needs to witness the falsification for him to be embarrassed. The discovery alone that he is not quite the agent he thinks he is and ought to be seems sufficient to embarrass him.

6 Wittgenstein, *Philosophical Investigations*, #243.

Effects and Strategies

When we set out on this exploratory journey, we mentioned that the neglect of embarrassment as a topic of philosophical attention has meant that, apart from the need for an audience, embarrassment's relational properties have been largely unexplored. But embarrassment is a state that is caused in distinctive ways and has distinctive effects. Exploring these characteristic relations ought to give insight into both the cognitive makeup of embarrassment and the creatures who experience it.

It is from its effects that embarrassment gets its name: embarrassment encumbers, impedes, or bars agency. Thus, the expression "an embarrassment of riches" means a case in which a wealth of options frustrates one's ability to choose from among them. For instance, even though he was hungry, Tom was embarrassed by the riches of the salad bar. Embarrassment's ability to disrupt agency is a feature shared with other emotions. Fear, for example, can clear the agency decks, so that whatever was on the agent's agenda is displaced by what we are afraid of. Displacement of a goal by the object of fear may only paralyze agency. But, in certain contexts and circumstances, fear may prompt fear-avoidance behavior. In such cases, fear displaces whatever goal we may have had and replaces it with the goal of avoiding the object of fear. These features of fear give it survival value. Unless it is your job or you think you can make a valuable contribution, it would be unwise of you to seek out the locale marked by a suicide bomber. Fear is not intrinsically bad. T-shirt slogans that advertise "No fear" are radically misguided, for some things are rightly feared. That nothing is to be feared is a common misinterpretation of Franklin Roosevelt's remark that "the only thing we have to fear is fear itself." As he makes it clear in his speech, what he opposes is unreasoning irrational fear that saps a nation or an individual of its vital sources for renewal.

Embarrassment is akin to fear in that it may be merely disruptive, a bar to agency, an encumbrance, and can thus clear the agency decks. It need not make demands on agency, and very likely no demands with the urgency that fear sometimes carries. However, because it is unpleasant and sometimes even painful, embarrassment may, again in certain contexts, be the cause of embarrassment avoidance behavior. "I felt so embarrassed that I wanted to hide," reports the acutely embarrassed. Freud and others have argued that embarrassment may have psychological effects including deliberately ignoring who or what embarrasses us and pressing on with the business at hand, as well as the repression of the object of embarrassment. Embarrassment may also be a prompt to reasoning about strategies for dealing with it. And in its practical upshots we find part of what distinguishes embarrassment from guilt, since where guilt incurs a debt to another, embarrassment incurs a debt to the self. If I wrong someone, I may be embarrassed, but the wrong incurs a debt to me, perhaps to take measures to correct what I perceive to be a fault of mine.

But this is not quite right. For now it looks as if we have shame rather than embarrassment on our hands. How do they differ? Briefly, one salient difference between them is precisely that while embarrassment often involves a sense of innocence, shame involves seeing oneself at fault for some deliberate wrongdoing. Errol Bedford brings out this point with reference to the man who, as a child, was the model of Barrie's character Peter Pan.[7] One can understand this man being somewhat embarrassed about this fact, but it would be difficult to understand his being ashamed of it. The reason for this seems to be that being a model for Peter Pan is not a matter of his fault, and it is hard to imagine how he could construe it as such. Shame then involves a sense of guilt or wrongdoing, embarrassment a sense of guiltless awkwardness. To be embarrassed is often to be at a loss for what to say or do—at a loss for words or action—to experience a sudden sense of diminished agency. So, the embarrassed person resolves to take steps not to put himself, or be put into similar situations, to brush up on protocol and so on; while the person who is ashamed resolves to correct what he sees to be a fault of his.

The mechanisms at work in these effects of embarrassments tell us something about its content—what we can be embarrassed about—as well as about the nature of embarrassable creatures. One plausible explanation of embarrassment's effect on agents is that in embarrassment the agent's attention is drawn away from whatever occupied him—action, practical reasoning, and the like—and is focused instead on the agent himself as agent. But it is not merely a distraction: embarrassment prompts the agent into self-scrutiny, and the embarrassee is now forced to take a look with an evaluative eye, not simply at some action, but on the self *qua* agent. Since practical matters require attention, the distraction that is characteristic of embarrassment—this shift in attention away from what one has been doing and to the self—seems to be sufficient for the effect of paralysis, however momentary. This is not to say that agents may not learn to control or limit the degree to which embarrassment is agency-paralyzing. Perhaps self-control includes the ability to allow agency to proceed despite the distraction that embarrassment brings.

Whatever else is true of embarrassment, it must, by virtue of some of its features, be sufficient to move the agent's attention from the doing to the

7 Errol Bedford, "Emotions and Statements About Them," in *The Social Construction of Emotions*, Basil Blackwell, Oxford, 1986.

doer. One natural suggestion is that becoming aware that one has an audience—not just that one is not alone, but that others observe and evaluate one—is enough to make one self-conscious rather than, or in addition to, conscious of what one is doing. Thus, the plausibility of the claim that an audience, together with the belief that one has a critical audience, is a necessary condition of embarrassment. As many of our examples show, however, this shift in awareness may take place not only without an audience, but even without the belief that one has an audience. Should I anticipate having an audience that I do not have, or imagine that, contrary to fact, I am public and not private, may be enough to produce embarrassment's characteristic features. Moreover, merely remembering that I had so anticipated or had so imagined may likewise produce the same effect. Thus, it isn't obvious that another scrutinizing agent is a necessary condition of at least this feature of embarrassment.

The normative aspect of the publicity condition in the standard view of embarrassment is that "real" embarrassment requires not only the belief that one is being observed, but also that one is being judged, and judged negatively. Again, as many of our examples show, the normative assessment of the self as agent—one of the marks of embarrassment—does not seem to require that another agent think badly of one, nor even that one think badly of oneself. That is, one need not think of oneself as having failed to satisfy some standard, one's own or one's community's, to address the self normatively. Suppose one is embarrassed by a compliment. The compliment may be spoken too loudly, or by someone who wishes to ingratiate, or by someone who pretends to understand what is involved in my achievements but does not really. So, embarrassment need not involve having failed to live up to some standard, since in this particular case, one is praised precisely for having lived up to it.

Rather, a point like the following suggests itself. Coming to reflect on oneself, rather than on what one is doing, or trying to do, causes one to see that there is something evaluative in the offing, namely, behavior understood by the agent as revelatory of the self qua agent. Thus, the impending behavior is seen as a test of agency, of how one performs or whether one performs at all, which will reveal to others and to oneself how good an agent one is. That much, we argue, may be sufficient to explain the critical self-assessment characteristic of embarrassment.

One of embarrassment's presuppositions is the belief that one's behavior is revelatory and therefore evaluative of the self. Embarrassment adds a further normative dimension to the revelatory nature of behavior: what embarrasses you, or whether you are beyond embarrassment, tells all of us about the sort of normative creature you are. Here is an example which may be distressingly self-revelatory: I profess to believe that nudity is nothing to be embarrassed about, so I happily agree to attend the nudist colony's open house. Upon arrival I am distressed to learn that I am embarrassed, that my beliefs lack conviction.

What an agent does in the face of embarrassment will indicate something about the scope and strength of his rationality and, perhaps, the limits of his autonomy. Suppression is perhaps the crudest of strategies. If it was a mistake or an accident that embarrassed you, then revising the relevant beliefs and desires is one strategy. If so, then whether you do so will be an index of you qua rational agent. Where one is embarrassed by what one is unable or unwilling to change, agents may resort to rearranging their normatives, a kind of rationalizing, perhaps extending to self-deception, intending to thereby prevent future embarrassments.

Embarrassment as Means

Consider: Even though I am convinced that nudity is nothing to be ashamed of, I know it embarrasses me and so, in an attempt to correct this, I attend the nudist colony's open house, intending this as a means to produce in me the courage of my convictions. Again, I testify at the AA meetings where the embarrassment is intended to buoy my conviction to stay on the wagon. In these cases, embarrassment, like praise, blame, reward, and punishment, may be used as a device of control. So, just as I might try to embarrass you into some behavior or other, I may use self-embarrassment in an attempt to control myself when other more direct means of self-control have failed. That I may be forced to resort to such measures to control myself may be a further source of embarrassment for me, showing as it would that I am not the fully autonomous agent that I should like to be.

Concluding Remarks

These examples of embarrassment, some admittedly more controversial than others, have revealed the riches of embarrassment: not only as illustrations of the uses of the concept but also as driving our project, together with a sense of where conceptual problems may lie. We have argued that the social conception of embarrassment is mistaken, that while an audience may not be sufficient, ceteris paribus, for embarrassment, it is not necessary, at least not for normative, self-evaluative, self-scrutinizing agents. This is not to say that the standard view is wrong in its entirety: it is not uncommon for inadequate theories to have part of the picture right. By insisting on the role of another, the standard view underestimates the complexities of our normative lives.

Embarrassment shows that our accounts of ourselves and others are accounts of self-evaluating, self-scrutinizing agents; that our presumption is in favor of privacy, but that privacy may be betrayed by behavior; that while we may be opaque in some respects to others and to ourselves, that opacity may be breached in moments of embarrassing self-revelation.

ENVOIS: TWO MOMENTS OF EMBARRASSMENT

The reader may have noticed that we speak of two distinct moments of embarrassment in modern philosophy: those that were embarrassing for their authors, and those that should have been embarrassing for them but weren't. The former is descriptive; the latter is prescriptive. Vide Rousseau. One might object that we move too freely back and forth between these moments, even though only our former claim casts light on the texts we examine; the latter shows nothing more than that we think that the philosophers in question were mistaken in their views. Saying that they should have been embarrassed when they weren't indicates mere disagreement but does not give new insight.

To resolve this problem, we approach it from the author's—as well as from the critic's—point of view. Beginning with the author, consider a case of retrospective embarrassment where the author committed a faux-pas, or made a mistake, thought it to be trivial and refused to pay attention to it at the time. Replaying the scene in his mind, it dawns on him that he unwittingly violated his own, as well as shared norms, and that he was in fact embarrassed and should have acknowledged it.

And now to the critic's or other's point of view. Suppose an author puts forth a theory and a supporting argument. A critic says the author should be embarrassed because the justification is flawed for putting forth the theory or the way he argues because the justification offered has all sorts of fault lines. Thus far, this is mere disagreement—a conflict between two claims. To strengthen and clinch the charge "If you were not embarrassed, you should have been," the critic needs to show the author or the reader how the situation warranted embarrassment; that due to some negligence—lack of self-reflection, weakness of will or self-deception—he violated his own standards and acted against the social norms as well as his own. The author repressed or at any rate was not fully aware of being embarrassed, even though he now acknowledges that he should have been.

While this sort of criticism is external in the sense that it comes from another person, it is also internal insofar as it refers to the author's own standards and norms. Hence, this sort of criticism is not an arbitrary imposition of the critic's own norms. In such a situation, the critic is our better self—our unstifled conscience.

BIBLIOGRAPHY

Appelquist, Hanne Ahonen. *Wittgenstein and the Conditions of Musical Communication*. Acta Philosophica Fennica, Volume 85. Helsinki: Hakapaino Oy, 2008.

Árdal, Páll. *Passion and Value in Hume's Treatise*. Edinburgh: Edinburgh University Press, 1966.

Austin, J.L. *How to Do Things with Words*. Oxford: Clarendon Press, 1962.

Ayer, A.J. *Language, Truth, and Logic*. 2nd ed. London: Gollancz, 1946.

Baier, Annette. *A Progress of Sentiments: Reflections on Hume's* Treatise. Cambridge, MA: Harvard University Press, 1991.

Beck, Lewis White. *A Commentary on Kant's Critique of Practical Reason*. Chicago: University of Chicago Press, 1960.

Bedford, Errol. "Emotions and Statements About Them." Rom Harré, editor, *The Social Construction of Emotions*, pp. 15–31. Oxford: Basil Blackwell, 1986.

Boeker, Ruth. "Locke and Hume on Personal Identity: Moral and Religious Differences." *Hume Studies*, Volume 41, pp. 105–135, 2015.

Campbell, Peter and Béla Szabados. "Wittgenstein on Self-Deception in Science, Psychology and Philosophy." *Wittgenstein-Studien*, Volume 4, pp. 143–170, 2013.

Castelfranchi, Cristiano and Isabella Poggi. "Blushing as a Discourse: Was Darwin Wrong?" W.R. Crozier, editor, *Shyness and Embarrassment: Perspectives from Social Psychology*, pp. 230–254. Cambridge: Cambridge University Press, 1990.

Cerbone, David. *Wittgenstein on Realism and Idealism*. Cambridge: Cambridge University Press, 2023.

Coval, S.C. and Peter Campbell. *Critique of the Liberal Conception of Persons*. Lewiston, New York: Edwin Mellen Press, 2010.

Davidson, Donald. "Deception and Division." J. Elster, editor, *The Multiple Self*, pp. 79–92. Cambridge University Press, 1986.

Davidson, Donald. "Paradoxes of Irrationality." Richard Wollheim and J. Hopkins, editor, *Philosophical Essays on Freud*, pp. 289–305. Cambridge: Cambridge University Press, 1982.

Davidson, Donald and Jaakko Hintikka. Editors. *Words and Objections*. Dordrecht, Netherlands: Reidel, 1969.

Darwin, Charles. *The Expression of Emotion in Man and Animals*. Darwin-online.org.uk, 1872.

Dent, Nicholas. *Rousseau*. London and New York: Routledge, 2005.

Descartes, René. *Meditations* on *First Philosophy*. EarlyModernTexts.com, 1641.

de Sousa, Ronald. *The Rationality of Emotion*. Cambridge, MA: MIT Press, 1987.

de Sousa, Ronald. "Emotion." Edward Zalta, editor, *Stanford Encyclopedia of Philosophy*. Stanford, CA: 2018 edition.

Drury, Maurice. "Conversations with Wittgenstein." Rush Rhees, *Ludwig Wittgenstein: Personal Recollections*, pp. 113–184. Oxford: Basil Blackwell, 1981.

Eliot, George. *Daniel Deronda*. New York, New York: Penguin Random House, Modern Library, 2002. Originally published in 1876.

Elster, Jon. *The Multiple Self*. Cambridge: Cambridge University Press, 1986.

Elster, Jon. *Ulysses and the Sirens*. Cambridge: Cambridge University Press, 1979.

Feynman, Richard. "Cargo Cult Science." Commencement Address at Cal Tech, *Caltech's Repository*, pp. 1–12, 1974.

Fogelin, Robert. *Wittgenstein*. London: Routledge & Kegan Paul, 1976.

Follesdal, Dogfinn. "Developments in Quine's Behaviorism." *American Philosophical Quarterly*, Volume 48, pp. 273–282, 2011.

Goffman, Erving. *Interaction Ritual: Essays on Face to Face Behaviour*. Penguin Random House, 1982.

Goffman, Erving. *The Presentation of the Self in Everyday Life*. New York, New York: Anchor, 1959.

Gordon, Robert M. *The Structure of Emotions*. Cambridge: Cambridge University Press, 1987.

Haack, Susan. "Two Faces of Naturalism." *Synthese*, Volume 94, pp. 335–356, 1993.

Hahn, Hans, Otto Neurath, and Rudolf Carnap. *The Scientific Conception of the World. The Vienna Circle*. (Also known as the *Manifesto of the Vienna Circle*.) Online, 1929.

Haller, Rudolf. *Questions on Wittgenstein*. Lincoln: University of Nebraska Press, 1990.

Harré, Rom. "Embarrassment: A Conceptual Analysis." W.R. Crozier, editor, *Shyness and Embarrassment: Perspectives from Social Psychology*, pp. 181–204. Cambridge: Cambridge University Press, 1990.

Heal, Jane. "Wittgenstein and Dialogue." *Proceedings of the British Academy*, Volume 85, pp. 63–83, 1995.

Hume, David. *My Own Life*. Hume Texts Online. https://davidhume.org.

Hume, David. *A Treatise on Human Nature*. Hume Texts online. https://davidhume.org.

Juhos, Béla. "Moritz Schlick." Paul Edwards, editor in chief, *Encyclopedia of Philosophy*, Volume 7, Reprint ed. New York, New York: MacMillan Publishing and The Free Press, 1972.

Kant, Immanuel. *Critique of Pure Reason*. 2nd ed. Translated by Norman Kemp Smith. London, England: Palgrave MacMillan, 2007.

Kant, Immanuel. *Notes and Fragments*. Edited by Paul Guyer. Translated by Curtis Bowman, Paul Guyer, and Frederick Rauscher. Cambridge: Cambridge University Press, 2010.

Kenny, Anthony. "Wittgenstein on the Nature of Philosophy." Brian McGuinness, editor, *Wittgenstein and His Times*, pp. 1–26. Oxford: Basil Blackwell, 1982.

Kim, Jaegwon. "What is Descriptive Epistemology." *Philosophical Perspectives, Volume 2*, pp. 381–405. Atascadero: Ridgeview Publishing, 1988.

Kuusela, Oscar. "Carnap and Wittgenstein: Tolerance, Arbitrariness and Truth." https://www.mdip.com, 2024.

Lugg, Andrew. *Wittgenstein on Colour, 1916–1950*. Cambridge: Cambridge University Press, 2025.

Lyons, William. *Emotion*. Cambridge: Cambridge University Press, 1980.

McGuinness, Brian. *Approaches to Wittgenstein*. New York: Routledge, 2002.

McGuinness, Brian. "Freud and Wittgenstein." Brian McGuinness, editor, *Wittgenstein and His Times*, pp. 27–43. Oxford: Basil Blackwell, 1982.
McGuinness, Brian. *Wittgenstein: A Life. Young Ludwig.* Berkeley: University of California Press, 1988.
McGuinness, Brian. *Wittgenstein in Cambridge: Letters and Documents 1911–1951.* Oxford: Blackwell Publishing, 1995.
Mele, Alfred. *Irrationality: An Essay on Akrasia, Self-Deception and Self-Control.* Oxford: Oxford University Press, 1987.
Mele, Alfred. "Twisted Self-Deception." *Philosophical Psychology*, Volume 12, pp. 117–37, 1999.
Modigliani, André. "Embarrassment, Facework and Eye Contact." *Journal of Personality and Social Psychology*, Volume 17, pp. 15–24, 1971.
Moore, G.E. "Wittgenstein's Lectures in 1930–1933." Ludwig Wittgenstein, *Philosophical Occasions*, edited by James Klagge and Alfred Nordmann. Indianapolis and Cambridge: Hackett Publishing Company, 1993.
Nagel, Thomas. "What is it like to be a Bat." *The Philosophical Review*, Volume 83, pp. 435–450, 1974.
Nussbaum, Martha. *Upheavals of Thought: The Intelligence of Emotions.* Cambridge: Cambridge University Press, 2001.
Oakley, Justin. *Morality and the Emotions.* London and New York: Routledge, 1992.
Passmore, John. *Hume's Intentions.* Cambridge: Cambridge University Press, 1952.
Pears, David. *Motivated Irrationality.* Oxford University Press, 1984.
Pears, David. *Wittgenstein. Fontana Modern Masters.* Glasgow, Scotland: Fontana Modern Masters, Fontana/Collins, 1971.
Pears, David. "Wittgenstein's Treatment of Solipsism in the Tractatus." *Critica Revista Hispano-Americana de Filosofia*, Volume 6, pp. 57–84, 1972.
Penelhum, Terence. "Pleasure and Falsity." *American Philosophical Quarterly*, Volume 1, pp. 81–91, 1964.
Penelhum, Terence. *Hume.* London: Palgrave MacMillan, 1975.
Penelhum, Terence. *Hume: The Self, The Will, Religion.* Oxford: The Clarendon Press, 2004.
Pinsent, David Hume. *A Portrait of Wittgenstein as a Young Man: From the Diary of David Hume Pinsent.* Oxford: Blackwell, 1990.
Prinz, Jesse J. *Gut Reactions: A Perceptual Theory of Emotions.* Oxford, Oxford University Press, 2004.
Proust, Marcel. *Remembrance of Things Past. Swann's Way.* Translated by C. K. Scott Moncrieff. London: Chatto & Windus, 1960.
Purshouse, Luke. "Embarrassment: A Philosophical Analysis." *Philosophy, The Journal of the Royal Institute of Philosophy*, Volume 76, pp. 515–540, 2001.
Quine, W.V.O. "Has Philosophy Lost Contact with People?" *Theories and Things*, pp. 190–193. Cambridge, MA: Harvard University Press, 1981.
Quine, W.V.O. "Naturalized Epistemology." *Ontological Relativity & Other Essays*, pp. 69–90. New York: Columbia University Press, 1961.
Redpath, Theodore. *Ludwig Wittgenstein: A Student's Memoir.* London: Duckworth, 1990.
Rhees, Rush. *Ludwig Wittgenstein: Personal Recollections.* Oxford: Basil Blackwell, 1981.
Ricks, Christopher. *Keats and Embarrassment.* Oxford University Press, 1974.
Robinson, Jennifer. *Deeper than Reason.* Oxford University Press, 2005.
Rousseau, Jean-Jacques. *Confessions.* Penguin Classics, 1953.

Rousseau, Jean-Jacques. *The Reveries of the Solitary Walker. English Translation with an Interpretive Essay by Charles E. Butterworth.* Indianapolis: Hackett, 1992.
Schlick, Moritz. *Problems of Ethics.* Translated by David Rynin. New York: Prentice-Hall, 1939.
Schroeder, Severin. "Schopenhauer's Influence on Wittgenstein." B. Vandenabeele, editor, *A Companion to Schopenhauer*, pp. 367–385. Oxford: Blackwell, 2012.
Shields, Carol. *Stone Diaries.* Random House Canada, 1993.
Smith, Benedict. "Hume and Liberal Naturalism." M. De Caro and D. Macarthur, editors, *The Routledge Handbook of Hume*, pp. 26–35. London and New York: Routledge, 2022.
Solomon, Robert. *The Passions.* New York, New York: Anchor/Doubleday, 1976.
Stanley, Liz. "The Writing of David Hume's My Own Life: The Persona of the Philosopher and the Philosopher Manqué." *Auto/Biography*, Volume 14, 2006.
Stenius, Erik. *Wittgenstein's Tractatus: A Critical Exposition of Its Main Lines of Thought.* Oxford: Basil Blackwell, 1960.
Stern, David. "Wittgenstein and Carnap on Physicalism: A Reassessment." Philsciarchive .pitt.edu/2860/, 2006.
Stern, David. Editor. *Wittgenstein in the 30s: Between the Tractatus and the Investigations.* Cambridge: Cambridge University Press, 2018.
Stern, David. *Wittgenstein on Mind and Language.* Oxford: Oxford University Press, 1995.
Strawson, Peter. "Freedom and Resentment." *Proceedings of the British Academy*, Volume 48, pp. 1–25, 1961.
Stroud, Barry. "Naturalism and Scepticism in the Philosophy of David Hume." Paul Russell, editor, *The Oxford Handbook of David Hume.* Oxford: Oxford University Press, 2016.
Szabados, Béla. "Embarrassment and Self-Esteem." *Journal of Philosophical Research*, Volume 15, pp. 341–349, 1990.
Szabados, Béla. "Reading Rousseau Through the Eyes of Embarrassment." *British Journal of Aesthetics*, Volume 34, pp. 266–277, 1994.
Szabados, Béla. "Wishful Thinking and Self-Deception." *Analysis*, Volume 33, pp. 201–205, 1973.
Taylor, Gabriele. *Pride, Shame, and Guilt.* Oxford: Oxford University Press, 1985.
Thrane, Gary. "Shame." *The Journal for the Theory of Social Behaviour*, Volume 9, pp. 139–166, 1979.
Tomassi, Paul. "From Toothache to Embarrassment: Wittgenstein on Emotion." *Philosophical Papers*, Volume 28, pp. 187–206, 1999.
Whitehead, A.N. *Process and Reality.* New York, New York: The Free Press, 1979.
Wilson, Catherine. "Self-Deception and Psychological Realism." *Philosophical Investigations*, Volume 3, pp. 47–60, 1980.
Wittgenstein, Ludwig. *Blue and Brown Books.* Oxford: Basil Blackwell, 1964.
Wittgenstein, Ludwig. *Culture and Value.* Translated by Peter Winch. Revised edition of the text by Alois Pichler. Oxford: Basil Blackwell, 1994.
Wittgenstein, Ludwig. *Lectures: Cambridge 1930–1932.* Edited by Desmond Lee from the Notes of John King and Desmond Lee. Oxford: Basil Blackwell, 1980.
Wittgenstein, Ludwig. *Philosophical Investigations.* Translated by G.E.M. Anscombe. Oxford: Blackwell Publishing, 2001.
Wittgenstein, Ludwig. *Philosophical Occasions.* Edited by James Klagge and Alfred Nordmann. Indianapolis and Cambridge: Hackett Publishing Company, 1993.

Wittgenstein, Ludwig. *Public and Private Occasions.* Edited by James Klagge and Alfred Nordmann. Lanham: Rowman & Littlefield Publishers, 2003.

Wittgenstein, Ludwig. *Remarks on Colour.* Berkeley: University of California Press, 2007.

Wittgenstein, Ludwig. *Remarks on the Philosophy of Psychology, Volumes I and II.* Edited by G.H. von Wright and Heikki Niemann. Translated by C.G. Luckhardt and M.A. Aue. Chicago: The University of Chicago Press, 1988.

Wittgenstein, Ludwig. *Tractatus Logico-Philosophicus.* Translated by D.F. Pears and B.F. McGuinness. London: Routledge and Kegan Paul, 1961.

Wittgenstein, Ludwig. *Zettel.* Edited by G.E.M. Anscombe and G.H. von Wright. Oxford: Blackwell, 1967.

Wollheim, Richard and J. Hopkins. Editors. *Philosophical Essays on Freud.* Cambridge: Cambridge University Press, 1982.

Wright, Georg Henrik von. *Wittgenstein.* Oxford: Basil Blackwell, 1982.

INDEX

www.ingramcontent.com/pod-product-compliance
Ingram Content Group UK Ltd.
Pitfield, Milton Keynes, MK11 3LW, UK
UKHW041922260426
470374UK00003B/8

9 781839 997662